Hiram Martin Chittenden

Gordon B. Dodds

Hiram Martin Chittenden
His Public Career

For

Brian Booth

with best wishes

from

Gordon

6 Dec 92

The University Press of Kentucky

To My Parents

ISBN: 0-8131-1283-4

Library of Congress Catalog Card Number: 72-91664

Copyright © 1973 by The University Press of Kentucky

A statewide cooperative scholarly publishing agency
serving Berea College, Centre College of Kentucky,
Eastern Kentucky University, Georgetown College,
Kentucky Historical Society, Kentucky State University,
Morehead State University, Murray State University,
Northern Kentucky State College, Transylvania University,
University of Kentucky, University of Louisville, and
Western Kentucky University.

Editorial and Sales Offices: Lexington, Kentucky 40506

Contents

[ILLUSTRATIONS FOLLOW PAGE 92]

Preface

When I first went up to the University of Wisconsin to commence doctoral studies in history, I was quickly introduced by my mentor to that indispensable monograph *The American Fur Trade of the Far West,* standing impressively in its three volumes on the shelves of the library of the State Historical Society. In time curiosity about the author of such a masterpiece led to the short article about Hiram Martin Chittenden in the *Dictionary of American Biography,* but for many years other studies prevented my following up this excellent introduction. When I resumed the project of investigating Chittenden's life, I found him to be a man worthy of interest in aspects of his career other than that best known to scholars.

Hiram Martin Chittenden (1858-1917) was one of the largely unrecognized group of army engineers who worked in the American West after the conclusion of the great age of the early explorers and surveyors, so graphically described by William H. Goetzmann in his *Exploration and Empire.* Chittenden published the first definitive report advocating the federal construction of irrigation projects, built the tourist roads in Yellowstone Park, made the survey of the boundaries of Yosemite Park, and planned the Lake Washington Canal.

In addition to his notable personal achievements Chittenden is significant for being a representative of an area largely untouched by students of the American West. One of the federal agencies with the largest impact upon the West is the Corps of Engineers, although there are very few biographies of officers of this branch of service. While there has been some monographic treatment of the era between the age of exploration and empire and the modern controversies over dam building, these studies have been almost exclusively of the Panama Canal and of the flood control projects. Chittenden's career illustrates many of the problems of an officer of the Corps of Engineers and thus encompasses a series of case studies of this influential agency. It further suggests the work of countless yet anonymous professionals, in and out of government service, whose work changed the face of the nation.

In the interstices of his professional career Chittenden discovered time to become an outstanding historian of the West. He produced three large historical works in addition to a guidebook about Yellowstone National Park. *History of Early Steamboat Navigation on the Missouri River,* the *Life and Letters of Father Pierre-Jean De Smet, S.J., 1801-1873,* and *The American Fur Trade of the West* are notable achievements. To the scholar of the West Chittenden's career as a historian is best known, although in this biography only one chapter deals with this facet of his life while the bulk of the work concentrates upon matters pertaining to his public career as an engineer.

After his premature retirement from military service and the engineering profession, Chittenden passed the final seven years of his life in Seattle where he became the first president of the new Seattle Port Commission. He also found time in these years to write for a national audience upon themes such as conservation and the prevention of war.

Throughout his career as engineer, politician, and writer, Chittenden in both public and private affairs exemplified the optimism, passion for service, and devotion to duty that characterized men and women of the reform movement of the late nineteenth and early twentieth centuries. His world was one of progress and evolutionary change, a world tempered by his own personal misfortunes from time to time, but not one that destroyed his progressive faith. In this respect he again serves as an exemplar of the professional and business men of the troubled era of the clash between the reality of modern industrialism and complexity and the nostalgia for past agrarianism and simplicity. Like many of them, Chittenden never lost faith that the nation, indeed all humanity, would clear its problems for a more radiant future.

This biography, although it was not intended to be so originally, is largely of the public man—the engineer, the writer of reports and histories, the government servant bent on discerning and shaping the competing interests of his various constituencies. At times, from memories of friends or children, a casual reference in a diary, or the letter of a friend, the private man appears, but the glimpses are tantalizingly brief and no one is more conscious than his biographer that the records of Chittenden's life lack many of the elements necessary to give a full dimension to the man. Out of necessity, provided by the historian's all too frequent fate of discovering that the great bulk of the personal correspondence and records was destroyed, not from malice but from a desire to be rid of accumulated debris, this is almost solely a biography of Chittenden's achievements and philosophy rather than of his personality, a focus that is regrettable but unavoidable.

Whatever the particular merits and demerits of this biography of Hiram Martin Chittenden, I hope that it will at least serve the purpose of opening up new areas of study for scholars of Western history. Chittenden's life touches upon many significant but untapped themes, untapped I would imagine both because of the bulk and the scattered nature of the data concerning them. Certainly much can be done by historians in the study of the civil work of the Corps of Engineers in the West. The history of irrigation and reclamation, national, state, and local, is largely unwritten. Many aspects of the philosophy and practices of the progressive conservationists have not been told. The beliefs and achievements of military men other than in time of war, and in pursuits other than on the battlefield, may yield fruitful results for the historian. The study of nature in a larger sense than formal conservation of useful resources has been investigated fruitfully by scholars like Hans Huth in *Nature and the American: Three Centuries of Changing Attitudes* and Roderick Nash in *Wilderness and the American Mind* but much remains unworked. The whole nature of the changing concept of American science as it entered the twentieth century is barely known. Chittenden's career touched all these problems; in some of them he made solid contributions, in all of them his work furnishes an incentive for historians to go deeper than this biography can suggest.

My greatest debt in the preparation of this biography is to my wife Rosemary who accompanied me upon many of my research travels, read the manuscript with a discerning eye, and performed many of the laborious tasks of editing and indexing. Without her aid this book would have been impossible for me to write.

Vernon Carstensen read the entire manuscript with his unequaled editorial skill and saved me from many errors of fact and interpretation. As on innumerable occasions in my scholarly career I have incurred an irredeemable obligation to him. Certain portions of the manuscript benefited immeasurably from the criticism of several other scholars of the American experience: the late William L. Davis, S. J., Herman J. Deutsch, Gene M. Gressley, Aubrey L. Haines, Thomas D. Morris, and Donald C. Swain. Their assistance is here acknowledged with deep gratitude. All errors remaining after running the gauntlet of these historians are of course my own. Other students of the national or regional history of which Chittenden was a part were also helpful to me in many ways. Robert E. Burke, Robert G. Dunbar, Eugene Exman, Harold D. Hampton, Robert V. Hine, William Lilley III, Bob Randolph O'Brien, and Thomas W. Paterson helped me more perhaps than they know. Judith Holland Sarnecki and Harlow T. Spaan were courteous, efficient, and careful research assistants. General Chittenden's three children, Eleanor Chittenden Cress, Hiram Chittenden, and Theodore P. Chittenden, all patiently answered innumerable questions about their father and his career. Otis D. Richardson kindly contributed helpful information about his father.

Because of the wide range, geographical and intellectual, of Hiram Martin Chittenden's career, librarians and archivists of many institutions have been called upon for information about his life and works. All have responded in the best traditions of their profession. Those who have been particularly helpful to me are Richard C. Berner and Mildred K. Sherwood of the University of Washington; Bruce Le Roy of the Washington State Historical Society; Stanley W. Brown, Helen T. Fineran, Robert Kvasnicka, and especially Harry T. Schwartz of the National Archives; Robert E. Fessenden and Millard H. McClung of the Oregon Historical Society; Annette N. Bartholomae, Edmond P. Gnoza, and Myra E. Wilson of the Portland State University Library; Edward P. Rich and Egon Weiss of the United States Military Academy; Dorothy M.

McKean of the Portland District of the Corps of Engineers; Warren M. Morris of Knox College; Hazel E. Mills of the Washington State Library and Frances H. Stadler of the Missouri Historical Society.

At several other institutions members of the staff have been of assistance to me, many of them anonymously, but invariably usefully. I take this opportunity to thank the men and women in the libraries or research departments of the *Atlantic Monthly,* the *Christian Science Monitor,* Columbia University, Cornell University, the Huntsville, Alabama, Public Library, the Illinois State Historical Society, the Minnesota Historical Society, Monmouth College (Illinois), the Montana State Historical Society, the Multnomah County Library, the Northern Pacific Railroad, the Port of Seattle, the Seattle Chamber of Commerce, the Seattle District of the Corps of Engineers, the Seattle Municipal League, the Seattle Municipal Reference Library, the South Dakota Historical Society, Stanford University Library, the Wyoming State Archives and Historical Department, Yale University, and the Yellowstone National Park Association.

Permission to use materials in the Bancroft Library of the University of California is gratefully acknowledged. I wish to thank the editors of the *Journal of American History* and the *Pacific Historical Review* for permission to reproduce material published in other forms in their journals. Financial assistance for research was generously contributed by the American Council of Learned Societies, Knox College, and Portland State University. A substantial contribution toward publication was also made by Portland State University. Typing of the manuscript was skillfully done by Maud Alexander, Sharon M. Axtell, Carolyn W. Coyner, and Nancy A. Maurer.

1.

A Western Engineer Emerges
1858-1896

The two army officers made a disparate pair as they conversed in their compartment on the Northern Pacific express crossing the Great Plains beyond St. Paul. The older man, short, voluble, and opinionated, was obviously the leader. His companion, tall, quiet, and self-contained, listened dutifully to the comments of his superior while the train rolled westward in the early June of 1891. They talked mostly of their destination, Yellowstone Park, a symbol of past achievement for the elder and of future challenge for the younger. As their train passed into Montana and drew nearer the hamlet of Cinnabar, the junction point for the park, Major William A. Jones, Corps of Engineers, United States Army, certainly ruminated aloud about his first visit to Yellowstone in the summer of 1873 when as a young lieutenant he had commanded a party reconnoitering north of Fort Bridger to find a line for a military road between the Union Pacific Railroad and the park's southern boundary. His expedition had been most successful and had culminated in the discovery of the magnificent Togwoheap Pass through the Wind River Mountains. Jones thought well of his accomplishments, past and projected, and his endless advice chafed the younger engineer officer seated beside him.[1]

For Lieutenant Hiram Martin Chittenden the Yellowstone station was to be his first individual responsibility and Major Jones's braggadocio hardly gave him confidence about mastering his new assignment. Indeed Hiram Chittenden was already depressed about the seeming futility of a military career and had even been driven during the past winter to write several pages of gloomy verse about his prospects. Although Chittenden, unlike Major Jones, was never confident of his own abilities, he had already demonstrated independence and intelligence long before he and Jones descended to the platform at Cinnabar in a driving rainstorm to begin the season of road building in Yellowstone Park.[2]

Born on October 25, 1858, to a farming couple, William and Mary Wheeler Chittenden, residents of Yorkshire Township, Cattaraugus County in western New York state, thirty-five miles southeast of the thriving lake port of Buffalo, Chittenden had enjoyed a boyhood that later generations might fancy a pastoral idyll. Hiram and his brother Clyde, two years younger, attended a one-room red schoolhouse, fished and hunted, tapped the sugar maples, filled the woodbox, swam and skated at the millpond, and in other ways disported themselves as rustic urchins. But where Hiram differed from most of his fellows was in his early passion for education and his later aspiration for a professional career that would free him from the rigors of farm life. The boy's parents, approving his zeal for learning, soon arranged his transfer to a superior country school in the adjacent district and, when Hiram was sixteen years old, enrolled him at the Ten Broeck Free Academy in the town of Franklinville, ten miles from the family farm. For the next four years Hiram alternated his studies at the academy with stints on the farm to pay his tuition fees, and onerous as were the tasks of haying and harvesting, they were amply justified by the opportunities at the Ten Broeck Academy where he met his future wife, Nettie Parker, of neighboring Arcade, and obtained not only a sound classical training but also a desire for higher education to foster a legal career. To help finance the last he endured one more hardship of great frustra-

---

1 HMC, "The Yellowstone," Hiram M. Chittenden Papers (Washington State Historical Society), hereafter cited CPHS; William A. Jones, *Report upon the Reconnaissance of Northwestern Wyoming, Including Yellowstone National Park, Made in the Summer of 1873* (Washington, D.C., 1875); William H. Goetzmann, *Exploration and Empire: The Explorer and the Scientist in the Winning of the American West* (New York, 1966), pp. 409-12.

2 Toward the end of his life Chittenden privately published a book of verse that contained some of his earlier poems. The later introductions to the poems supply some important biographical information. HMC, *Verse* (Seattle, Wash., 1916).

tion, the teaching of a district school in Seymour for a few months after his graduation from the academy.[3]

In the Horatio Alger mode Hiram's labor and ambition were rewarded in the summer of 1878, not once but twice, when he won by competitive examination a tuition scholarship at Cornell University and was offered an appointment by his congressman to the United States Military Academy. The West Point opportunity, with its prospects of an engineering career and a free education, preempted Hiram's earlier ambition to become an attorney, although he never lost his interest in the legal profession. He accepted both appointments, which, as it turned out, opened up eight years of higher education and professional training within the borders of his native state. Cornell came first, for realizing that the Military Academy curriculum flowed narrowly into military and engineering channels, Chittenden decided to broaden himself for a few months in Ithaca, concentrating upon languages, literature, and history before transferring to West Point.[4]

This decision was wise, for Cornell University, when Chittenden arrived in the fall of 1879, was a stimulating place for any rural youth. Although the finances of the university were in the doldrums, the competence of the faculty, the intellectual controversies over the Darwinian challenge to religious orthodoxy, and the academic and social freedoms of students all fulfilled the hopes for educational innovation of the university's founder, Ezra Cornell, and of its president, the scholarly and urbane Andrew Dickson White, at that time on leave as American minister to Berlin. During his two terms at Cornell Chittenden took courses in Latin, German, and mathematics and received his first systematic introduction to his future

[3] Genealogical information on the Chittenden family has been provided the author in a letter from Ethel K. Carves, Cattaraugus County Historian, August 24, 1968. The sources for Chittenden's early life before December 1878, when he began a diary, are two autobiographical sketches and a later diary entry. The first and briefer sketch was written in October 1879; the second was written in March 1908. Both are found in CPHS. He later gave a brief synopsis of a portion of his early life in HMC, "Diary," January 1, 1890, CPHS; Chittenden's experiences as a teacher are in HMC, *Verse*, pp. 36-38, and in his "Diary" entries for these years, CPHS.

[4] Unless otherwise noted, the details of Chittenden's entrance examination and his years at Cornell and his appointment to West Point are in his diary entries from these years and from that of January 1, 1890, all in CPHS.

profession of historical studies in lectures and colloquia presented by vice president William C. Russel, who had absorbed the seminar method and the spirit of scholarly investigation then being translated from German to American universities. Outside the classroom Chittenden hiked, debated, attended lectures, visited the law courts, and participated in the usual town-and-gown imbroglios of nineteenth-century university life. All in all he was content with his two terms at Cornell and was indeed sometimes uneasy about his plan to transfer to the dour atmosphere and the circumscribed regimen of the Military Academy. Upon departing for home to await the reporting date at West Point, he wrote a diary entry that summed up his experiences in Ithaca: "I left the school with a number of warm friends and a [sic] quite an attachment to the University."[5]

Quite the opposite were his initial sentiments at West Point. Coming down the Hudson on the steamship *Vibbard* after staying a few weeks at the farm reading for the entrance examination, Chittenden arrived at the Military Academy in late spring of 1880. "When I stepped from the steamer," he recorded in his diary, "I felt just a little lonely owing to the character of the place to which I had come." West Point was formidable, no question of that. Its grim and ancient buildings high above the Hudson symbolized the rigor of its system: conservative, disciplined, precise, and self-satisfied, the very antithesis of Cornell.[6]

Chittenden worried a good deal during his first days. In his diary and in letters to his family he expressed concern about the pettiness of military discipline in "Beast Barracks," about the coarseness, irreligion, and profanity of his fellow plebes, and about hazing in the impending summer camp. Most of all he worried about passing the entrance examination in academic subjects and the physical examination, the latter of concern to him because since youth he had been troubled by

5 The best account of Cornell in these years is in Morris Bishop, *A History of Cornell* (Ithaca, N.Y., 1962), especially pp. 197-223; "Diary," March 28, 1880, CPHS.

6 Data for Chittenden's career from the time of his departure from Cornell through his graduation from West Point are drawn from his diary entries unless otherwise noted.

chronic throat hemorrhages. However, he surmounted both tests and was off across the plain to summer training at Camp Heintzleman on the first of July. Chittenden's uncertainties about the Academy persisted for several months after the close of summer camp as he continued to doubt the wisdom of his transfer, to distrust the state of his health, and to feel the burden of the relentless pressures of military minutiae. But sometime after his first Christmas, surely by February 1881, homesickness and discontent were almost gone, and he could write hastily to his mother: "Once in a while I wish that I might be home just a little while. But my work is so hard that it doesn't leave me much time to think about other things."[7]

Academic activity at West Point was heavily technical in nature and included only a sprinkling of courses in the humanities and social sciences. Mathematics was the core subject supplemented by the other natural sciences, military engineering, and the art of war. Chittenden additionally gained a reading knowledge of Spanish and French, studied the mechanics of English, and read ethics for his humanities program while his lone subject in the social sciences was world history, a course taken in his senior year. His military program comprised the tactics of artillery, cavalry, and infantry, use of small arms, horsemanship, and fencing. Practical fieldwork in various encampments occupied the summers, and drill was omnipresent at all seasons. In the limited time free from study, classroom, and parade ground, Chittenden went on outings with a Bible class to Constitution Island, gathered chestnuts, took long walks, and frequented the Academy library where he read independently in Shakespeare, Scott, Francis Bacon, Byron, Milton, and various British and French historians with special attention to David Hume. He perused the daily press and subscribed to a French newspaper, *Le Courrier des Etats-Unis*. Maintaining his interest in law, he also read as much as possible in William Kent's *Commentary on American Law*.[8]

[7] HMC to William F. Chittenden, June 22, 1880; HMC to Clyde Chittenden, June 28, 1880; HMC to Mrs. William F. Chittenden, July 3, November 28, 1880, February 6, 1881; an unaddressed, undated fragment from HMC during summer camp 1880, all in the United States Military Academy Library.

[8] HMC's academic work and extracurricular activities are listed in *Official*

Chittenden's final year at the Military Academy was his most gratifying one. He had no demerits and was first in his class in discipline. In a class of thirty-seven, he finished in third place in general merit, a position that earned him a coveted commission in the Corps of Engineers. And thus at the traditional graduation exercises in June 1884 he could reflect on a profitable career at the Academy, for he had not only obtained the desired college education without personal expense but also had acquired the rudiments of engineering and could now anticipate two professional careers: army officer or civil engineer. His love for Nettie had remained constant, his health was no worse than upon entrance, and his mind had grown through extensive reading in spite of his parochial surroundings. In later life Chittenden always retained fond memories of the Military Academy, for it had fulfilled his expectations and he those of the institution.[9]

West Point's expectations, although numerous, did not include the assumption that its graduates were complete engineers, and the new second lieutenants who were assigned to the Corps of Engineers were given a three-year course following graduation at the Engineer School of Application at Willets Point, a post situated in the harbor of New York City. Chittenden reported to his new station on October 1, 1884, after an enjoyable leave of three and one half months largely spent with friends and relatives in Cattaraugus County. His next three years were even fuller than his career at the Military Academy, but with the difference that his trials were lightened by the "sweet disposition" of Nettie whom he had married at Arcade, New York, on December 30, 1884. A large portion of his work at Willets Point was partially familiar to him, for much of it was the study of various engineering topics although in more concentrated form than at West Point. Civil and

Register of the Officers and Cadets of the U.S. Military Academy, 1881 (Poughkeepsie, N.Y., 1881), p. 17, hereafter cited *OR; OR* 1882 (Poughkeepsie, N.Y., 1882), pp. 14, 27; *OR* 1883 (Poughkeepsie, N.Y., 1883), pp. 12, 27; *OR* 1884 (Poughkeepsie, N.Y., 1884), pp. 10, 24, 26; *The Centennial of the United States Military Academy at West Point, New York, 1802-1902,* 2 vols. (Washington, D.C., 1904), 1: 251-58; Williston Fish, *Memories of West Point, 1877-1881,* 3 vols. (Batavia, N.Y., 1957), passim; Stephen F. Ambrose, *Duty, Honor, Country: A History of West Point* (Baltimore, Md., 1966), p. 197.

[9] *OR* 1884, pp. 10, 24, 26.

military engineering, submarine mining, astronomy, photography, and meteorology composed the academic program, with the summers being spent in field application of these subjects. In a related area of intellectual endeavor Chittenden at last attained his youthful goal of legal study and arranged to read law with an attorney in neighboring Flushing to prepare for admission to the bar.[10]

In spare moments the Chittendens took advantage of cosmopolitan New York to see the great actors of the Shakespearean stage: Edwin Booth in *Hamlet,* Lawrence Barret in *Julius Caesar,* and Henry Irving in *The Merchant of Venice.* They heard the *Mikado* and occasionally attended the Plymouth Congregational Church where Henry Ward Beecher, a "great and good man" to Chittenden, formulated his synthesis of orthodoxy and evolution. From time to time the young couple entertained visitors and attended dances and other festivities on the post. Gradually Chittenden gained a modicum of social confidence and his intellectual competence was recognized in rapid succession from December 1886 to March 1887 in his promotion to first lieutenant, his admission to the bar of New York State, and his selection to lecture to the students of the Yale Sheffield Scientific School on the topic "Moving, Supplying, and Sheltering Troops." Shortly after completing this series of achievements, he left Willets Point on July 7 for duty as engineer officer of the Department of the Platte, stationed in Omaha, thus departing New York State for the first extended period of time in his twenty-nine years of life. His goal of becoming a competent military engineer had been attained and the challenge of applying his professional training lay at hand.[11]

Whatever he might have anticipated, Chittenden did not

[10] Hiram M. Chittenden, #3839-A.C.P.-1884, Records of the Adjutant General (Record Group 94, National Archives), hereafter cited ACP; HMC's years at Willets Point are described in *Annual Report of the Chief of Engineers* (hereafter cited *ARCE* [Washington, D.C., published annually]), 1885, 1: 427-29, 432-35, 450-53; *ARCE,* 1886, 1: 476-79, 481-83, 490; *ARCE,* 1887, 1: 416-27; ACP; and in his diaries for these years in CPHS; marriage certificate, CPHS.

[11] The certificate of admission to the bar is in CPHS; Sheffield Scientific School, *Biennial Report 1887-89* (New Haven, Conn., 1889), p. 15; ACP; Acting Chief of Engineers to Adjutant General, August 26, 1887, Records of the Office of the Chief of Engineers (Record Group 77, National Archives), hereafter cited RG 77.

find the opportunities of his first two assignments as an engineer officer particularly stimulating. Under the famed Indian fighter General George Crook, he spent a year attached to the headquarters of the Department of the Platte (a district comprising Iowa, Nebraska, Wyoming, Utah, and a portion of Idaho) making a map of the district, surveying several military reservations and rifle ranges, mapping and platting the posts, and dispensing maps and surveying instruments to the officers of the department. His competent execution of these tasks led General Crook to ask that he be retained for another year of service. The Chief of Engineers overruled this request, however, and assigned Chittenden to duty with the recently created Missouri River Commission that had been founded in 1884.[12]

In establishing the Commission, Congress had intended for it to plan for the systematic navigational improvement of the river and thus to supersede the traditional piecemeal "improvements" of a pork barrel nature. In practice Chittenden's work during the next two years belied this theory as he passed the working seasons of 1889 and 1890 largely aboard the government vessel *Josephine*, based at Fort Benton on the upper Missouri, engaged in damming, dredging, and surveying various portions of the river below Benton. Even though his wife and sister lived on the steamer during one season, the amenities that they contributed barely sufficed to make up for the apparent futility of his work. Most of Chittenden's efforts expended on behalf of this once great commercial thoroughfare did little to further navigational improvement because of an existing situation of poor river management.[13]

12 *ARCE*, 1888, 4: 2818-19; HMC to Chief of Engineers, January 25, 1888, #361/A1, RG 77; HMC, "Report of Operations, June 30, 1888," #2605/A, RG 77; HMC, "Report of Operations, August 31, 1888," #3431/A, RG 77; HMC, "Report of Operations, January 31, 1888," #475/A, RG 77; HMC to Chief of Engineers, January 25, 1888, #372/A, RG 77; Chief of Engineers to HMC, March 6, 31, 1888, #874/A, #1290/A, RG 77; John R. Brooke to Adjutant General (telegram), September 28, 1888; Adjutant General to Commanding General, Department of Platte, October 2, 1888, both ACP; Headquarters, Corps of Engineers to Inspector General, December 7, 1888, #188, RG 77.

13 *ARCE*, 1889, 4: 2760-61; *ARCE*, 1890, 4: 3419-20, 3422; HMC, *Verse*, pp. 77-79; William E. Lass, *A History of Steamboating on the Upper Missouri River* (Lincoln, Nebr., 1962), pp. 153-58; *ARCE*, 1890, 4: 3421; *ARCE*, 1891, 6: 3724, 3831; HMC, "Individual Report, April 21, 1890," ACP.

Following the success of the railroad, whatever river commerce remained was used by local citizens to justify federal expenditures for dikes and levees allegedly to improve commercial navigation. In actuality these structures served for local flood control and did not advance the overall development of the river valley. The hypocrisy and futility of this program and his participation in it galled Chittenden, and his first historical article, a history of Fort Benton, concluded with a plea that the United States abandon its expenditures for navigation and flood control purposes and replace them with an equivalent amount spent for irrigation. Yet he saw little hope that the region's citizens would abandon their time-honored subsidies: "But the dwellers of the valley being periodically pacified by these paltry pittances from the public purse, the paramount problem of making the river build up that country and convert these arid and barren wastes into productive farm-lands will go on unsolved." Such speculations were bold indeed from a junior officer in a Corps whose major methods of river control work had been almost unchanged for decades.[14]

Although he had accepted the recurring throat hemorrhages as no more than nagging annoyances, Chittenden found his professional frustrations compounded by an attack of typhoid fever in the early fall of 1890. After putting off his fears as long as possible, he finally consulted an army physician who recommended a six months leave of absence, an interlude that the Chittendens turned into a delayed honeymoon trip to Europe. Chittenden spent five months in France polishing his knowledge of the French language begun at West Point and indulging in a course of readings in science, history, and evolutionary philosophy. On returning to the United States in the spring of 1891, he learned from the office of the Chief of Engineers that although he had been slated for a station in Alabama, a vacancy had turned up in Yellowstone for which he had been selected. Assignment to this obscure post, low on the list of priorities of the Corps, was hardly a compliment

14 Hiram M. Chittenden, "The Ancient Town of Fort Benton in Montana: Navigating the Upper Missouri River," *Magazine of American History* 24 (1890): 409-25 (quotation, p. 425).

to Chittenden and the rigorous working conditions of the park might even be disastrous to one of his marginal physical health. Yet he lacked the rank or status to protest and found himself under the command of Major Jones at St. Paul with the summer duty of building roads in the nation's first national park.[15]

The first few days in Yellowstone were even worse than the gloomy Chittenden anticipated. He and Major Jones traversed the route from the depot at Cinnabar to the park headquarters at Mammoth Hot Springs over a trail jelled into gumbo by spring downpours, a vivid manifestation of the challenges awaiting the park road builder. During this depressing journey, Jones continued to extol, as he had aboard the train, the virtues of his civilian assistant, Ed Lamartine, a one-time sawyer at the government lumber mill in the park, into whose guiding hands he urged Chittenden to place himself. After a brief stay at Mammoth—a squalid collection of cavalry barracks, a small hotel, and some wooden office buildings—the party proceeded to the Lower Geyser Basin from whence Congress had recently ordered a road constructed to the West Thumb of Yellowstone Lake by way of Craig Pass. By now weather and ill health had confined both Jones and Chittenden to the primitive Basin Hotel while the untrained Lamartine at the major's orders made a cursory survey and soon announced triumphantly that he had located the new road. Everyone then returned to Mammoth, Jones left for his headquarters at St. Paul, and Chittenden, relieved at the major's departure, faced his problems.[16]

These were awesome. Nature had provided severe obstacles to road construction in the form of uneven terrain, towering mountains, thick forests, shifting soil, sudden freshets, and a short summer. Society had provided a people to match the unpromising environment. During Chittenden's term of service, poachers roamed through the park, someone set fire to the superintendent's haystack, outlaws robbed a stage bound

15 HMC to Adjutant General, October 31, November 20, 1890, both ACP; HMC, *Verse*, pp. 14, 20-29; HMC, "Individual Report, December 17, 1891," ACP; HMC, "The Yellowstone," CPHS; HMC to J. G. D. Knight, January 5, 1892, #158, RG 77.
16 HMC. "The Yellowstone," CPHS.

for Yellowstone twenty miles from the north entrance, and bandits held up other visitors on the very border of the park. Even most men eligible for work on road construction were transients trying to scrape together enough money from government service to finance their trip through the park. Inadequately clad for the rigors of the altitude, disinclined to discipline, they were hired without scrutiny because of lack of time and, finding the work too taxing, soon quit their jobs.[17]

Congress had provided little except a hampering administrative structure. Its appropriations had been parsimonious, averaging annually the sum of $22,463.24 for the years 1883-1888, although in 1889 it had increased this amount to $50,000 and to $75,000 for the years 1890 and 1891. Furthermore, Congress often did not vote appropriations until July or August, and these appropriations had to be expended during the fiscal year. Therefore the engineers had limited working time and were forced to rush work in the late summer and early autumn or in the few working weeks in the spring before the year expired. Congress had also required that an officer of the Corps of Engineers build the roads while the administration of the park remained in the hands of an acting superintendent, an officer of cavalry, who reported to the Secretary of the Interior. Division of authority thus made Chittenden subject to the official scrutiny of Major Jones, his superior in St. Paul, and to the unofficial but omnipresent observation of Captain George S. Anderson, the acting superintendent on the ground, who later confided that when he first met the fragile Chittenden he had expected him "to last about two weeks."[18] In spite of its own negligence the House Appropriations Committee in early 1891 had given Yellowstone Park an enormous amount of unfavorable publicity by blaming the low visitor attendance of the previous year—300 persons—on the poor condition of the park roads although a late and inclement spring was also partially responsible. But if Congress slighted the park, others had it very much in mind, so from time to

17 U.S., Department of the Interior, *Report of the Secretary of the Interior,* 1892, (Washington, D.C., 1892), 3: 642, 644-45, 649-57; *ARCE,* 1893, 6: 4398; *Livingston* (Mont.) *Enterprise,* August 22, 1891; HMC, "The Yellowstone," CPHS.
18 *ARCE,* 1892, 4: 3438-39; HMC, "The Yellowstone," CPHS.

time various interests tried to reduce the boundaries, "improve" its attractions by concessions of dubious value, obtain rights-of-way for railroads, and generally reshape it to the detriment of its natural beauty.[19]

To attack his host of challenges, Chittenden had only his own independence and courage, the extent of which he did not yet appreciate, and a sound plan for the roads laid down by a talented predecessor. Captain Dan C. Kingman of the Corps of Engineers had drawn up a comprehensive plan for road construction in the park in 1883, eleven years after Congress had created it. Kingman's program involved building roads of uniform width and grade, high quality material, and aesthetic appeal to connect the points of interest within the park. The Grand Loop, as it became known, linked Mammoth Hot Springs, the Geyser Basins, and Yellowstone Lake and then led back to Mammoth by way of the Grand Canyon. (See map.) By the time Chittenden first assumed duty in the park, he found that approximately sixty miles of dirt road had been constructed on the Grand Loop circuit. Roads completed, although not up to Kingman's standards, made up the routes from the northern entrance of the park to the Geyser region and from the Norris Geyser Basin to the Grand Canyon of the Yellowstone River. Uncompleted roads ran from the Geyser Basin to the Grand Canyon via Hayden Valley and from Mammoth to Yancey's. Little construction had been attempted over the most mountainous portion of the Loop, extending from Yancey's to the Grand Canyon.[20]

During the next two seasons Chittenden supervised a work force ranging up to 130 men that opened up fifty-three miles of new road, thirty-nine miles of which were completed, undertook survey work, and made numerous repairs on the existing system. His worst experience came in the first three months when the novice commander was harassed by Lamartine's incompetence and dishonesty. Jones's train was hardly out of

19 U.S., Congress, House, Subcommittee on Appropriations, *Hearings on . . . Sundry Civil Appropriation Bill for 1892*, 51st Cong., 2d sess., January 24, 1891, p. 73; *Livingston* (Mont.) *Enterprise*, July 18, 1891; John Ise, *Our National Park Policy: A Critical History* (Baltimore, Md., 1961), pp. 40-44.
20 Bob Randolph O'Brien, "The Yellowstone National Park Road System: Past, Present and Future" (Ph.D. diss., University of Washington, 1965), pp. 43-46, 52-61, 79, 92-93; *ARCE*, 1892, 4: 3433-34, 3444-45.

sight when Lamartine was in Chittenden's office to present him with an expensive fishing outfit. Both regulations and Chittenden's integrity prevented him from accepting the gift from his assistant, yet he could not be absolutely sure that it represented a bribe to overlook incompetence. Chittenden extricated himself, tactfully though expensively, by buying the outfit from Lamartine. Having thus disposed of this awkwardness, Chittenden went to work on his first project, the road through Craig Pass.[21]

Chittenden and Lamartine took command of separate survey parties at each end of the line and, because of the limited working season, hastened ahead with the inadequate equipment available. Moving through heavily forested and rugged terrain, with his only instruments a hand level and a strong stick about five feet in length, Chittenden found a line for a road, with a grade less than 5 percent, that crossed the continental divide through Craig Pass. There he encountered Lamartine's approaching party simplifying its task by clearing an existing Indian trail as the site for the road rather than choosing an aesthetic route that also had a manageable grade. The disgusted Chittenden had to call off the work party until, personally retracing his subordinate's route, he completed the survey to the summit. Lamartine's slovenly performance was the first of several errors that culminated in Chittenden's dismissing him in three months. Later Jones rehired Lamartine in 1893 after Chittenden had left the park. It is characteristic of Chittenden that, in the midst of slogging towards Craig Pass, he paused in awe at the discovery of a beautiful little lake, so perfect that he composed a poem celebrating its radiance.[22] Chittenden's work in this survey and throughout the park during the year greatly impressed Superintendent Anderson who praised him profusely in his own annual report, a well-meaning gesture that backfired when Major Jones read Anderson's tribute and dashed off a letter in response to it:

My dear Anderson
I quote as follows from your annual report:
"Lieut. Chittenden, U. S. Engineers in charge of the work is

[21] *ARCE*, 1892, 4: 3438-44; HMC, "The Yellowstone," CPHS.
[22] HMC, "The Yellowstone," CPHS; HMC, *Verse*, pp. 53-57.

zealous untiring, and remarkably efficient in its prosecution and will certainly make a fine showing by the end of the year." Don't you think, old fellow, that giving away all the glory to a subordinate at the expense of the Boss is calculated to stir up the latter's feelings.

I know very well that you have not intended to do me an injustice, but how would you feel were I to officially report that your 1st Sergeant was entitled to all the credit for the beautiful discipline of your Company? I don't ask you to glorify me. Nor do I ask you not to glorify Chittenden. He has done very well. Only do it so as not to throw an odious light on.

Yours very truly,
    W. A. Jones.[23]

Chittenden's second road building crisis arose when he returned to Yellowstone for his second season on June 18, 1892, accompanied by his wife Nettie and their first child, five-month-old Eleanor. This crisis, exemplifying in severe form the usual difficulties of divided administration, occurred because of the zeal of Captain George L. Scott, one of the cavalry officers stationed in the park. While Chittenden was away, Scott had busied himself on the twenty-mile stretch of road between Gibbon Canyon and the Excelsior Geyser by removing boulders from the retaining wall and depositing them in the roadway to repair erosion damage. This well-intended project went awry when the record spring floods, unchecked by the wall, magnified the previous destruction. The floods also destroyed other stretches of the road system, so Chittenden's reputation as a road builder progressively shrunk with the washing out of each culvert and retaining wall. Although the situation seemed impossible to rectify because the next congressional allocation of funds would not come until midsummer, Chittenden promised to make good the damages if he could somehow raise the money to pay the working force.[24]

He persuaded Captain Anderson to contribute $500 of his appropriation and raised another $500 from the Yellowstone

23 W. A. Jones to George S. Anderson, September 17, 1891, in the Yellowstone National Park Archives (Yellowstone National Park, Wyoming), hereafter cited YNPA.
24 HMC, "The Yellowstone," CPHS; HMC to George S. Anderson, July 15, 1892, June 27, 1893, YNPA.

Transportation Company and from Frank J. Haynes, the park photographer. With Chittenden in the lead singling out the most necessary places for repair, the hastily assembled work party started out over the Grand Loop from the Upper Basin in an effort to complete the work before the seasonal arrival of the tourists in early July. The chief impediment was the ignorance of the workmen, so Chittenden frequently had to double back, dismount, and instruct the men in the art of handling pick and shovel or ax and saw. Nevertheless all went well until the work party reached Yellowstone Lake and discovered that the meat had not caught up with the men, some of whom threatened to strike, others to quit. With whatever eloquence he could summon Chittenden talked the men into remaining for at least half a day and, aided by the enterprise of the cook who caught a mess of trout for lunch, the food crisis was resolved with the arrival of the beef in time for supper. By working straight through for fourteen days, including two Sundays and the Fourth of July, Chittenden's men completed the work as promised. Chittenden's engineering reputation seemed restored.[25]

His relief was illusory, however, for the Interior Department officials had caught wind of the road problems and dispatched a special inspector, Eugene F. Weigel, to investigate them and other conditions in the park. Major Jones was convinced that one of the cavalry officers had informed on the engineers to embarrass them, but in any case it was Chittenden's bad luck that when Weigel arrived he was impressed by Captain Scott but was unable to confer with Chittenden's friend, Superintendent Anderson, who was absent on leave. Weigel's ensuing report recommended that the Corps should in the future take care to hold over enough funds for spring repair work and praised Captain Scott for reopening the roads during the past spring. Needless to say, this estimate of their work disconcerted Chittenden and enraged Jones, both of whom defended their administration and assailed Weigel and Scott, but the storm over the investigation soon blew over.[26]

25 HMC, "The Yellowstone," CPHS.
26 Eugene Weigel to John W. Noble, Secretary of the Interior, August 15, 1892, #5677/1, endorsement by HMC, October 17, 1892, RG 77.

Throughout the trials of his two seasons of road building Chittenden's appreciation of natural beauty persistently confirmed the truth of Kingman's earlier view that distinguished park roads from earlier highways. In annual reports to the Chief, Chittenden contended that it was not necessary to build new roads since most of the scenic attractions of the park were now accessible. What was required was to refurbish the existing roads to a high standard of quality that included not only sound construction but pleasing appearance. The road with the best effect, he wrote, was "winding, following the valleys and avoiding the hills, thus by its short views ahead giving the tourist a sense of expectancy, instead of treating him to the long perspective of a monotonous roadway ahead of him." The tourists' pleasure, not the shortest distance between two points, should be the controlling principle and roads so constructed would add to the reputation of the United States and its government in the minds of the visitors who came to Yellowstone from all over the globe.[27]

Desire to protect the park also led Chittenden to help thwart a raid by mining and realty interests controlled by the Northern Pacific Railroad that since 1883 had been attempting to gain a right-of-way from Congress through the northeastern area of the park from Cooke City to the mines along the river valley or, alternatively, to reduce the boundaries of the park to permit the building of the railroad. Although resisted continually by superintendents and engineer officers, the plan cropped up repeatedly. The current measure was one introduced by Senator Wilbur F. Sanders of Montana to permit the construction of a railroad from Cinnabar to Cooke City and to cut off all the park north of it. Chittenden criticized this measure in his annual report and, to emphasize his opposition, wrote a separate letter to the Chief of Engineers urging him to combat both portions of the bill. He argued that the construction of the proposed railway would both mar the scenery and set an ominous precedent, for no sooner would the northern crossing be legitimized than another railroad would pressure for a right-of-way across the southwestern section of the park where lay the lowest pass across the Conti-

27 *ARCE*, 1892, 4: 3449 (quotation, p. 3451).

nental Divide. At the very least, he declared, if it were necessary to permit the road, the land surrounding it should be retained in the park to prevent rampant commercialism from following its tracks. He stated that the interests favoring the project at Cooke City were not formidable and implied that the Chief would not be expending much political capital in resisting their encroachment upon the park.[28]

Chittenden's conscience did not permit him to rest easy with these efforts, and he sought a national audience in March by publishing—anonymously for obvious reasons—a long letter in *Harper's Weekly* entitled "Legalized Vandalism." Reduction of the park's area for a railroad, he wrote, "is surely very much as if a physician should propose to cure a felon on the finger by amputating the patient's arm." The park was national property, he concluded, and should not become the prey of the local communities surrounding it. Still exercised about the threat, Chittenden, along with Captain Kingman, W. Hallett Phillips of the Department of the Interior, and Theodore Roosevelt, the organizer of the Boone and Crockett Club, published articles on the controversy in *Forest and Stream*. The series of articles was published subsequently as a separate pamphlet entitled *A Standing Menace: Cooke City vs. the National Park*. Shedding his diffidence, Chittenden enclosed a copy of this pamphlet in a personal letter to President Benjamin Harrison urging him to veto the railroad bill if it passed the Congress. Branding the proposal the "most audacious attempt to sacrifice public to private interests that I have ever seen," Chittenden declared that the distance of the park from heavy centers of population made it difficult to rally public sentiment against the railroad. Fortunately the anti-railroad forces, although they saw the bill pass in the Senate on May 10, 1892, were able to prevent it from coming to a vote in the House.[29]

28 For the history of these measures see Ise, *National Park Policy*, pp. 42-43; H. Duane Hampton, *How the U.S. Cavalry Saved Our National Parks* (Bloomington, Ind., 1971), pp. 113-20; "Report of Lieut. H. M. Chittenden, January 26, 1892," #3513/1, RG 77 (not all this report was published in *ARCE*); HMC to J. G. D. Knight, January 5, 1892, #158, RG 77.

29 A Friend of the Park, "Legalized Vandalism," *Harper's Weekly* 36 (March 12, 1892): 258; *A Standing Menace: Cooke City vs. the National Park* (New York, 1892); HMC to the President of the United States, December 16, 1892,

Chittenden also took the leadership against another proposal that authorized the introduction of a railroad into Yellowstone. The roads in the park, because of the limited budget, were all dirt, not even graveled, and on the hot summer days were miserable for travel. Tourists who had come great distances at heavy expense were able to view Old Faithful or the Yellowstone Canyon only through clouds of dust. To still their clamor the park transportation and hotel enterprises suggested the construction of an electric railroad that would be smokeless, noiseless, and dustless. Chittenden originally leaned toward this solution to the dust problem provided that the railroad be built and operated by the government, but he adamantly opposed construction by private interests for fear that in the park, as elsewhere in the nation, it would be impossible to regulate private carriers. However, by the time he left the park he had dropped his support of even the faint possibility of government railway construction because his conversations with tourists and their responses to questionnaires he had sent them in the previous winter convinced him that they overwhelmingly preferred good graveled roads to any other means of transportation.[30]

In the spring of 1893 Chittenden's first tour of duty in Yellowstone ended with a new assignment to Louisville, Kentucky, to assist in the maintenance and operation of the Louisville and Portland canal. News of the transfer was disappointing, for Chittenden felt he had the park work well in hand and, gnawed by concern about the circumstances of his transfer, he wrote to Superintendent Anderson after his arrival at Louisville, asking Anderson to check with the Chief's office to see if he had been relieved on account of personal delinquencies. He concluded his letter: "If you can give me any light you need not hesitate out of any consideration for my feelings. It is at least not gratifying to think that a man like Jones has got the whole thing in his hands. He appears greatly elated over it." If Anderson responded to this request, his

#7146/1, RG 77; Hampton, *How the U.S. Cavalry Saved Our National Parks*, pp. 115-17.
30 "Report of Lieut. H. M. Chittenden, January 26, 1892," #3513/1, RG 77; HMC to Chief of Engineers, August 8, 1892, #3513/9, RG 77; *ARCE*, 1893, 6: 4400; HMC to George S. Anderson, December 24, 1892, YNPA.

letter is unfortunately not extant, but he himself had no doubts of Chittenden's merit, having earlier written to the Chief of Engineers (without Chittenden's knowledge) when he first heard about his transfer: "I hope you will see your way to a revocation of the order,—or rather the assignment of Lt. C. to *full* charge of the work there, under a limited supervision by the Supt. of the Park. . . . I make this plea purely in the public interest,—still I wish to add that I regard Lt. C. as one of the most competent & efficient officers I have ever met."[31]

So far as personal arrangements were concerned Chittenden was pleased with his new station at Louisville. He wrote to Anderson: "I am fixed in great shape here. I have a fine house (gov't) in the center of the prettiest grounds in Louisville, with a great many conveniences and appurtenances which I would not begin to secure with my salary. So, domestically speaking, I am well fixed." He was far less pleased with his engineering duties that consisted of executing dredging operations, building two drawbridges over the canal, supervising routine maintenance and construction projects, and gathering commercial statistics about the use of the canal. Although of fairly commonplace nature, his year's work at Louisville did provide some engineering experiences that would be useful to him at later stages in his career.[32]

Chittenden's major achievement at Louisville and at his next station at Columbus, Ohio, was the composition of a history of Yellowstone National Park that he first published in Cincinnati in 1895 under the title, *The Yellowstone National Park: Historical and Descriptive.* Writing the book gave Chittenden the opportunity to satisfy a long-standing urge to write professionally that was traceable to his Cornell days. Although his personal experiences and his love for Yellowstone Park were the basis of the book, Chittenden's characteristic passion for accuracy and thoroughness required that he consult many other people in his research, and in the first stages of the project he was most fortunate to fall in with two ex-

[31] HMC to George S. Anderson, March 28, 1893, YNPA; George S. Anderson to Thomas L. Casey, March 26, 1893, #1433/1, RG 77.

[32] HMC to George S. Anderson, June 6, 1893, YNPA; *ARCE*, 1893, 3: 2543-47; *ARCE*, 1894, 3: 1935-42.

perienced authors, Elliott Coues, scientist and editor, and George B. Grinnell, conservationist and ethnologist, who became his constant intellectual companions in the writing of the book. Coues was especially encouraging and helpful. Chittenden also wrote to scores of others, including Arnold Hague of the Geological Survey; Nathaniel P. Langford, one of the creators of the park and its first unsalaried superintendent; and Superintendent Anderson, who was a principal source for data on the nomenclature of the park, statistical information on the number of visitors, and a record of congressional appropriations.[33]

Progress on the manuscript was slowed by this interminable correspondence, by awaiting the birth of his second child, Hiram, Jr., on August 4, 1894, and by the preparations for his promotion examination for the rank of captain which he attained on October 2, 1895. Feeling guilty at one point about his slow pace and his repeated queries, Chittenden apologized to Anderson: "I am afraid that you think I have been a good while at this work; but I came to the conclusion some time ago that I might better not do it at all than not to do it carefully. So I have tried to study out every detail and get it into shape so that it might be an authority." The problem of finding a publisher led to conflicting advice from his friends, for Anderson and Grinnell advocated government publication while Coues suggested a private firm. Chittenden finally decided against a government document for "not one person in fifty knows even how to proceed to get hold of such a book and not one in ten thousand would even hear of its existence." At Coues's suggestion he contracted with the Robert Clarke Company of Cincinnati, which in December 1895 published *The Yellowstone National Park*, dedicated "To the Memories of John Colter and James Bridger, Pioneers in the Wonderland of the Upper Yellowstone."[34]

Many years later Chittenden described his book as "some-

33 HMC, "Historical Work," CPHS; HMC to George S. Anderson, November 7, 1894, YNPA. In the YNPA there are many letters from HMC to Anderson referring to his correspondence with many authorities on the park.

34 HMC to George S. Anderson, March 28, December 19, 1895, YNPA; HMC, *The Yellowstone National Park: Historical and Descriptive* (Cincinnati, Ohio, 1895), p. iii.

what amateurish and freakish" but with his usual modesty he
underestimated its merit. *The Yellowstone National Park* was
well written and comprehensive and included a history of the
park area from the time of the Indian occupation, a survey of
its natural features, a sketch of the park administration, and a
description of the features the tourist would observe on a
journey around the completed portions of the Grand Loop.
Mindful of his recent struggles, he did not neglect to include
a defense of the integrity of the park against the mines, railroads, and other industries that sought special concessions
within it. Although leavened with a sprinkling of anecdotes,
the book was a substantial piece of work that found widespread
critical approval when first published and a continuing reader-
ship that justified revisions by Chittenden in 1903 and 1915
and subsequent editions after his death in 1924, 1927, 1933,
1940, and 1949. In 1961 the historical portion was published
separately by the University of Oklahoma Press in a new
edition. Sustained interest in *The Yellowstone National Park*
is not surprising, for the book is clearly if not graphically
written, contains an abundance of factual material, and inter-
relates successfully the historical and descriptive sections.
Throughout, the author's enthusiasm for the park is tempered
by his knowledge of its history, and although an obvious
partisan of Yellowstone, Chittenden never exaggerates or
misinterprets the attractions of the park or the tourists'
difficulties in viewing them.[35]

Begun while Chittenden was stationed at Louisville, the
manuscript was taken by him to his next station, Columbus,
Ohio, where he finished it while embarking on his examination
of the canal routes in Ohio for the Corps. The canal survey
proved both more interesting and more valuable for Chittenden's career than his earlier river and harbor work on the
Missouri and Ohio. The survey was engendered by a law
pushed through Congress by Senator Calvin S. Brice of Ohio
asking the Corps to investigate possible canal routes between
the Ohio River and Lake Erie and to assess the engineering
feasibility and the commercial advisability of constructing

---

[35] HMC, "Historical Work," CPHS.

such a canal. The statute called for the appointment of a Board of Engineers to make the survey but the members of the board, alleging the press of other duties, sought an executive secretary and gave the job to Chittenden on November 19, 1894. The board soon decided to narrow its task and to confine its labor to three routes, the Cleveland-Marietta, the Sandusky-Portsmouth, and the Toledo-Cincinnati routes. In actuality, the executive officer conducted the survey, a project that proved eventually of little use to either state or nation (as was true of most river and harbor surveys), but of great value to the development of Hiram Martin Chittenden as engineer and historian.[36]

Chittenden benefited in several ways from the Ohio canal survey. He had the responsibility of putting four survey parties into the field and giving them general guidelines for their report. This task, although not so exasperating as dealing with Ed Lamartine, did provide further experience in dealing with subordinates. He had to supervise the preparation of a great many maps for an atlas for each of the three routes surveyed and to see that drawings to illustrate the text were furnished. Much time was spent gathering commercial data from chambers of commerce, facts about the ideal size of vessels from ship-builders, and historical information on the Ohio canals from government documents. He wrote to county surveyors, con-sulted proceedings of engineering societies, and studied reports of boards of trade.[37]

After fourteen months of work in field and office Chittenden drew together the threads of his research and prepared his final report, a ninety-five-page document, with accompanying atlases, which he presented to the board on January 20, 1896, for transmittal to Congress. This lucid essay argued that it would be feasible to build a canal along any of the three routes —although he preferred the Sandusky-Portsmouth one—and advisable to build one provided Congress deepened the channel of the Ohio River for connecting traffic. The members of the

36 *ARCE*, 1896, 5: 2976-77; Benjamin LeFevre to O. M. Poe, August 27, 1894, #7464/1339, RG 77.
37 *ARCE*, 1896, 5: 2973, 2977, 2997-3006, 3043-44, 3046-47, 3059-91; HMC to Thomas L. Casey, April 17, 1895, #10709/2, RG 77.

board praised Chittenden's diligent labors, but Congress did not authorize the construction of the Ohio-Erie canal primarily because of the spread of railroads and their opposition to free water transportation. Chittenden thus left Ohio in 1896 with a sense of frustration, but he soon became involved in a different kind of survey, concerning irrigation and flood control rather than commercial navigation and involving the examination of arid rather than humid country.[38]

[38] "Report of Hiram M. Chittenden, Corps of Engineers, Executive and Disbursing Officer of the Board," in *ARCE*, 1896, 5: 2996-3091.

2.

Pioneer in Reclamation
1896-1902

When Chittenden was reassigned to the Missouri River Commission in March 1896, after the completion of the Ohio canal survey, he did not anticipate that he was on the verge of acquiring a national reputation in the field of reclamation. Opening his mail in St. Louis on an August day, he discovered that he had been ordered by the Acting Chief of Engineers to conduct a survey to locate prospective reservoir sites in Colorado and Wyoming and to investigate the functions of reservoirs in general. The genesis of Chittenden's new assignment was an amendment to the River and Harbor Act introduced by Senator Francis E. Warren of Wyoming and adopted by Congress June 3, 1896. The Secretary of War on July 30 allocated $5,000 for these purposes. Senator Warren frankly described his intentions in a letter to the Wyoming irrigation engineer Elwood Mead: "Of course the amendment itself is of very little if any value, but it is an entering wedge and a sort of notice served on the Senate that we in the arid region propose to be looking after the river and harbor bills hereafter." Two weeks later he wrote again to Mead, "We have got to keep this reservoir and irrigation business red hot all the time and as fast as we discard or wear out old schemes we must have new ones, for we must rivet and retain public attention and opinion to the matter."[1]

By the time Chittenden took up his new and challenging task, the principle of reclamation through irrigation was well known to the American public. The prehistoric Indians of the Southwest, the invading Spaniards, the Mormons of the Enclosed Basin, and private American interests in California and

Colorado had presaged the national irrigation movement of
the last quarter of the nineteenth century. In 1878 had appeared John Wesley Powell's report *On the Lands of the Arid
Region of the United States,* a blueprint for the use of the
arid and semi-arid sections of the nation through congressional
enactments that classified the public lands and permitted
ranchers and settlers to establish irrigation districts. In the
1880s the Corps of Engineers actually proposed construction of
a federal reservoir dam near El Paso on the Rio Grande.
Although neither the Powell programs nor the El Paso dam
scheme was executed, the idea of federal participation in
irrigation projects was well publicized by the 1890s when new
interests added their force to this thrust.[2]

In this decade Congress requested reports on irrigation from
the Geological Survey and the Signal Corps, congressional
committees investigated various reclamation possibilities, and
the Department of the Interior made recommendations for land
classification. In 1892 a Montana irrigation convention resolved in favor of federal governmental assistance in terms
anticipatory of the Newlands Act, and in the following year
the governor of that state recommended that the legislature
petition Congress on its behalf. In 1894 Congress passed the
Carey Act, which gave one million acres of the public domain
to each of the western states and territories if they agreed to
irrigate them by closely supervising private venture capital, a
measure widely hailed but disappointing in its results in that
little land was irrigated under its terms. Private individuals
were also organizing in the 1890s to pressure government
toward a greater role in reclamation. The leading spirit of this
crusade was William E. Smythe who founded the *Irrigation
Age* journal in 1890 and two years later summoned the first
National Irrigation Congress. Initially Smythe and his allies
fought for federal land grants to the states, but after the

1 *ARCE*, 1898, 4: 2815-19. Francis E. Warren to Elwood Mead, May 12, 27,
1896, Francis E. Warren Papers (University of Wyoming Library), hereafter
cited FEWP.
2 Walter P. Webb, *The Great Plains* (Boston, 1931), pp. 348-58; J. W. Powell,
*Report on the Lands of the Arid Region of the United States with a More
Detailed Account of the Land of Utah,* 2d ed. (Washington, D.C., 1879); Wallace
Stegner, *Beyond the Hundredth Meridian: John Wesley Powell and the Second
Opening of the West* (Boston, 1962), pp. 202-42, 310-13.

disillusion produced by the Carey Act, they turned to advocacy of direct federal construction.[3]

Chittenden's influence upon reclamation began with the speedy preparation of a plan for the survey and the quick approval of the plan by his superiors in order to meet the usual demand of Congress for immediate results.[4] He began the first phase of his work at his desk in St. Louis by gathering data on reservoirs from foreign and American libraries and from as many irrigation engineers as he could contact through correspondence. Then, as soon as ice closed the Missouri and halted river and harbor projects, Chittenden left for the first of three trips into the arid regions on December 9, 1896.[5] A week later he arrived in Phoenix after stopovers in Denver and Santa Fe and passed the next three days attending the meetings of the Irrigation Congress. Chittenden's chief personal benefit from these sessions was the opportunity to meet and talk with many individuals active in the irrigation cause including F. H. Newell of the United States Geological Survey, J. D. Schuyler, a distinguished irrigation engineer, and C. C. Wright, author of the famous California statute of 1884 approving the creation of local irrigation districts. His greatest discouragement throughout the session was his impression that the delegates and their guests were too naive politically and too divided internally to obtain federal aid, but he was pleased when the convention adopted a resolution in favor of federal construction of storage reservoirs. Following the close of the convention he departed by train for California, accompanying

[3] U.S., Congress, House, Select Committee on Irrigation of Arid Lands in the United States, A. W. Greely, *Report on the Climatology of the Arid Regions of the United States, with Reference to Irrigation,* 51st Cong., 2d sess., 1891, H. Exec. Doc. 287; U.S., Congress, Senate, Committee on Appropriations, *Report to Accompany H.R. 10884,* 51st Cong., 1st sess., 1890, S. Rept. 1466, pp. 46-136; Montana, House, *Journal,* 3d sess., 1893, pp. 24-25; U.S., Congress, Senate, Special Committee on the Irrigation and Reclamation of Arid Lands, *Report to Accompany S. 2104,* 51st Cong., 1st sess., 1890, S. Rept. 928, 2 vols.; Webb, *Great Plains,* pp. 356-58.

[4] HMC to Amos Stickney, August 7, 1896, #16519, RG 77.

[5] HMC to Secretary of State, August 25, 1896, #16893/1; HMC to Chief of Engineers, November 13, 1897, #14937/13, both in RG 77; HMC to Elwood Mead, August 17, 25, 1896, January 30, 1897; HMC to Francis E. Warren, November 18, 1896, all in Elwood Mead Papers (Wyoming State Archives and Historical Department), hereafter cited EMP; Chittenden described this trip in an unpublished manuscript entitled "Journey of Trip to Pacific Coast," in CPHS.

several leaders of the irrigation movement including Wright, Schuyler, and George Maxwell of San Francisco, the great propagandist of the reclamation crusade and later founder of the National Irrigation Association. At Los Angeles Chittenden said farewell to his new and valuable acquaintances and embarked on a vigorous tour of irrigation works that carried him in the next few days to San Diego, Escondido, Riverside, back to Los Angeles, and ultimately to San Francisco. He was active in that city, for he visited George Maxwell and Colonel Charles R. Suter of the Corps of Engineers and one day was called on by Mrs. Frances Fuller Victor, the historian, with whom he spent three enjoyable hours in conversation about the history of the west. Traveling by way of Salt Lake City and Cheyenne, he arrived home in St. Louis on January 8.

After his return to his office, Chittenden spent the inclement season reviewing the information he had gathered on his recent trip, organizing the working force for his forthcoming surveys later in the year, and attending to his routine duties on the Missouri River Commission, while Senator Warren fretted about his apparent lack of progress.[6] In May and August of 1897 he sent two parties under F. B. Maltby and Fred Bond, respectively, to help gather the data from which he would make his synthesis, and in late April left again for the arid regions himself.[7] He stopped for conversations with engineers at Council Bluffs and Cheyenne and thence moved on to Denver where he was especially cheered by an evening with Elwood Mead, who assured Chittenden that he wished him well in his project. On the fifth of May, having completed his preliminary inquiries, Chittenden was en route to the first of the prospective sites, that on the South Platte River.

Making his headquarters at the village of Turnbull, Chittenden traveled by wagon and on foot and reached the site of the reservoir in a thundershower in the later afternoon. Impressed as usual with the beauty of the mountains, the energetic and ambitious Chittenden reviled the lethargic inhabitants of Turnbull, a community rapidly becoming a

6 Francis E. Warren to Elwood Mead, February 6, 1897, FEWP.
7 *ARCE*, 1898, 4: 2834, 2879-86; HMC, "Journal of Trip to Wyoming and Colorado in May 1897," CPHS.

ghost town after a brief flurry of gold mining and realty speculation. "They would sit together on the steps of some deserted store," he wrote in his journal, "and mourn the timidity of capital in not seeking so promising a field. They all said that even a common prospector with no other capital than his pick, shovel, pan, and carpet, could make $2.00 per day. I wondered why some of them did not go at it." After dinner and a bed in a "questionable hotel" he took the stage to Platte City and then journeyed by train to Denver and Laramie from whence on the following day, along with an old classmate from Franklinville and the Laramie city engineer, he proceeded by wagon thirty miles up the Laramie River to visit the prospective site on that stream. After this punishing trip, Chittenden at midnight boarded the Union Pacific train for Rawlins to begin a day typical of the rigors of his western survey work.

From Rawlins he left by stage at 4:30 in the morning for Devil's Gate on the Sweetwater River passing through the Ferris Mountains in the cold and wind to find, successively, repellent food at a lonely ranch, desolate sandhills, and the unpromising town of Ferris. He stayed near the Devil's Gate at Tom Sun's ranch, a two-mile walk by moonlight from the stage stop. The two-day wagon journey of 130 miles, even he confessed, had tired him and justified his unaccustomed nine hours of sleep at the ranch. The next day he and Sun went to the Devil's Gate, a "perfect site for a reservoir dam," yet in his journal he seemed more impressed with the beauty of the surrounding countryside and its historical importance. He wrote, "The view from the summit of this rocky ridge entirely satisfied me that it is the locality mentioned by Irving as being passed by the Astorians October 28, 1812. I could not wonder that they stopped to reform and feast for one day when they came to the beautiful valley above this spot, for a more delightful scene I have not often witnessed." He noted also, as a historian would, the famous monument of Independence Rock along the Oregon Trail six miles in the distance and in the afternoon he and Sun visited it. Later in his journal Chittenden expressed disappointment that the earliest names carved upon the rock had been weathered away.

A few days later Chittenden and another rancher rode into the Platte Canyon, which Chittenden identified as the "Fiery Narrows" of the returning Astorians who passed through this country in the fall of 1812. Although he admired the interesting geological formations of the Canyon and the miles of beautiful prairie plum flowers, he did not find the place worthy of comment for irrigation purposes. What struck him most along the Platte was the presence of the Oregon Trail that paralleled the stage route for most of the journey to his next destination of Casper: "Romance and tragedy were written in every mile and the deep and abiding impression which the pilgrimage made along the surface of the earth is but a symbol of the deeper and more lasting impression which it wrought upon the life of the nation." From Casper Chittenden ultimately reached Cheyenne where he had a rewarding conversation with Governor De Forest Richards and then boarded the train for St. Louis, arriving home on May 17.

After another interval of office work, Chittenden made the third and final trip connected with the reservoir survey in August 1897.[8] Following a brief riding and fishing vacation with his wife and children in Estes Park, Chittenden left his family and continued alone to Greeley, Colorado. He made another visit to Cheyenne for more consultations and map study, and then took a short train trip to Wheatland, Wyoming, thirty miles from the crumbling remains of Fort Laramie. Chittenden visited the fort and filled two pages of his journal with musings about its history and about the endeavors of the various frontiersmen who had used its services. The next day, however, Chittenden was back to irrigation. In the company of Clarence Johnston, engineer for the Wyoming Development Company and later Wyoming state engineer, he surveyed the works of this organization and then pushed on to Sheridan, Wyoming, for some trout fishing and a visit to another abandoned army post, Fort McKinney. The next three days were spent in visits to Cloud Peak Lake and Lake De Smet, both of

---

[8] Sources for this trip are HMC, "Trip of August 1897," CPHS; HMC, "Some General Impressions," *Irrigation Age* 13 (1899): 195-202; Elwood E. Mead, "Some of the Agricultural Problems and Possibilities of Northern Wyoming—Impressions of a Camping Trip," *Irrigation Age* 13 (1899): 109-15, 149-57.

which impressed Chittenden as possible reservoir sites and
he deemed them worthy of further detailed survey by Maltby's
field party.

On August 18 Chittenden joined a party of sixteen men to
explore the country between Sheridan and Jackson Hole. The
first stage of the journey over the Big Horn Mountains was
uneventful although Chittenden found his destination colorful: "Arrived at Meeteetse at noon. This is one of the most
abandoned towns I ever saw. Saloon business was the only
prosperous one. Every hotel kept a sporting woman for the
convenience of boarders. The first night we were treated to
a succession of revolver volleys probably designed to excite
the alarm of the tenderfeet." After spending a few days
camping for pleasure in the area around Meeteetse the party
returned to that town, refitted, and laid in supplies for regular
camping, as the country they were about to investigate was
devoid of ranch homes.

On the twenty-seventh the party started westward, crossing
the Owl Creek Mountains and coming in sight of the beautiful
Wind River range at sundown. Their aesthetic pleasure was
marred, however, by fear that the notorious Hole-in-the-Wall
gang of that vicinity might assail them. The travelers spent
the next two days ascending the Wind River and then crossed
southwesterly over the Gros Ventre River and into the valley
of the Green, "that famous stream," whose history Chittenden
undoubtedly recalled from his study of the fur trade. On
September 2 the party doubled back to reach Jackson where it
divided, all going on to Yellowstone Park except Chittenden
who took the stage to Victor, Idaho. At departure time Chittenden felt cold symptoms which were hardly allayed by the
twenty-five mile ride to his destination across Teton Pass in a
heavy rainstorm that necessitated a ford of the Snake River.
At Victor, Chittenden engaged a stage driven by "one of
the most profane, vulgar, and repulsive men I have met," an
alleged grandson of the Mormon apostle Parley P. Pratt, but
a man who impressed Chittenden with his knowledge of the
art of stage driving. Ending his stage journey at Pocatello he
joined the main line of the Union Pacific and returned to
Cheyenne where he conferred with Senator Warren for two

days about the state of reclamation activities in Congress. Then he rejoined his family at Denver to return to St. Louis on September 11.

Before completing his report, however, Chittenden had some politicking to do based on his conversations with Warren. On September 27 he wrote to his friend Mead, then attending the meeting of the Irrigation Congress at Lincoln, Nebraska, and urged him to see that the Congress pass a resolution favorable to Senator Warren's reservoir survey project. He also expressed hope that the Congress would repeat its resolution of the previous year in favor of construction of storage reservoirs by the United States, but hastily explained to Mead that he should not infer from this suggestion that Chittenden advocated federal control of the irrigation works and their distributing systems, projects that he felt were within the purview of state and local governments. Three days later he again wrote to Mead, referring to a communication from Senator Warren which gave him the fear that the senator considered him "something of a special advocate of gov't. reservoir construction." Chittenden assured Mead that he was not a special pleader and that his forthcoming report would examine all sides of this question, but he concluded: "of course personally I believe in it."[9]

Chittenden finished his report on November 6, 1897, less than two months after his final return from the field. The completed essay, including three appendixes written by his assistants, was published in a *House Document* in 1897 and in the *Report of the Chief of Engineers*, 1898.[10] It remains a classic report that is tightly organized, lucidly presented, amply documented; it is without superfluity yet contains essential engineering, economic, and physiographic data drawn from a wide range of sources, both historical and contemporary, in the United States and abroad. Chittenden opened the report by declaring at once that his surveys of Wyoming and Colorado proved that reservoir construction was both practicable from

9 HMC to Elwood Mead, September 27, 30, 1897, EMP.

10 *ARCE*, 1898, 4: 2817-922; U.S., Congress, House, Committee on Irrigation of Arid Lands, *Preliminary Examination of Reservoir Sites in Wyoming and Colorado*, 55th Cong., 2d sess., 1897, H. Doc. 141.

an engineering position and desirable for the purposes of industry and commerce.

Specifically, he summarized his investigations of three reservoir sites in Wyoming and two in Colorado. In Wyoming he had assessed the Laramie River site about five miles southwest of Laramie, the Sweetwater River site near the center of the state, and the Piney Creek system in the west central region. In Colorado he had investigated the South Platte site and the Loveland site, each respectively fifty miles southwest and fifty miles north of Denver. His detailed investigations resulted in his advocacy of dams for all the reservoir sites and his preference for two sites, one in each state, the Piney Creek system and the South Platte, if Congress were unable to authorize immediate construction of all five. Whatever sites might be chosen by Congress, however, Chittenden strongly recommended that it should embark upon no project without obtaining absolute control of it. The government, he insisted, should acquire the site and the rights to the streams filling the reservoirs and should complete construction without state or private assistance.[11]

Following his analysis of the five sites, Chittenden in the remaining section of his report turned to a consideration of the theoretical function, practical application, and financial costs of reservoirs in general. Nature had supplied man with running streams, he wrote, but the flow of most was unreliable and inconsistent, alternating droughts and floods. For centuries, the engineer had attempted to control rampaging waters but with little success. Chittenden struck at this series of failures (and indirectly at his own Corps of Engineers) by condemning man's preoccupation with the symptoms rather than with the causes of floods. Concentration upon levees and channel excavations was unscientific, for the true scientist should engage in the task of assuring uniformity of flow, not the control of flood waters.[12]

Man could learn from nature how she controlled stream flow, but he could not always emulate her, although he had been attempting to do so since the infancy of the ancient

11 *ARCE,* 1898, 4: 2820-44.
12 Ibid., p. 2845.

civilizations of the Near East. The reservoirs built by man had served many purposes, he continued: to feed canals, to foster navigation on natural streams, to prevent floods, to furnish water for cities, to provide power, and to yield water for irrigation. But the fundamental purpose of each was to control the flow of streams so that it might be, so far as possible, equalized throughout the year.[13]

In accordance with the mandate of Congress, Chittenden next attacked the great and popular question of the relationship of reservoirs to the prevention of floods. Reservoirs, he wrote, need not be empty to function as flood deterrents, for even when full they served to slow down a flood and thus protected people below a dam by giving them adequate advance warning of danger. On the other hand, reservoirs were not to be considered panaceas for flood-endangered regions. In the first place, after a period of extended rainfall, even the largest reservoir filled eventually and the outflow equaled the inflow to it. In illustrating such a situation, Chittenden made an exact comparison to the influence of forests upon stream flow. The forest would restrain stream flow until it became saturated; subsequently it would have no more restraining influence than bare ground. Second, there existed cases in which a reservoir actually magnified flood dangers and destruction. On a large watershed, under natural conditions, flood waters from several tributaries might reach the principal stream at different times; however, because of the delaying process of reservoirs, tributaries equipped with them might send their waters into the main channel at the same time, thus increasing the flood dangers. In other words, the reservoir in and of itself was not the answer to flood control, although if properly managed it might be of great value to humanity.[14]

After proving to his satisfaction that reservoirs were not only desirable but necessary for the economic development of the arid West, Chittenden then faced the significant question of who should construct them. He canvassed five possible solutions and summarily rejected two, the private individual

13 Ibid., pp. 2849-52.
14 Ibid., pp. 2852-55.

and the private corporation, chiefly because neither could profitably build as large a reservoir dam as a site would efficiently demand. Chittenden also rejected Major Powell's plan for cooperative irrigation districts as a practical failure wherever it had been attempted, and he refused to accept state construction because large streams flowed across state lines and affected the destiny of many regions beyond the one where the dam was built.[15]

For Chittenden, reservoir construction was clearly a federal task, analogous to existing national forest policy: "If it is properly a Government function to preserve the forests in order to conserve the flow of streams, surely it can not be less a Government function to execute works which will conserve the flow even more positively and directly. Granting all that can be said of forests in this connection, they certainly can never prevent the June rise, and it is precisely this waste flow which reservoirs will help to save." The federal government also had an economic stake in building its own reservoirs since it was the largest landowner in the arid region, possessing, for example, over 90 percent of the land of Wyoming. To store the waters would appreciate the revenues of the nation.[16] Chittenden was careful to make clear that the United States should build only the storage dams, not the distributing canals, and that it should not control water rights. The only exception he granted was that the largest projects, involving vast interstate canals, would necessarily be built by the federal government.

In reasoning in this manner, Chittenden was not abandoning his usual faith in federal action even though limiting it in this way, for he did declare that if the government had embarked upon a "comprehensive policy" fifteen or twenty years earlier, then it "might have been productive of much good; but that opportunity had passed." State laws, state policies, and a professional corps of state water engineers had filled the void in the intervening years and thus circumscribed the national role. In sum, Chittenden advanced far beyond Powell, who never proposed federal construction, but he did not himself advocate a full "comprehensive policy" at this time and, in his hesitancy,

15 Ibid., pp. 2864-68.
16 Ibid., pp. 2868-70 (quotation, pp. 2869-70).

he did not go so far as the Newlands Act and its subsequent revisions.[17]

During the next few years following publication of the report, Chittenden labored with military duties, routine tasks of rivers and harbors, his second tour of duty in Yellowstone Park, and his book about the fur trade. Nevertheless he also exerted every effort to advance the cause of government construction of irrigation works. He began by planning a paper at the request of Elwood Mead for the annual meeting of the National Irrigation Congress in September 1898. His essay, reduced to a letter to the delegates and read *in absentia* at the Congress because of his Spanish-American War duties, was designed to meet the objections raised to his report, particularly those sections urging federal construction. He stated in the letter that government was different from private business and thus need not build dams for immediate profit. Nor did he accept the opinions of those who wished the government to recoup construction costs by charging for the water it stored. He was adamant about the principle that the increment to natural waters from reservoirs should be as free as increases from rainfall.[18]

Chittenden also plunged with characteristic vigor into the political issues of construction by assailing as too dilatory the Newlands bill then before Congress, a measure that proposed the appropriation of $250,000 for surveys of the arid lands. He wanted work to begin at once. Although disingenuously stating that it mattered not to him, he suggested that authorization for reservoirs might follow the same procedure as the development of a river and harbor project. Local interests proposed a plan that was appraised by the Corps, and then Congress selected from the approved projects. In clinching his point, Chittenden anticipated the multiple-use argument of the conservationists and their plea for unified control of waters: "A stream is a stream—one thing, from its mouth to its source. . . . It would seem to be at least a natural arrangement, that the department

17 Ibid., pp. 2870-71.
18 HMC to Elwood Mead, August 20, 1898, EMP; *Seventh Annual Session of the National Irrigation Congress Held at Cheyenne, Wyoming, Sept. 1, 2, and 3, 1898* (Cheyenne, 1899), pp. 21-24. The essay was also published in *Irrigation Age* 13 (1898): 32.

which controls the public works on part of the streams should control all."[19]

Chittenden's report was specifically endorsed at this meeting of the Irrigation Congress in a resolution of that body: "We favor the preservation and development of our natural resources by the construction of storage reservoirs by the Federal Government for flood protection and to save for use in aid of navigation and irrigation the flood waters which now run to waste and cause overflow and destruction, as recommended in the report of Colonel Hiram M. Chittenden, and we argue the adoption of the recommendations of this report as to the construction of storage reservoirs in the arid regions as a part of the national policy of internal improvements." Senator Warren, in a paper delivered at the Congress, also praised the Chittenden report and the passage of the Newlands Act of federal construction of irrigation projects, who endorsed it as a historical landmark and accepted Chittenden's proposal that the federal government should deal with reservoirs as it did with river and harbor improvements.[20]

In the five-year period between the publication of the Chittenden report as did George Maxwell, the publicist for 1902, the report gained increasing attention and support from many individuals and organizations that favored national reservoir construction. George Maxwell founded a pressure group, the National Irrigation Association, to agitate for federal construction. The Trans-Mississippi Commercial Congress supported the principles of the report in its convention in 1899 while Frederick H. Newell, chief hydrographer of the United States Geological Survey, in the same year singled out the report to support his advocacy of federal construction of reservoirs for flood control. Senator Warren was busy introducing bills for reservoirs in the Piney Creek and South Platte watersheds and obtaining the passage of a resolution asking the Secretary of Agriculture to investigate the commercial value of irrigation in the United States. Several news-

[19] *Seventh Annual Session of the National Irrigation Congress,* pp. 24-25 (quotation, p. 25).
[20] Ibid., p. 151; Francis E. Warren, "What Congress Is Doing in Aid of Irrigation," ibid., pp. 79, 145.

papers favored the Chittenden program and their editorials were presented in testimony before congressional committees. Chambers of commerce fell into line.[21]

Senator Warren also introduced an amendment to the river and harbor bill in 1899 which was a direct result of the report and which was prepared in consultation with Chittenden. Warren in fact hoped that Chittenden would be chosen to execute the work if the measure became law. This amendment had two parts, the first of which appropriated $50,000 for the construction of the three reservoirs on Piney Creek advocated by Chittenden. The second part authorized a preliminary survey of at least one reservoir site in each of the arid or semi-arid states. Warren relied heavily on Chittenden's report in defending this amendment and quoted from it extensively although he twisted it somewhat by implying that construction of reservoirs on the upper Missouri would reduce flood waters on the lower Mississippi. Such a notion was hardly what Chittenden believed.[22]

When the House of Representatives rejected the amendment, after it had passed the Senate, and its conference committee also refused to accept it, Warren and his western colleagues began a filibuster to kill the entire river and harbor bill unless the conference representatives from the lower house gave in. During his speech Warren again, by extensive quotation, publicized Chittenden's views. Finally, yielding to the desperate pleas of his colleagues who feared the loss of their river and harbor projects, Warren abandoned both filibuster and amendment, although he could take some consolation from the battle, as he wrote to Mead:

[21] *Official Proceedings of the . . . Trans-Mississippi Commercial Congress . . . 1899* (Wichita, Kans., 1899), pp. 164-65; F. H. Newell, "Report of Progress of Stream Measurements for the Calendar Year 1898"; U.S., Geological Survey, *Annual Report,* 1899 (Washington, D.C., 1900), 4: 39, 349-50; there is an extensive compilation of newspaper views on irrigation contained in U.S., Congress, House, Committee on the Public Lands, *Hearing on H.R. 12230 and H.R. 12844,* 56th Cong., 2d sess., January 23, 1901, which include favorable mention of Chittenden's report on pp. 96, 98, 103; U.S., Congress, Senate, *Congressional Record,* 55th Cong., 3d sess., 1899, 32, pt. 2: 1445, 1598; U.S., Congress, House, *Congressional Record,* 56th Cong., 2d sess., 1901, 34, pt. 4: 297-306.

[22] Francis E. Warren to HMC, February 13, 1899, FEWP; U.S., Congress, Senate, *Congressional Record,* 55th Cong., 3d sess., 1899, 32, pt. 3: 2268-82.

We have doubled and trebled, yes we have increased the interest more than twenty fold and perhaps fifty fold in irrigation and arid lands and the necessity of doing something to protect us in the West and to reclaim these lands—through the fight we have made in both these matters, but mainly on the reservoir question. I had them on the tender [sic] hooks all the day and night of the 3rd of March . . . and it was brought to the attention and consideration of every member of the House as well as the Senate that I had them where the hair was short for the time being; that they were liable to lose their river and harbor bill through their meanness to us.[23]

Chittenden was present at the Irrigation Congress held in Chicago in the fall of 1900 and shared the platform with Gifford Pinchot, the forest conservationist, George Maxwell, and Willis Moore, the head of the United States Weather Bureau. In 1900 General Nelson Miles, the most prominent officer in the United States Army and a long-time proponent of irrigation, published an article specifically supporting Chittenden's plea for federal construction of reservoirs in the arid regions. In 1901 Congressman Franklin W. Mondell of Wyoming testified before the House Committee on Irrigation that if Congress were unwilling to enact a comprehensive irrigation scheme, then it should begin in piecemeal fashion with already surveyed projects as in Wyoming and Colorado.[24]

In an article in the *North American Review* in February 1902, Chittenden assailed the critics of public construction who argued that federal aid was un-American and flatly stated that the building of reservoirs would enable the government to control the disposition of water and thereby avoid the historic evil of private monopoly of natural resources. He even returned to the proposition, heretical for one of his profession, that river and harbor work on the Missouri River was a waste of time and money and that on the upper waters of that stream

23 U.S., Congress, Senate, *Congressional Record*, 55th Cong., 3d sess., 1899, 32, pt. 3: 2817-43; Francis E. Warren to Elwood Mead, March 6, 1899, FEWP; Francis E. Warren to HMC, February 13, 1899, FEWP.

24 "Nation as Arid Law Reclaimer," *Irrigation Age* 15 (1900): 74; Nelson A. Miles, "An Unwatered Empire," *Irrigation Age* 15 (1900): 157; U.S., Congress, House, Committee on Irrigation of Arid Lands, *Hearing on H.R. 12844 and H.R. 13846*, 56th Cong., 2d sess., January 31, 1901, p. 71.

not half a dozen steamboats had passed in the last eleven years since he was first assigned to work on river improvement there. Now was the time, he argued, for federal aid to be diverted, at least on many rivers, from aid to navigation to aid to agriculture, because the true value of the West to the nation lay in that sphere, not in subsidies to largely nonexistent commerce.[25]

The Newlands bill passed the Congress and was signed by President Theodore Roosevelt on June 17, 1902, but Chittenden modestly attributed its success to western congressmen and cautioned that the projects authorized under it should be built slowly and carefully so that its enemies would gain no new weapons to assail it. Certainly he underrated his own role in bringing about this important statute that was a turning point in the national government's resource policies, but those individuals directly involved in the agitation for the law realized his role in larger proportions.[26]

Senator Thomas J. Walsh of Montana declared that "the report of Captain Hiram M. Chittenden on the storage of flood waters marked a new era in the national irrigation movement. It was probably the strongest single influence which turned the thought of our people toward the policy of national construction of reservoirs." F. H. Newell, the chief engineer of the Reclamation Service established in the Newlands Act, also ascribed great importance to the Chittenden report: "Following the report of Captain Chittenden, an attempt was made by Senator Warren and his colleagues to secure an appropriation in the river and harbor bill with which to begin this work. The continued agitation of this matter had great influence in the ultimate consideration of the reclamation law." William E. Smythe listed the Chittenden report among the great landmarks of irrigation history, for it "at last gave us a definite ideal to work for."[27]

[25] HMC, "Government Construction of Reservoirs in Arid Regions," *North American Review*, No. 543 (February 1902): 245-58.

[26] U.S., Congress, Senate, *Congressional Record*, 57th Cong., 1st sess., 1902, 35, pt. 3: 2221; U.S., Congress, House, *Congressional Record*, 57th Cong., 1st sess., 1902, 35, pt. 8: 259; HMC to Gilbert McClung, September 29, 1902, in *Official Proceedings of the Tenth National Irrigation Congress . . . 1902* (Colorado Springs, 1902), pp. 88-89.

[27] Thomas F. Walsh, "The Humanitarian Aspect of National Irrigation," in

From the perspective of a later period Chittenden's role in the adoption of the policy contained in the Newlands Act remains significant. He was the first person of influence to suggest that the United States government directly construct a reservoir system in arid regions. He spurned the contemporary western sentiments, personified by Senators Warren and Carter and Congressmen John F. Shafroth and Franklin W. Mondell, that the public lands should be turned over to the states or that the irrigation works once built by the United States should then pass to the states or to private enterprise. He demanded that interstate waters be controlled by the federal government and that water rights and land rights should be joined.

Chittenden's report appeared at a time when significant numbers of citizens were fearful of the impending closing of the traditional agricultural frontier and were desperately searching for alternatives. It crystallized sentiments and gave the proponents of federal construction a platform, although Chittenden rather uncritically accepted the plea to develop more farmland without making any effort to predict scientifically if there would be a need for those crops requiring further irrigation works. He was perhaps unduly pessimistic about the inability of private enterprise to finance single-purpose agricultural irrigation projects and conversely he overestimated the benefits to agriculture of large multi-purpose projects in the era before subsidized farming, special tariff benefits for irrigated crops, and the boom in prices afforded by the First and Second World wars. Although it is true that Chittenden, unlike many who felt that the settlers alone could finance the cost of irrigation works under the Newlands Act, realized that manufacturing and hydroelectric industries would have to bear the major share of the cost of the works, he still emphasized their benefits to agriculture. Like many Americans who had left the farm for the opportunities of the city, Chit-

---

Official Proceedings of the Tenth National Irrigation Congress . . . 1902, p. 22; F. H. Newell, "History of Irrigation Movement," U.S., Department of the Interior, Reclamation Service, *Annual Report of the Reclamation Service*, 1902 (Washington, D.C., 1903), p. 38; William E. Smythe, "The Influence on Irrigation of the American Ideal," Eleventh National Irrigation Congress, *Official Proceedings 1903* (Ogden, Utah, 1903), p. 190.

tenden was committed to preserving the agrarian heritage of
the nation when he wrote in words reminiscent of William
Jennings Bryan's Cross of Gold speech: "The industrial growth
of any country and its capacity for a high civilization depend
in an eminent degree upon its agricultural development.
Manufacturing and commercial interests may fluctuate, mines
may become exhausted, but the progress of the seasons per-
petually renews the productivity of the soil, and only the
indolence of man or the perversity of Government can impair
this elementary source of wealth and power."[28]

Chittenden personally relished the prospects promised by
the Newlands Act and yearned to participate in their realiza-
tion. After visiting the Irrigation Congress at Ogden in 1903,
he wrote in his diary: "How gladly would I relinquish my
position in the Army if I would have charge of a work like
that."[29] But indirectly his mark was upon all future irrigation
projects, for Chittenden was among those men who were
stressing the necessity for new methods of resource development to preserve the nation's agricultural heritage. His views
resembled, and in some cases anticipated, the ideas of that
small band of federal civilian employees, Pinchot, Newell,
W J McGee, and others, who would in the new century found
the organized conservation movement, a crusade that ironically
came to number Chittenden among its enemies. Like the
conservationists Chittenden shared the contemporary hope,
indeed confidence, that trained, scientific intelligence, represented by engineers and other applied scientists, could solve
the public problems of the post-frontier era.

[28] Stanley R. Davison, "The Leadership of the Reclamation Movement, 1875-
1902" (Ph.D. diss., University of California, Berkeley, 1952), passim; HMC,
"Government Construction of Reservoirs," p. 245.
[29] HMC, "Diary," September 22, 1903, CPHS.

3.

Assignments Multiply
1897-1906

Toward the close of the working season of 1897 Chittenden and his superior, Colonel Amos A. Stickney, were called before a subcommittee of the United States Senate Committee on Commerce that was investigating the causes of the spring floods of that year on the Mississippi River and its tributaries to discover preventive measures. The subcommittee was also concerned about the extent of commercial traffic engendered by waterways improvements in the West. In response to questioning by Senator Knute Nelson of Minnesota, Chittenden stated that he had little faith in the popular theory of controlling floods on the lower Mississippi by constructing reservoirs on the upper Missouri. The bulk of the Mississippi floods, he declared simply, came from the Ohio and its tributaries, not from the Missouri, but his experience with reservoirs in Ohio and in the Far West in the past three years enabled him to assert firmly that if a large number of reservoirs were built on the Ohio and on the Missouri, flooding on the two rivers, and the Mississippi, would be substantially abated, but the immense cost of a sufficient number of these works made them unfeasible. The only comfort he could give to the committee members was to urge the continuation of the traditional levee system on the Mississippi, although with some slight improvements.[1]

Regarding the second part of the subcommittee's charge Chittenden took a position that was less traditional in terms of the Corps of Engineers. He contended that the existing traffic on the Osage, Gasconade, and Missouri rivers was purely local, although he argued that Congress could make the two smaller streams navigable for the entire year at but small cost. Chittenden then bluntly informed the subcommittee that by congressional direction the scattered improvements made by the Missouri River Commission were designed to protect local property against flooding and erosion rather than to improve navigation for commercial advantage.

On the central question of whether or not federal expenditures for commercial improvements were worth the cost, Chittenden responded at some length. He stated without hesitation that federal expenditures in terms of existing commerce had not been profitable, but he argued that if the Missouri were developed comprehensively—as was the original charge of the Commission—then "there would be an important regular commerce on the river. There is every reason to think that such would be the case." Although this position was somewhat contradictory to his earlier opinion that no amount of federal subsidy could revive river commerce killed by the railroad, it is explicable by Chittenden's conversion to a view widely held at the end of the century, and one that he stressed to the senators on the Committee, that the real value of stimulating waterways traffic was to regulate railroad rates by providing competition. In any case, regardless of the merits of these theories of river development, Chittenden had little opportunity to test them because the Spanish-American War presented him with a grim substitute for past routine.

On May 9, 1898, twelve days after Congress declared war on Spain, Chittenden was appointed lieutenant colonel of United States Volunteers and assigned the position of chief engineer of the Fourth Army Corps. By his own confession, Chittenden had some misgivings about his qualifications to handle this important position, undoubtedly because of his lack of experience in commanding troops, but he welcomed field duty and eagerly awaited orders.[2] Finally, on June 1 he was told to leave St. Louis to report directly to Major General John J. Coppinger, the commander of the Fourth Army Corps in

[1] Chittenden's testimony is in U.S., Congress, Senate, Committee on Commerce, *Floods of the Mississippi River: Report to Accompany S.R. 76*, 55th Cong., 3d sess., 1898, S. Rept., 1433, pp. 131-38.
[2] HMC to John M. Wilson, April 27, 1898, #23244, RG 77.

Mobile, by the fastest means of transportation.[3] By the time he reached Mobile, however, he had to wire the Chief to send the equipment for the corps to Tampa, Florida, for the training base had been changed to that city.[4]

Chittenden moved with his corps to Tampa on June 8, where its mission was to participate in the training of troops for the invasion of Cuba and Puerto Rico, but if he anticipated playing a vital role in training troops for combat operations, he was to be greatly disappointed. Indeed, Chittenden was not even involved in engineering work for much of the first two months of his service but was instead given the inglorious and onerous job of paying the bills for the mass of hastily ordered and hence poorly recorded engineering equipment now pouring into the embarkation station for shipment to the Cuban front.[5] In the evening, sitting around the campfire in front of the big tent with the other officers of General Coppinger's staff, Chittenden listened to one of them read the war news. Although the results of military and naval actions were successful, the means to these triumphs greatly displeased Chittenden and his fellow members of the general staff, who felt that the military authorities in Washington were trifling with the lives of the soldiers.

During his periods of evening relaxation, when he wrote to his family and kept his diary current, Colonel Chittenden found much else to brood about. John Coppinger was a veteran of the Civil War who, along with the staff officers of other branches, had little use for members of the Engineers Corps ("one of the penalties of graduating with honors from West Point," he wrote sarcastically). Chittenden incongruously caught a cold in the tropical heat that otherwise threatened to prostrate him, felt disappointment that the Fourth Corps was not being sent to Cuba or Puerto Rico, and became contemptuous of the orders and counterorders, the assignments

3 HMC to Chief of Engineers, June 1, 1898, #26244/3, RG 77; HMC, "Diary," June 10, 1899, CPHS.

4 Unless otherwise cited, the following account of Chittenden's service in the Spanish-American War is drawn from HMC to John M. Wilson, January 20, 1899, unnumbered, RG 77.

5 This affair is described in HMC to Adjutant General, July 25, 1898, #27875/2; William M. Black to Adjutant General, August 26, 1898, #27875/3, both in RG 77.

and reassignments, that frustrated the work of his engineering unit. On one occasion, his diary significantly records an evening spent with the Book of Job.

To a man of Chittenden's passion for service, consciousness of reputation, and zeal for order, the war had been a lengthy fiasco of little credit either to his corps or to himself. Never wholly discouraged, however, he wrote on August 1, 1898, a remarkable letter to General John M. Wilson, Chief of Engineers, that so typifies its author that it deserves quotation. Frustrated and heavily overburdened with thankless tasks, Chittenden saw one honorable way to use the war to perform a notable service to the nation. He wrote:

The present course of events indicates that an opportunity for active service in this war will not be afforded to the officers of the staff of the 4th Army Corps . . . I am ambitious for work, and if nothing offers in the military line, I hope that there may be something in the civil line—for which, indeed, my past experience better qualifies me.

In the event of an early peace, and of our acquisition of the Island of Puerto Rico, it has occurred to me that it would be a very desirable and useful thing, both to the President and to Congress, to know definitely what this island is, its topography, roads, rivers, harbors, coast, cities, etc. etc. I wish that I might have an opportunity to make such a survey—it would really mean more to me than almost any other service, and would leave me more than satisfied with my share in this war . . . I have always taken a great interest in the history of explorations of the far west by officers of our Corps and have regretted that there seemed to be in the future no opportunity for similar work.

I believe that a very complete survey of the Island of Puerto Rico can be completed, and a report concluded, in time for use at the latter part of the next Session of Congress. Such a survey and report would embrace a good contour map of the island, showing all important features, cultivable and cultivated lands, and, in fact, all matters a careful map is expected to contain. The report should embrace an historical sketch of the island, with a complete description of its present condition—its geography, fauna, flora, resources, industries, rivers, people, institutions etc. etc. It should be illustrated by a judicious selection of photographs.[6]

[6] HMC to John M. Wilson, August 1, 1898, #27825, RG 77.

General Wilson replied that he knew of no more qualified officer in the entire army to undertake such a task, but that if the island were retained in the peace settlement, its survey would be undertaken by the civilian Coast and Geodetic Survey rather than the War Department.[7]   Undoubtedly disappointed by General Wilson's reply, Chittenden perhaps took some consolation in the fact that he was to be transferred to a new station.

On August 10 he departed, without reluctance, from Tampa to accompany the Fourth Corps to its new post at Huntsville, Alabama, where it was to continue its training mission. Perhaps at this new station Chittenden would have more satisfying work than that of Tampa which he described to his friend Elwood Mead: "I am greatly disappointed in the lot which fell to me in this war of not seeing any war service. But it may be best, for bullets or sickness might have disqualified me for future work. My actual duties have been of the most vexing character and not in any sense to be compared with those which I have had heretofore."[8]

Chittenden's chief mission at Huntsville was to select camp sites for infantry and cavalry units and to supply these camps with water, but in addition he became responsible for much road repair. He supervised the preparation of a topographical map of the entire valley and made maps of the different encampments. He was in charge of miscellaneous construction and repair work by the engineer troops and collected from various sources a good set of engineering instruments. As a final chore he had to undergo the frustration of supervising the transportation of surplus equipment from Tampa, Florida, to Willets Point, New York, when the war ended.[9] As part of his official duties Chittenden performed a useful service to the city of Huntsville. Both the government camps and the municipality required an addition to the water supply and Chittenden constructed a new waterworks, the one permanent accomplishment he left to the people of the Huntsville valley.[10]

[7] John M. Wilson to HMC, August 3, 1898, ibid.

[8] HMC to Elwood Mead, August 20, 1898, Papers of the State Engineer, Wyoming State Archives and Historical Department, Cheyenne.

[9] HMC to John M. Wilson, September 3, 1898, #27048/27, RG 77.

Although Chittenden found the experience of camp life in Alabama preferable to that of Florida, he never fully adjusted to the way of the military. His diary gives the impression that he did not fit into the camaraderie of Coppinger's staff, whose members delighted in teasing him about being a teetotaler, chaffing him unmercifully about his "debauch" the night he drank "about a teacupful" of champagne when the mess table was toasting a fellow officer's promotion. Yet General Coppinger praised his engineering ability, one of the few consolations of life at Camp Wheeler.[11]

The most welcome balm was the visit of his family. On October 1, Chittenden obtained leave to travel to Detroit where he met his wife and children and then accompanied them to Camp Wheeler via stopovers at Cincinnati and Louisville. His family boarded with Mrs. Chapman, who ran a dairy in Huntsville, until their departure for Michigan in December. Their stay was pleasant, including outings in the surrounding countryside and musical evenings in town, and during it Colonel Chittenden celebrated his fortieth birthday on October 25, which event was not so pleasant. On that date he told his diary: "I wanted to have my two books on western history finished now and should have had the war not interfered. Its recompenses have been small return for the delay I have suffered in a work I valued at no small importance."[12]

On January 30, 1899, the break with the life of regular routine military duty became permanent as Chittenden's tour of active duty ended. He lingered a few days in Huntsville to complete his work for the city (which finally paid him $500 for it), reading in his evening hours Prescott's *History of the Conquest of Mexico*. On Lincoln's Birthday he was ordered back to St. Louis, for which assignment he was "most pleased," and he arrived at the Burr Hotel in that city on another anniversary, February 15, a date that was suitably noted in his diary:

---

10 Elizabeth H. Chapman, "Changing Huntsville, 1890-1899" (Master's thesis, Columbia University, 1933), pp. 32-33, 49-50; City of Huntsville, "Minute Book," September 20, October 4, 18, 1898.

11 HMC, "Diary," August 31, September 24, 1898, CPHS.

12 Ibid., September-December, 1898, passim, CPHS.

Today is the anniversary of the destruction of the Maine. . . . The outcome of the war has been most gratifying to me. I cannot share at all in the sentiments of those who are opposed to carrying our flag to the islands of the sea. . . . Nations like individuals grow with years and the truly rational view is to foster such growth in every legitimate way. If our institutions of government are what we claim for them, why should it be such a calamity to the inhabitants of the Philippines to extend them there. . . . To my personal ambitions the war was a disappointment in that it did not give me the slightest opportunity for foreign service. . . . While the work I performed may have been quite as essential and important as any I might have done in an active campaign, and while it is work absolutely necessary to be done, still it is not of a character to attract public attention, and the meed of fame, so dear to the soldiers [*sic*] ambition is not to be found in such duty.[13]

He was grateful that his superiors had praised his work and that he had done useful service for the city of Huntsville, but he could hardly have been satisfied with his military service that ended with his discharge from the United States Volunteers on February 25, 1899.[14]

Chafed by the boredom of his Spanish-American War service and disheartened by failure to obtain the Puerto Rican project, Chittenden returned to St. Louis and the Missouri River Commission in the summer of 1899. He resumed his work on the upper Missouri, Osage, and Gasconade rivers and, although in general he found it no more appealing than before the war, he did draw some assignments that were either challenging or provocative. The first of these was to resume the construction of Lock and Dam Number One on the Osage River which he had begun before his military service, an undertaking that Congress had authorized as long ago as 1890. As funds permitted, Chittenden worked on this project for the next seven years and had almost completed it when on January 29, 1906, "to the great surprise of all concerned" (as a subsequent report mildly put it) pier number three suddenly sank beneath the waters of the Osage carrying with it about twenty feet of the completed dam. Chittenden's embarrassment at the collapse

13 Ibid., January 30, February 8-9, 12, 15, 1899, CPHS.
14 Ibid., June 11, 18, August 12, November 21, 1899, CPHS.

of the dam was certainly matched by his relief that he had already been transferred to Seattle when demands for an investigation became vehement. His successor did make a thorough survey of the fiasco of the dam and concluded, rather gently, that Chittenden had made some mistake in estimating the character of the river bottom, but he said he could not be precise about the nature of the error.[15]

Far more pleasurable for Chittenden was his work as chief engineer of a monument in Sioux City, Iowa, honoring Sergeant Charles Floyd, a trusted member of the Lewis and Clark Expedition who had died near that city on the outward journey and who was the first American soldier to die west of the Mississippi. A private group, the Floyd Memorial Association, raised most of the construction costs of the monument, and Congress contributed the balance as well as the services of Chittenden as architect and engineer. Between trips to Yellowstone, in the summers of 1900 and 1901, he worked on this small replica of the Washington Monument, a project appealing to his historical interest in western exploration, and completed it in time for dedicatory ceremonies on Memorial Day, 1901. Subsequently the Floyd Memorial Association presented Chittenden with an honorary membership, a handsomely bound thirteen-volume set of the *Life and Works* of Francis Parkman, and a resolution that properly labeled his services to the construction of the monument as a labor of love. The Corps also recognized Chittenden's work by choosing a model of the Floyd Monument as one of its exhibits at the St. Louis World's Fair in 1903.[16]

The year of the fair also saw Chittenden serving his first assignment on a board of engineers, a committee of officers

15 "Special Report of Conditions of Osage River Lock and Dam, Missouri, June 27, 1906," #10588/62, RG 77.

16 Reuben Gold Thwaites, *Original Journals of the Lewis and Clark Expedition, 1804-1806,* 7 vols. (New York, 1904-1905), 1: 114; *In Memoriam, Sergeant Charles Floyd, Second Report of the Floyd Memorial Association* (Sioux City, Iowa, 1901), pp. 1, 8, 18, 20-22, 36-37, 61-62, 100; *ARCE,* 1901, 1: 687-88; 5: 3827-33; HMC to John M. Wilson, April 11, 1900, #30331/28, RG 77; HMC to John M. Wilson, May 7, 1900, #30331/31, RG 77; Francis M. Davis to HMC, July 5, 1901, #30331/40, RG 77; inscription on flyleaf of Parkman volumes owned by HMC, in possession of his daughter Eleanor C. Cress; HMC to G. L. Gillespie, July 15, 1901, #36070/12, RG 77.

appointed by the Chief of Engineers to examine serious problems of a political or engineering nature that were beyond the competence or jurisdiction of a district engineer. In May 1903 the Kansas River (locally called the Kaw) flooded disastrously in its worst outbreak since 1844. Chittenden was chosen as the junior officer of a board of three to investigate the causes of this flood and in the fall of the year he participated in field investigations and in public hearings in Kansas City, Missouri, and in communities along the lower Kansas and Missouri rivers. The report of the board concluded that the floods were caused by the heavy May rainfall and were magnified by the railroad bridges across the river at its mouth and by the building of commercial enterprises, especially the stockyards, on the West Bottoms at the mouth of the Kansas. The board reported, with Chittenden's concurrence, that storage reservoirs were too expensive to construct and that the time-honored method of levees combined with a reduction in the number of railroad bridges would provide protection for the two Kansas Cities. But local sentiment opposed even this expenditure, the plan was rejected, the bridges were rebuilt, and the floods continued.[17]

Even before this plan had been defeated by the forces of apathy and parsimony, Chittenden was disenchanted with his work diking, bridging, revetting, and snagging the three rivers entrusted to his care. His greatest disappointment was the failure of Congress to appropriate sufficient funds for the systematic improvement of the Missouri River for irrigation, flood control, or navigation. In the year 1902 there were only twenty-one vessels on the entire stretch of the upper Missouri, 1,660 miles from Sioux City to Stubbs Ferry, Missouri, the head of navigation. As an important carrier of commerce the upper Missouri was dead, and in 1902 Congress abandoned its hypocritical lip service to a comprehensive program of river development by killing the Missouri River Commission, a stark denouement to a farseeing plan that led Chittenden to press

[17] The report of the board is published as U.S., Congress, Senate, *Kansas (Kaw) and Missouri Rivers*, 58th Cong., 2d sess., 1904, S. Doc. 160; Secretary of War to Chief of Engineers, March 22, 1904, #40262/115; Charles L. McClurg to Secretary of War, October 24, 1903, #48993, both in RG 77.

some new ideas about the use of river basins upon the Chief
of Engineers in his annual report for the fiscal year 1903.[18]

Chittenden began this report by calling the Chief's attention
to the rumor circulating throughout the upper Missouri
country that all work on the river would be abandoned now
that the Commission had met its demise. Using this rumor
as an opening to justify a full report about conditions on the
upper river, he argued that a policy of abandonment—should
it be adopted—would be disastrous to life and property along
the river. Rather than passively permitting this tragedy to
occur, he recommended that the Corps take steps to alter
radically its water resource programs in the region. Chittenden
did not blame the Corps for the decline of commerce on the
river, but he did declare that the amount of traffic was so
insignificant that the government had no obligation to spend
more money upon it for commercial purposes except for
routine snagging and dredging operations. Chittenden recommended that the government, in lieu of devoting all its
attention to these historic and largely futile pursuits, maintain
its rights to supervise bridge construction and to develop
harbor lines on the river.

More important, it should launch a new program of far-
reaching impact whose purpose avowedly would be flood control to protect the properties of the valley. This new enterprise
should be done frankly and explicitly and not as a devious
adjunct to navigational improvements. The difficulties and
dangers of the Missouri were unique, unlike even the Mississippi, for at least that stream had a consistent course at
certain places while the channel of the Missouri was ever-
shifting, and thus consistently and continuously destructive so
that it could not be controlled by any agency except the national government. As in the case of western reservoirs Chittenden regarded various other possibilities as demonstrably
impracticable. Private landowners, singly or in combination,
were interested only in their property and lacked the resources
even there to make all but the cheapest repairs. Municipalities

18 *ARCE*, 1900, 1901, 1902, passim, contain the data on Chittenden's river
work in these years. The original draft of the report is HMC, "Policy of Future
Improvements," in Box 2136, Gifford Pinchot Papers (Library of Congress).

and counties could build only within their boundaries and the states would never protect the banks of an interstate waterway, for they feared their upstream neighbors would not do their equivalent share of river protection. The United States remained the only source of protection for the banks and lowlands of the Missouri where it had the same responsibility for protecting against floods in the national interest as it did for constructing river and harbor improvements for navigation. As Chittenden bluntly summarized his program for the government: "It should abandon the policy upon which the work has hitherto been conducted, but not the work itself; which should be entered upon anew on a more rational basis." He brushed aside the constitutional objection because flood control works would also fulfill navigational purposes which the government clearly was empowered to further.

Chittenden had no indication of the reception of his proposals until the *Annual Report* was published in February 1904. When he discovered that his heretical ideas about the future of the Missouri River had been excised, he confided to his diary that he saw the point of the Chief's action and rebuked himself for being impolitic in criticizing his predecessors too vigorously.[19] Yet he refused to allow his thoughts about the river to remain stifled and seized the occasion of a paper on the subject of "Technical Methods of River Improvement" by S. Waters Fox, his former assistant on the Missouri, to publish his views as part of the discussion of the Fox essay in the *Transactions* of the American Society of Civil Engineers. In this comment he reiterated his ideas about the forces causing the decline of river commerce and the ineffectuality of the government's continuing its improvement work for navigational purposes alone. In a more popular form, and in more colorful language, he assessed the worth of the government navigational improvements: "The result? So far as its influence upon the commerce of the valley is concerned the same as if this money had been raised to build a railroad in Greenland. Not a boat more has followed the river than if the work had not been done." He did say that the work had been

19 HMC, "Diary," February 10, 1904, CPHS.

useful in flood control and in developing theories of river control and predicted again that the river's great benefit to humanity would be in stimulating irrigation.[20] But in spite of Chittenden's persistence his theories worked no immediate change in the top echelons of the Corps of Engineers and he come to believe that the Corps was downgrading his Missouri River work in retaliation for his radical ideas.[21]

In a larger context Chittenden's ideas for treating the entire Missouri River as a unit for flood control and irrigation in 1903 was a long stride toward the even more comprehensive plans for full multiple-purpose development of river basin water to include navigation, flood control, forest conservation, power production, and irrigation. These plans were to become popular in another four or five years through the speeches and writings of Gifford Pinchot, W J McGee, F. H. Newell, and others, and would culminate in the creation of the Inland Waterways Commission in 1907 and its subsequent offshoots. Certainly Chittenden's ideas were taken seriously by the advocates of multiple-purpose resource use. Herbert Quick, a popular novelist and inland waterways advocate, somehow obtained a copy of the unpublished report of 1903, passed it on to Marshall O. Leighton of the Geological Survey, who gave it to Gifford Pinchot with the comment: "This report was never published and it is understood that it was suppressed for certain reasons which you may well imagine. It is suspected that the original is on file in the office of the Chief of Engineers, U.S.A. Thinking that perhaps you may not have seen it, I send this copy."[22] Presumably it would make excellent ammunition against the tradition-bound Corps as well as reinforcing the intellectual foundation of the multiple-purpose conservation theorists. In any case the suppressed report was known to members of the Inland Waterways Commission and

[20] Fox, "Technical Methods of River Improvement as Developed on the Lower Missouri River, by the General Government, from 1876, to 1903," *Transactions of the American Society of Civil Engineers* 54 (1905): 280-326. HMC's discussion of this paper is in ibid., pp. 336-42; HMC, *History of Early Steamboat Navigation on the Missouri River: Life and Adventures of Joseph La Barge*, 2 vols. (New York, 1903), 2: 447-48 (quotation, p. 423).

[21] HMC, "Diary," February 10, 1904, CPHS.

[22] M. O. Leighton to Gifford Pinchot, November 12, 1907, Box 2137, Gifford Pinchot Papers.

may have played a part in the formulation of its seminal report published in 1908. At the very least Chittenden's report was a contributory force to the general climate of opinion then developing in favor of fuller use of water resources.

The report of 1903 and its sequel in the *Transactions* demonstrate Chittenden's flexibility and his willingness to challenge the orthodox thinking of the Corps. His hatred of waste and inefficiency, a sentiment that was the hallmark of the engineer, forced him to speak out against the old system that was of benefit only to a few localities and their supporters in Congress. His service with the national government gave him a broader allegiance than that of local property owners and a confidence in the probity and competence of the federal employees, particularly those in the Corps.

In the summer of 1905 General Alexander Mackenzie, the Chief of Engineers, gave Chittenden his second assignment as a member of a board of engineers, this time as chairman. His task was to inquire into the operations of the five reservoirs at the upper reaches of the Mississippi River in northern Minnesota. Chittenden was a natural choice for chairman because of his experience on the Kansas River board and because of his familiarity with the reservoir system. Chittenden had come to know the upper Mississippi when stationed in the St. Paul district office from 1891 to 1893. He had returned to this area in 1901 when he was in charge of improvements on Lock and Dam Numbers One and Two between St. Paul and Minneapolis, the operation of the reservoirs, and other minor river and harbor work in the district. Although the chairman-ship of a board was a distinction for Chittenden, who had been appointed to the rank of major on January 23, 1904, it could not have come at a less propitious time, for he was completing road work in Yellowstone and also was suffering great physical pain and intermittent paralysis in his back and legs, a condition that had been growing worse during the past few years. Still he had to accept the assignment, unless he asked to be excused, and every excuse, granted or otherwise, could be a blot upon an officer's record. So Chittenden plunged ahead and gathered his fellow board members, Captain William V. Judson and Major Charles L. Potter, for an organizational session at St.

Paul on August 14, 1905, to examine the issues and to plan the itinerary of the board.[23]

Following authorization of the project by Congress in 1880, two dams were completed in 1884, and by 1905 there were five completed reservoirs, Winnibigoshish, Leech, Pokegama, Sandy, and Pine, stretching from 413 to 185 miles above St. Paul on the Mississippi and its tributaries. The function of the reservoirs was to entrap the spring floods and to release them in the dry season so that navigation and milling along the length of the river from the reservoirs to the Twin Cities could proceed efficiently regardless of the season of the year.[24]

To some the system was more effective in theory than in function. In late May 1905 the citizens of Aitkin, Minnesota, were flooded and approximately $50,000 of their property was destroyed.[25] They demanded that Major George M. Derby, district officer in St. Paul, close the dams to reduce the flood waters. Constituents pressured Senator Knute Nelson for action and he wrote to the Chief of Engineers to see if the reservoirs were magnifying the flood. When the Chief called for an explanation, Major Derby stated that no operation of the reservoir system could satisfy all the different enterprises on the upper Mississippi. These enterprises numbered seven: the steamboat operators above and below St. Paul; the logging mills at, below, and above Minneapolis; the riparian owners on the river; and the riparian owners on the shores of the reservoirs. Derby contended that he had managed the reservoirs to appease to some extent all the groups except the riparian owners along the reservoir shores, who had been compensated by Congress in 1890 for the overflow of their lands.[26]

After the flood waters receded, the rumor began to circulate in the Twin Cities and to the north that interested parties were agitating to force the government to abandon the reservoir

[23] Chief of Engineers to HMC, July 22, 1905, #49126/14, RG 77; "Report of Board of Engineers upon Matters Connected with the Operation of the Reservoirs at the Headwaters of the Mississippi River," *ARCE*, 1906, 2: 1443, hereafter cited as "Report."

[24] Ibid., pp. 1444-45, 1447.

[25] Ibid., p. 1459.

[26] Knute Nelson to Alexander Mackenzie, May 16, 1905, #49126/14, RG 77, with endorsements by Major Derby.

system for their own nefarious purposes. William de la Barre, attorney for the water power companies in Minneapolis, wrote to former Congressman William D. Washburn, the father of the system, that speculators were in favor of abandonment so that they could obtain the flowage lands that, when dry, would revert to their original owners. Also in favor of this retreat was the Neils Lumber Company at Cass Lake that had built on flowage lands confident that the government would never flood its mills. The spokesman of the land grabbers, de la Barre wrote, was the *Duluth News Tribune* seconded by the Cass Lake newspaper. At Grand Rapids, he continued, the United States Paper Trust had a mill that was overbuilt and was demanding 2,000 more cubic feet per second than Major Derby could safely supply to them without sacrificing the other interests along the river. Seizing on another rumor de la Barre wrote that General Mackenzie was to appoint an investigating board of engineers and urged Washburn to write to the general to urge exactly that purpose. He also recommended that the commercial clubs or boards of trade in the Twin Cities commence counteragitation and concluded by stating ominously that Derby had informed him that their enemies had gained the support of influential men including officers of the government.[27] Derby himself meanwhile was supplying arguments to the Duluth Commercial Club attempting to place the blame for agitation upon land speculators.[28]

On July 22 Mackenzie appointed the board and made Chittenden the chairman whose orders were to listen carefully to the complainants and to see if they were justified in their objections to the policies of the district officer, always bearing in mind the purpose of the building of the reservoir system— the protection of navigation. Mackenzie concluded: "While the Chief of Engineers is thoroughly satisfied from the reports of the district officer that the past administration of the work has been in the best interests of the public, he desires to have available the record of an independent investigation to meet the criticisms which he anticipates at the next session of

27 William de la Barre to W. D. Washburn, July 19, 1905, #49126/26, RG 77.
28 George M. Derby to H. V. Eva, Secretary, Duluth Commercial Club, July 25, 1905, St. Paul District Letters Sent (Operations), 3, RG 77.

Congress, if not earlier."[29] Chittenden thus was to conduct a most unusual investigation. He was to discover evidence that would exonerate the district officer, whom he knew well and had previously corresponded with on cordial terms, and yet he had to conduct an impartial examination that would bring out all the facts. Even if his health had been good, the task would have been difficult, ensnared with political complications as it was.

On September 12 in St. Paul Major Chittenden opened the first of the board's public hearings. He first outlined the procedures for the hearing and then stated that its purpose was to test the accuracy of the complaints against the operations of the reservoirs by the district officer. Although he announced that the Chief of Engineers was satisfied with the conduct of the district officer, he promised to conduct the investigation "in a spirit of perfect fairness." After the completion of these preliminaries, the various complainants were called to testify in elaboration of their written briefs which had been presented previously.[30]

Much of the testimony of the adverse witnesses overlapped, but several strands stood out. All took pains to deny that they favored the abandonment of the reservoirs, a position uniformly attributed to them by their opponents. The agricultural, or possibly land speculation, interests about Aitkin contended that the flooding was greater because of the mismanagement of the dams than it would have been without the dams. As their attorney put it when assailing the government for constructing the reservoirs: "It has loaded these great water guns to the muzzle, and turning them upon 100,000 acres, has discharged them on the defenseless log huts and tarpapered dwellings of the homesteaders." Counsel for the Neils Lumber Company at Cass Lake argued that the company had suffered when the rising waters in the spring had flooded its mills. Major George L. Scott, the Indian agent for the vicinity, further testified that lands of the Indians had been inundated. Counsel for the people of Grand Rapids contended that the local lumber mills

[29] Office Chief of Engineers to HMC, July 22, 1905, #49126/14, RG 77.
[30] This description of the hearings is drawn from the transcript located in RG 77.

lacked water for logging and power and that the government, although correct in favoring navigation as its primary purpose in operating the reservoirs, discriminated in its distribution of incidental benefits to manufacturing.

The businesses satisfied with existing operations then took their turn. Defenders of Major Derby's methods were the water power plants at Sauk Rapids, the St. Paul Commercial Club, Congressman Frederick C. Stevens of St. Paul, Minnesota, the paper company at Sauk Rapids, the Little Falls Manufacturing Company, Senator Moses Clapp (with some reservations), the city of St. Cloud, the St. Cloud Water Power Company, Rome G. Brown of the water power interests of the Twin Cities, the Minneapolis Commercial Club, and former Congressman Washburn. These groups maintained that the reservoir system should not be abandoned and that the complete discretion of the district officer should be retained.

Following public hearings that lasted for three days, the members of the board dispersed to their respective stations to study the testimony and to gather additional information.[31] Years later Chittenden asserted that he could not accept the original draft of the board's report and was permitted to rework it to his satisfaction. Apparently Captain Judson was interested in deciding the issue narrowly by concentrating on Derby's operation of the system, but Chittenden took higher ground: "I was for seizing the opportunity and making the most of it, giving a comprehensive view with recommendations as to the future of the system."[32] In any case the last session of the board was held on November 27 to complete the report.[33]

The conclusions of this tribunal were as Chittenden desired, for there was no dissenting report.[34] The board first disposed of the complaints. It gave no comfort to the riparian interests, either white or Indian, above the dams. Similarly the board ruled against the paper mills at Grand Rapids. Finally, the board blamed the flood difficulties at Aitkin upon geography, not upon the reservoir system. After disposing of the specific

31 "Report," p. 1443.
32 HMC, "Upper Mississippi Reservoirs," CPHS.
33 "Report," p. 1443.
34 The recommendations of the board are in ibid., pp. 1452-74.

arguments of the original adversaries, the board launched into a defense of the reservoir system as a whole. It stated not only that the reservoirs benefited navigation of steamboats and logging rafts above St. Paul, but also that at that point on the river it was possible for the district officer to maintain a three-foot gauge nine years out of ten. Furthermore, in spite of some conflicting testimony, the board concluded that the reservoirs did raise the gauge even below Lake Pepin south of the Twin Cities. Businessmen on the river thus gained a considerable monetary benefit directly from the low rates for freight carried on the river and indirectly by keeping railroad rates along the river down to a reasonable level. Benefits incidental to navigation were also large; the board estimated that the milling companies obtained a benefit to the amount of $500,000 annually.

Turning finally to an appraisal of the operation of the reservoirs, the board recommended some slight changes in procedure that were hardly critical of Major Derby. Not surprisingly, the report pleased Derby, attorney Brown of the water power interests, and Senator Nelson, who, at the urging of Brown, wrote General Mackenzie demanding publication. The document did appear in 1906 in the *Annual Report of the Chief of Engineers*.[35] Controversy over the operations continued for a while but the reservoir system was preserved.

In this particular phase of his career Chittenden was shuttled not only from assignment to assignment but from region to region and the Far West was his next destination. When important decisions had to be made about the boundaries of Yosemite National Park, civilian and military officials, aware of Chittenden's services in Yellowstone, called upon him for expert assistance. Yosemite National Park was created in a piecemeal process that exacerbated the usual problems of the early national parks in the period before the creation of the National Park Service in 1916. The United States ceded the Yosemite Valley from the public domain to the state of California in 1864. The surrounding highlands were declared

35 HMC, "Upper Mississippi Reservoirs," CPHS; Rome G. Brown to J. T. McCleary, December 19, 1905, #49126/45; Knute Nelson to Alexander Mackenzie, January 19, 1906, #49126/48, both in RG 77; *ARCE*, 1906, 2: 1443-74.

a national park in 1890. Neither area was well governed for lack of adequate finances and appropriate regulations. Private companies still used the area for mining, grazing, and other commercial enterprises to the detriment of the natural wonders of Yosemite.[36]

As far as the federal authorities were concerned, the chief problem was the private land claims within the park. Various solutions had been offered for this problem over the years: purchase by the government, exchanges for other federal lands, and the redrawing of the park boundaries. The privately owned toll roads, providing the only access to the valley, were another major annoyance to park officials and tourists. Three toll roads had been constructed by 1875, fifteen years before the federal park was created, and their high fees and poor conditions fostered a demand that they be acquired by the United States. Numerous investigations were made by Congress, the War Department, and the Department of the Interior regarding the toll roads almost from the time of their first completion, but the investigations changed nothing until April 28, 1904, when Congress passed a statute appropriating $3,000 for a study of the park by the Department of the Interior to determine which of its lands should be returned to the public domain and to select a route for a highway from the park boundary into the center of the Yosemite Valley.[37]

Secretary of the Interior Ethan A. Hitchcock requested that Chittenden serve as the senior member of the commission to study the Yosemite region and the Chief of Engineers consented, stating that Chittenden's "service would be of more value than that of any other officer, he having had much experience on the class of work involved."[38] R. B. Marshall, a topographer in the United States Geological Survey, and Frank

[36] Unless otherwise cited, Ise, *Our National Park Policy*, pp. 51-80, is the source of this and the following paragraph.

[37] U.S., Congress, Senate, Committee on Forest Reservations and Protection of Game, *Report of Yosemite Park Commission*, 58th Cong., 3d sess., 1904, S. Doc. 34, pp. 1-2, hereafter cited *Report of the Commission*.

[38] Secretary of the Interior to Secretary of War, May 18, 1904 (and later endorsements), #3839-A.C.P.-1884, ACP; E. A. Hitchcock to Frank Bond, HMC, and R. B. Marshall, June 14, 1904, #2012, General Correspondence Yosemite National Park (Records of the National Park Service, Record Group 79, National Archives), hereafter cited GCYNP.

Bond, Chief of the Drafting Division of the United States General Land Office, were the other two members of the commission. Secretary Hitchcock's instructions followed the text of the enabling statute except that he asked the commission also to investigate the recent application of A. H. Ward to build a road up the canyon of the Merced River into the park to reach his mining properties.

Chittenden's party gathered at Wawona on June 24 to plan its expedition. Since the park region was unserved by roads for the most part, the commissioners planned a fifteen-day camping trip with horses and pack mules, a soldier cook, and four civilian assistants. On the eve of departure Bond reported their immediate plans to Special Inspector W. B. Acker of the Department of the Interior: "We start in the morning, 6 o'clock, and I do not anticipate pleasant posterior sensations at the close of the first 28 mile ride—not having been in the saddle for some years. The membership of the Commission is most agreeable and barring necessary inconveniences and daily wear and tear of horseback and mountain travel the trip will I hope be pleasant."[39]

The expedition went off efficiently and by the ninth of July the Sierra trip was finished. The commission moved its headquarters to San Francisco where it conducted interviews with politicians and with "John Muir, who represents the best sentiment of the country in favor of preserving the Park." Later the commissioners met with state officials in Sacramento and then dispersed to their homes to prepare the final report: Marshall to gather the detailed statistical information on private claims and other data in California, Bond to prepare the maps, and Chittenden to draft the final report.[40] On August 8 Chittenden came to California to confer again with Marshall about the California matters and was able to transmit the final report to Washington on August 31, a little more than four months after Congress had passed the law.[41]

The commissioners had little internal difficulty in drawing their conclusions for the report, the actual writing of which

39 Frank Bond to W. B. Acker, June 26, 1904, #3403, GCYNP.
40 *Report of the Commission*, p. 3.
41 Ibid., p. 4.

was left to Chittenden who summarized the activities of the commission and its findings and recommendations in twenty pages of text and a few appendixes.[42] The commission decided to reduce the boundaries of the park to eliminate many of the private claims within it; in effect, this was a recommendation made necessary because the parsimony of Congress and its receptivity to large economic pressures made it impossible to keep them out. The report proposed that the park be reduced by 429.26 square miles, a reduction that would eliminate the greater part of the private timber claims, and practically all the mineral lands, but would retain the water resources like the Tuolumne watershed including the Hetch Hetchy Valley.[43] Anticipating the outcries of the preservationists who came to national attention in the later Hetch Hetchy controversy, the commissioners rationalized their actions by arguing that "well-chosen reservoir sites in the upper valleys of these streams, if judiciously utilized under Government supervision, would add beautiful lakes to the landscapes, maintain the cataracts through the season, and at the same time conserve the water for the people below."[44] The report suggested that, as a safety valve, the excluded lands be immediately placed in the Yosemite Forest Reserve where they would obtain limited protection by the Secretary of the Interior.[45] This reshuffling of the boundaries included the proposal that the government incorporate as part of the park the Merced and Tuolumne groves, "as fine an example of the wonderful forests of the Sierra as to be found along the entire range,"[46] but the commission failed to include within the park several areas of great natural beauty: the Devils Postpile, Red Meadows, Rainbow Falls, and the Minarets, although the Devils Postpile and the Rainbow Falls were made national monuments in 1911. This boundary settlement proposed by the Chittenden commission was generally well received; however, in 1906 adjustments were made that added a total of forty-one square miles to the park.[47]

42 Ibid., pp. 2-4.
43 Ibid., pp. 4-9.
44 Ibid., p. 9.
45 Ibid., p. 5.
46 Ibid., p. 7.
47 Ise, *Our National Park Policy,* p. 70.

The Gillett Law of 1905 embodying the commission's proposals was passed by the Congress on February 7, 1905, by a unanimous vote of both houses.[48]

Concerning the toll roads and the proposed road building projects, the commission noted that none of the three existing toll roads into the park followed the entrance proposed by nature—the banks of the Merced River from the western entrance to the park. Assuming that an electric railroad would be built to this entrance, adoption of the Merced route would reduce the travel time from San Francisco to the valley from forty-five to nine hours. The private road construction companies had not employed this route because the cost of building along the riverbanks would require heavy expenditures for removing solid rock to make the roadbed. The commission recommended that the United States government build this road along the Merced from the park boundary into the valley. It also recommended against Ward's application.[49]

The commission was uncompromisingly hostile to the existing toll roads. It declared that "the power of private parties to lay tribute upon travel through a national park set apart for their free enjoyment is naturally repugnant to the feelings of everyone not financially interested. It is a public burden in several ways which should not be allowed to continue."[50] The commission suggested that the government should purchase only those parts of the existing roads that would integrate with its planned roads for the park and at current replacement costs.[51] This was a blow to the road corporations that (with the aid of congressional allies) wanted the government to buy all their roads at exorbitant rates.

Finally the commission made some suggestions not called for in the instructions. It suggested that park headquarters be transferred from the extreme southern boundary of the park to the valley for greater efficiency in law enforcement and that the sadly depleted supply of game be replenished, although it admitted that there was an insufficient supply of range for

48 Ibid.
49 *Report of the Commission*, pp. 10-14.
50 Ibid., pp. 14-15.
51 Ibid., p. 17.

wild animals. Most important, it joined the swelling chorus of voices led by John Muir and Robert U. Johnson of the *Century Magazine* that California retrocede its valley park to the United States to form a new, unified national park comprising both valley and high country.[52]

The commission closed its report to Congress with specific legislative recommendations, four of which were significant: 1) that all laws affecting the park be repealed to clear the slate; 2) that a set of regulations based on those for Yellowstone be established so that the park might be efficiently administered; 3) that the sum of $100,000 be appropriated for beginning the purchase of private claims; and 4) that the government appropriate at once the necessary moneys to start building a road up the Merced River Canyon.[53]

Chittenden believed that the filing of the commission's report would end his work in Yosemite, but in this he was mistaken, for in January 1905 he was on the alert in the renewal of a campaign that had started long ago in Yellowstone Park. A railroad, this time the Southern Pacific, was attempting to secure the passage of congressional legislation permitting the construction of an electric line in Yosemite. At once Chittenden dashed off a letter to Marshall in California urging him to contact "responsible people" in his state to wire their representatives to act against the bill and at the same time he wrote a four-page letter to Governor George C. Pardee of California in which he argued that the railroad bill was opposed by the great majority of park visitors.[54] Chittenden also shrewdly reminded the governor of President Roosevelt's opposition to legislation injurious to the park.

The matter came to a head in July when Congressman James C. Needham of California wrote to Chittenden asking the position of the commission concerning a proposal of the Southern Pacific to build an electric line from Wawona into the valley. This proposition would necessitate a further

52 Ibid., pp. 18-19; Ise, *Our National Park Policy,* pp. 71-74.

53 *Report of the Commission,* p. 20.

54 HMC to Marshall, January 23, 1905; HMC to "My dear Governor," January 23, 1905, both in R. B. Marshall Papers (University of California, Berkeley), hereafter cited MP. Used by permission of the Director, The Bancroft Library, University of California, Berkeley.

revision of the park boundaries for the right-of-way and Chittenden wrote Needham that he would have to consult his fellow commissioners before responding to his request. Chittenden circulated a draft of his response to Marshall and Bond in which he strongly recommended on engineering grounds that the Southern Pacific build along the south fork of the Merced rather than over the divide (the "hill route"), the route that it was planning.[55] He also pointed out the political difficulties in again redrawing the park boundaries and the most serious problem of all, namely, the impossibility of convincing Congress to appropriate money for two government wagon roads within the park to meet the two railroad lines that ended at the border. If the company insisted, however, in spite of this advice, then Chittenden was willing to cut a little off the park along the Wawona road.

Apparently his colleagues on the commission made some suggestions, and he drafted a second reply to Needham on September 1. This echoed the sentiments of the first letter in more polished language and again enclosed the telling postscript of the first which showed his and the other commissioners' real fear: "P.S. I note on the map you sent me that the proposed route extends clear into the valley as far as to the Bridal Veil Falls. I take it, that this is not intended, as it is not so specified in the petition; but it significantly shows what was in the mind of the individual who sketched in the line. No such proposition could ever, in my opinion, succeed in Congress, for the whole United States would be against it."[56] Upon reading this second draft Frank Bond wrote him a cordial but firm note implying that Chittenden had been too lenient toward the Southern Pacific: "I have declined in my letter to Mr. Needham, written before starting west in July, to assent to any suggestion looking to a change in the western boundary of the park in any private or corporate interest whatever."[57]

Ever alert to his honor and to even presumed slights to his devotion to the public service, Chittenden replied to Bond

[55] Needham's original letter is lost but its contents are summarized in HMC to Marshall, July 22, 1905, MP.

[56] HMC to Needham, September 1, 1905, draft in MP.

[57] Frank Bond to HMC, September 18, 1905, copy in MP.

on September 29 (with a copy to Marshall in case he entertained the same doubts) that he was not proposing a change
in the park boundaries but only showing willingness as a last
resort to assent to it if the company insisted. He made two
major points in defense of his position. First he asserted that
the commission had erred in making the western boundary of
the park the eastern bank of the Merced River's south fork
because a railroad building along one bank might have to
cross for a short distance to the opposite side and encroach
upon park land. Bridges would also pose a problem in this
case. For these reasons it would have been better to place the
boundary elsewhere than on the river. To this view he also
summoned the support of Special Inspector Acker of the Department of the Interior. Second, Chittenden wrote to Bond
that the appropriations for Yosemite would largely be controlled by the congressional delegation from California and
hence it would not be wise to antagonize the delegation by opposing its proposal on this matter. Out of his long experience
and success in getting appropriations for Yellowstone, Chittenden wrote Bond, "It is better not to assume too extreme an
attitude in this thing lest our position become untenable and
we lose much in trying to save a little."[58] He knew that a
courteous response conceding a position that it would be
difficult for Needham and the railroad to maintain in the face
of public hostility was no loss to the interests of the park;
rather, on pragmatic grounds, it was a gain. A lifetime of
service with an eye to the Congress guided Chittenden accurately in this matter. The railroad did not enter the park.

The wisdom of the Chittenden policy of tact was proved
in another connection. In October, having allayed Bond's
suspicions, Chittenden was able to write Marshall that Needham had asked him to propose a bill for the proper administration of the park as the commission had recommended.[59] He
accordingly prepared one on October 18, 1905 (his experience
as a lawyer and in river and harbor works doubtless was of
help), drawing upon a variety of sources: the original enabling

<hr />

58 HMC to Marshall, September 29, 1905, MP; HMC to Bond, September 29,
1905, copy in MP.
59 HMC to Marshall, October 18, 1905, MP.

act for Yellowstone, the act admitting the state of Wyoming to the Union, and the general laws and appropriation bills for Yellowstone.[60] A few days after submitting the proposed administration bill, Chittenden reported that he had suggested to Needham that he drop the boundary change bill.[61] Later in 1905 Congress accepted the offer of the state of California, made the year before, to cede the Yosemite Valley to the United States. A single park now came into existence, one that incorporated both the high country and the valley, as the Chittenden commission, and many other groups and individuals, frequently had recommended.

Four years after Chittenden had filed his Yosemite report with the Secretary of the Interior, Robert Underwood Johnson, in preparing an article for *Century*, asked him a series of questions about the work of the commission. In his lengthy reply Chittenden claimed three accomplishments for it: the remarking of the park boundaries that Congress accepted completely (except for the slight and harmless changes in 1906), the retrocession of the valley, and the construction of a wagon road from the boundary to the center of the valley (although "by private parties under Federal permission").[62]

Chittenden's services were remembered with gratitude and in April 1905, Senator George C. Perkins of California asked the Chief of Engineers to assign Chittenden to the important post of California division engineer with headquarters in San Francisco. The Chief declined because Chittenden lacked sufficient rank and because his work on the Yellowstone roads was not completed. Two years later Secretary Hitchcock tried to obtain Chittenden's services for the construction of the government roads in Yosemite Park but was turned down by the Secretary of War because Chittenden was then engaged in important military engineering projects in Puget Sound.[63]

While in California at the time of the Yosemite investiga-

[60] HMC to Marshall, October 21, 1905, MP.

[61] HMC to Marshall, October 24, 1905, MP.

[62] HMC to Johnson, June 1, 1908, Robert Underwood Johnson Papers (University of California, Berkeley).

[63] George C. Perkins to Alexander Mackenzie, April 28, 1905, #55175; E. A. Hitchcock to Alexander Mackenzie, January 16, 1907 (with endorsements), #62103, both in RG 77.

tion, Chittenden also executed two minor projects in the state. The first of these involved the frequent floods on the Sacramento and San Joaquin rivers that had been endemic since the time of the original gold seekers and that had challenged engineers for decades. In the aftermath of the enormous floods of March and April 1904, a state river convention was called in San Francisco and its delegates passed a resolution calling for a government commission to recommend flood control measures. The Secretary of War appointed Chittenden to this body whose three members undertook an exhaustive survey, including fieldwork, in the last part of 1904 with Chittenden, who again was chosen secretary, presenting his final report on December 15. The commissioners advocated a program of levees rather than reservoirs for flood control on the two rivers, but the recommendations were never carried out because the Corps of Engineers scuttled the project as a flood control rather than a navigational improvement and the state of California also refused to provide the necessary funds.[64]

Before leaving California Chittenden did achieve a small success with another project. Senator Frank P. Flint of California asked the Secretary of War on behalf of the people of Riverside, California, if Chittenden could assist in the construction of a mountain road up Rubidoux Mountain in that city.[65] In 1905 the Chamber of Commerce had begun a tree planting project on the hill and Frank A. Miller, a member of the Chamber and a friend of Chittenden who had met him in Yellowstone Park, formed a private organization to secure title to the land. After completing the purchase, this association presented a plan for the road to the top and the public raised $21,000 to which Henry E. Huntington, the railroad heir, added

64 Robert Kelley, "Taming the Sacramento: Hamiltonianism in Action," *Pacific Historical Review* 34 (1965): 21-37; River Improvement and Drainage Association of California, *Bulletin Number One* (Sacramento, Calif., 1904), pp. 1-5, hereafter cited *RIDACB;* HMC, "The Sacramento Flood Problem," CPHS; "Report of the Commission of Engineers . . . upon . . . the Sacramento and San Joaquin Rivers . . ." in *Report of the Commission of Public Works to the Governor of California* (Sacramento, Calif., 1905), pp. 6, 11-14, 19-74; HMC, "Diary," September 25, 1904, CPHS; *RIDACB Number Four* (Sacramento, Calif., 1905), 1-31.
65 Frank P. Flint to Secretary of War, December 6, 1905 (and later endorsements), #57674, RG 77.

$29,000 for its construction. Although his health was bad and the work a physical trial, Chittenden spent part of his annual leave, from February 28 to March 10, 1906, in laying out a picturesque road for carriages and automobiles (his first work for that vehicle). On Washington's Birthday, 1907, dedication ceremonies were held with Jacob Riis, the journalist, giving the major address. Although Chittenden was not present at this occasion, his name was perpetuated at the highest point on the boulevard where several cannons and a naval anchor were displayed and the spot named Fort Chittenden, the third site now bearing his name in the West in addition to the Chittenden Bridge in Yellowstone and the Chittenden Locks in Seattle.[66]

During these crowded years of achievement and disappointment Chittenden was no automaton, relentlessly pursuing his professional objectives.[67] He devoted himself frequently to family activities while living in St. Louis from 1899 to 1901 and thereafter in Sioux City, where the Chittendens bought the first home of their married life in April of 1901. Nettie and the children always spent the summer working season with Hiram in Yellowstone Park, their favorite station without qualification. The elder Chittendens were quite gregarious, and they made many friends both in St. Louis and Sioux City. They were invited to various social gatherings—principally card parties—several times a month. From time to time house guests arrived, including Hiram's sister Ida, and the whole family enjoyed boat rides, trips to the world's fair in St. Louis, excursions to the levee, and other pleasant outings. In St. Louis Hiram and Nettie not only worked together on historical research but also relaxed together at special exhibits presented by the Missouri Historical Society and occasionally attended the opera. Rather infrequently Chittenden slackened his routine by hunting along the rivers, playing tennis, fishing, or by giving a talk on a historical theme to the Sons of the American Revolution or the Sioux City Round Table Club.

[66] Interview Eleanor C. Cress, August 3, 1968; *Riverside Daily Press*, December 31, 1906, February 22, 1907; HMC, "Diary," March 29, 1906, CPHS.
[67] This paragraph and the next are drawn from HMC, "Diary," 1899-1906, passim, CPHS.

His diary recorded his great satisfaction from unspectacular pleasures such as buying his sons a flute or bicycle and putting the Christmas gifts inside a teepee for the children to discover. Health problems—Eleanor's tonsils and young Hiram's pneumonia—caused anxiety for the parents, but apparently there were no major discipline problems and Chittenden's summary of his family's state on New Year's Day, 1905, holds for all these years, his own health condition the exception: "The rest of the family are all in good health, and are, I believe, as happy as any family in the land."

During the seven years of service after the Spanish-American War, Chittenden had exerted himself and maintained a high level of achievement. In their annual efficiency reports for these years Chittenden's superior officers, with one exception, praised him highly in all categories of work and in 1903 General Gillespie, the Chief of Engineers, recommended him for assignment to the General Staff. Inexplicably, in two years, 1904 and 1905, Colonel O. W. Ernst, division engineer of the Northwest Division, answered one question on Chittenden's evaluation form critically. Question number sixteen asked "Should he be intrusted with important duties requiring discretion and judgment?" to which Ernst responded: "I have some doubts upon the subject." During these years Ernst rated Chittenden good or excellent in all other categories, and in the year 1904 he did not see him at all, so there seems to be no objective reason for this critique that is the single black mark upon Chittenden's record although it did not injure him.[68] But, in spite of his accomplishments, these were also deeply frustrating years considering his labors on the Missouri, Osage, and Gasconade rivers. While Chittenden valued the road building work in Yellowstone Park, he needed a self-imposed task to supplement his periods of river and harbor drudgery and to salve his conscience about drawing his salary for that duty. This solution, as he described it many years later, was the writing of history: "Now began the experience which has been a source of astonishment to me ever since. I didn't care enough about the Missouri River to waste any unnecessary

[68] "HMC Efficiency Reports," 1897-1906, ACP.

energy thereon, for I felt as certain then as I do now that it would all be labor lost. I, therefore, had no compunction in directing as much of my time as I could to work which I believed would be of a great deal more use to my country-men."[69]

[69] HMC, "Historical Work," CPHS.

4.

Historian
1890-1905

Chittenden's passion for historical studies germinated as early as his college years and culminated ultimately in the production of three significant works on the history of the American West. Published within the space of three years were *The American Fur Trade of the Far West, History of Early Steamboat Navigation on the Missouri River,* and, in collaboration with Alfred T. Richardson, *Life and Letters of Father Pierre-Jean De Smet, S.J.* Chittenden's researches, in spite of his lack of formal historical training, yielded volumes reflecting the transitional historiographical era in which he wrote when the modern tenets of scientific research and the "New History" were blending with the older romantic interpretations. Regardless of its philosophy, however, his work commanded widespread attention among students of the West for decades and in the case of *The Fur Trade* is still regarded as definitive.

It is impossible to mark the moment when Chittenden first became interested in history, but it is clear that his preparation for historical writing was quite thorough by the time he was ready to write *The Fur Trade.* At Cornell he had received the rudiments of seminar training from Professor William C. Russel, and at West Point he had taken a course in history. His interest in law from his days at Ten Broeck Academy also demanded wide reading, especially when preparing for admission to the bar, and his familiarity with the rules of evidence was a help in historical writing. By the time Chittenden had left the Engineer School in 1887, his formal training, which he mourned as lacking in works of literature, had been supplemented by a self-study program running back to his days at Cornell that led him through the works of men who were great artists as well as informative writers, including Francis Bacon, Hugo, Hume, Milton, and Montesquieu. Although Chittenden's language training at West Point was one-sided—the study of written Spanish and French with no conversation—it was invaluable for one who was to go through thousands of documents in these tongues for his fur trade research.

Professional travel also prepared Chittenden for the writing of history. Not only had the Corps of Engineers given Chittenden the opportunity to see the West but also it had required that he report upon it. He had produced official reports of his annual labors for the Chief of Engineers as well as hundreds of succinct notes to the Chief's office. In addition Chittenden had published two massive special reports, the preparation of which had given him experience in synthesizing a mass of data from an enormous range of sources.

Chittenden's best preparation for his major historical writing was his prior experience as an author. Many years after beginning *The Fur Trade,* he wrote a fragment of an unpublished autobiography entitled "Historical Work" in which he traced the evolution of his literary ambitions. At one (unspecified) time he aspired to a career as a writer of fiction or of essays, but finally he fixed upon his true literary course:

My entry into the field of historic writing was purely accidental. I had become so discouraged over an [*sic*] prospect of ordinary literary work, and still my ambition was so strong to do something in that line, that I felt quite disheartened as to whether to drop all idea of such work or not. It is only when one runs up against the real thing, and finds how ignorant he is of the intimate experiences of life that he learns how little he is fitted for fiction and similar writings. . . . I had some faculty of expression, and if I had . . . some knowledge of facts I could have accomplished much more than I did. It was only when it came to things in which my line of information was special, that I could accomplish real work.[1]

---

[1] HMC, "Historical Work," CPHS.

His first "real work" in history was the publication of an article on Fort Benton in the *Magazine of American History* in 1890, which proved to be an interesting transition between his unpublished fictional efforts and his historical works. In the essay Chittenden examined the decline of Fort Benton as a river port, ascribing its fate to the advance of the railroad, and predicting that the United States government might more profitably expend its efforts on the Missouri River in irrigation rather than in navigation projects. A large portion of the article was a composite account of a "typical" journey on the Missouri that he had composed from consulting actual logs of several steamboat journeys. Although poorly organized, this short piece was the germ of Chittenden's interest in the history of the fur trade and steamboat navigation and was his first written expression of a belief in a multiple-purpose approach to river management.[2]

Writing the excellent guidebook about Yellowstone Park had forced him to delve into source materials and led him into a correspondence with two professional historians, Elliott Coues and Frances Fuller Victor. *The Yellowstone National Park* itself included memorable historical passages on the mountain men and the Indians, but acquaintance with Coues was Chittenden's "turning point" in the direction of future historical studies.[3] Thus, by the time Chittenden went to St. Louis in 1896 to work with the Missouri River Commission, his interest in the fur trade and its history was already manifest. Since that city had been the historic entrepôt of the trade, Chittenden, after consultation with Coues, decided—assuming the availability of records—to begin writing the history of the fur trade. An obvious need was source materials and Chittenden soon discovered that the Chouteau family, prominent in the western fur commerce, was still represented in the city. He got in touch with the descendants of the traders and was delighted to find that they would allow him to consult their massive quantity of surviving documents.[4]

2 HMC, "The Ancient Town of Fort Benton in Montana," *Magazine of American History* 24 (1890): 409-25.
3 HMC, "Historical Work," CPHS.
4 Ibid.

Permission gained from the Chouteaus, Chittenden set about his enormous task of research and composition. The Chouteau papers were the heart of his heuristics, and he doggedly began examining these letters, journals, and other business memorabilia that together made up about half a freight car of records. Chittenden reserved a small alcove at the boardinghouse where he lived with his wife and two small children and there prepared for the tasks of the historian. He dressed in workman's clothes every time he went to the Chouteau warehouse to select materials, for the records were buried in coal dust about three-fourths of an inch thick. Returning home, he made excerpts from the records with the aid of his wife, placing the brief ones on note cards and the longer ones in large notebooks. Since he had a full-time profession, his work was made possible only by the sacrifice of his evenings and weekends. Not unnaturally, his wife often protested that his labor would result in very little of benefit. But Chittenden persisted, even on the afternoon of the great St. Louis cyclone of May 27, 1896, when he left work for the security of the basement only at the last possible minute despite the repeated pleas of his wife.[5]

Insofar as his engineering obligations permitted, Chittenden sought out other source material. He went through the *Missouri Gazette* (later the *Missouri Republican*) line by line from its founding in 1808 until 1850 and found this journal indispensable. The *Missouri Intelligencer* was another key newspaper source, especially for the Santa Fe trade. Chittenden made the acquaintance of M. L. Gray of St. Louis, the administrator of the Sublette estate, who permitted him to consult the invaluable correspondence among the Sublette-Ashley-Campbell-Smith group that at one time formed the nucleus of the enterprise known as the Rocky Mountain Fur Company. He frequented the recorder's office in St. Louis for legal materials bearing upon the fur trade. He spent many hours in the Mercantile Library and the Missouri Historical Society perusing original documents and secondary works. On

5 Ibid.; John Devoy, *A History of the City of St. Louis* . . . (St. Louis, Mo., 1896), p. 60; interview with Eleanor C. Cress (HMC's daughter), August 3, 1968; HMC to Pierre Chouteau, December 30, 1896, June 2, 1898, Chouteau Collections, Missouri Historical Society, by permission.

Sunday afternoons in the company of his little girl he visited the aging river pilot Joseph La Barge to collect his reminiscences of the trade, years before oral history became fashionable. On leaves or in conjunction with his official work he visited a variety of sites including the John Jacob Astor Hotel on Mackinac Island, Michigan; the historical societies of Wisconsin, Missouri, Kansas, Nebraska, Iowa, Minnesota, and Montana; much of the upper Missouri country; and portions of Wyoming, Colorado, and New Mexico. By correspondence he consulted Elliott Coues and Frances Fuller Victor, skillful collaborator of Hubert Howe Bancroft and biographer of the mountain man Joseph Meek.[6]

It is uncertain when Chittenden turned from research to composition, but he finished the book and sent it to his publisher on May 18, 1900.[7] When the time came for submitting the manuscript, Coues, his wisest counselor, was dead. However Coues's approval of the fur trade project and his active encouragement had opened doors for Chittenden at the house of Francis P. Harper which had published several of Coues's editions of western journals.[8] *The Fur Trade,* bound in handsome green with gold lettering, appeared in 1902.

Other writers had devoted considerable pages to the fur trade, but never to the extent of a huge monograph upon the subject. When Chittenden looked for guidance among published works of history that touched upon the fur trade, he became aware of Washington Irving's classics, *Astoria* and *Captain Bonneville.* He knew too of Francis Parkman's epic account of the struggle between the French and the English for the North American continent. Parkman had influenced Theodore Roosevelt, whose four-volume *The Winning of the West* (1884-1896) was dedicated to Parkman and encompassed the conflicts between Indian and white man on the Appalachian frontier of the eighteenth century. Although there is no evidence that Chittenden had read Roosevelt, he did know

6 HMC, "Historical Work," CPHS; interview with Eleanor C. Cress, August 3, 1968; HMC, *The American Fur Trade of the Far West . . . ,* ed. Grace Lee Nute, 2 vols. (Stanford, Calif., 1954), 1: xxxi-xxxvi; hereafter cited as *Fur Trade.* Citations are to this most recent edition of the work unless otherwise indicated.

7 HMC, "Diary," May 18, 1900, CPHS.

8 HMC, "Historical Work," CPHS.

at least some of the works of Bancroft, whose massive set of works on the North American West was well underway when Chittenden began research in St. Louis in 1896. Three years before Chittenden began work Frederick Jackson Turner had written "The Significance of the Frontier in American History," but again there is no evidence that Chittenden had studied this seminal essay. Among the compilers and editors were Reuben Gold Thwaites, who had published his *Jesuit Relations and Allied Documents* (1896-1901), and Elliott Coues. But so far as a monograph of the fur trade was concerned, Chittenden had to make his own mold, an enormous task that explains, if it does not excuse, many of the book's weaknesses.[9]

Among other problems of writing on a largely unexploited topic, Chittenden had to hew proper guidelines for organization and proportion. He decided to work on a grand scale and when his work was finally published it appeared in three volumes, two stout ones of text supplemented by a slender volume of appendixes. In the five major sections of his book, Chittenden relied upon a combination of the chronological narrative and the thematic approaches to his subject. The first part of the book (seventy pages) is the shortest and deals with the organization and financing of the fur trade.[10] Following these introductory chapters, Chittenden presented the most important section of his work, entitled "Historical." Constituting almost one half of the book, it traces the origins of the fur trade in North America and develops in detail the histories of the major companies operating in the Trans-Mississippi West.[11] Part Three of *The Fur Trade* discusses "Contemporary Events Connected with the Fur Trade," and Part Four contains "Notable Incidents and Characters in the History of the Fur Trade."[12] The last part of the text, "The Country and Its Inhabitants," includes a scientific description

[9] For convenient surveys of frontier historiography, see Harvey Wish, *The American Historian: A Social-Intellectual History of the Writing of the American Past* (New York, 1960), pp. 181-208, and Michael Kraus, *The Writing of American History* (Norman, Okla., 1953), pp. 145-56, 271-93.

[10] HMC, *Fur Trade*, 1: 1-70.

[11] Ibid., 1: 71-482; 2: 483-553.

[12] Ibid., 2: 555-723.

of the mountains, plains, watercourses, flora, fauna, and Indian life of the Plains and Rockies. After the text comes a series of eight appendixes that encompasses source material such as the newspaper accounts of the "Flathead Deputation" of 1832 and miscellaneous materials including the author's lists of trading posts in the West.[13]

So far as can be determined from that era of anonymous book reviewers, the only two professional historians to scrutinize *The Fur Trade* were Frank H. Hodder of the University of Kansas and Frances Fuller Victor. Mrs. Victor, who was a personal friend of Chittenden and whom Chittenden tried to rescue from the poverty of her declining years, was only flattering, but Hodder brought out valid criticisms of Chittenden's book. As befitting a professional historian, Hodder attacked Chittenden's lack of bibliographic precision although his comments were generally favorable.[14] Chittenden certainly did not provide a careful estimate of the relative worth of the differing parts of his source collections although he did indicate which collections were the most important. In any case, these bibliographical omissions do not seriously impair the value of the book.

Judgment must be harsher in regard to the citation of his authorities. Chittenden used footnotes, of course, but not with the consistency nor quantity of the modern monographic author as is illustrated by his nineteen-page chapter on the important campaign made by Colonel Henry Leavenworth against the Arikara villages on the Missouri in 1823, in which he employed only four notes.[15] As a general rule, Chittenden used notes only when quoting or for the purposes of explicating at further length material alluded to in the text. This manner of referring to authorities was inadequate not only by later standards but also by those of his own generation, for many historical monographs published at the same time as *The Fur Trade* were far more specific in their citations.

The way Chittenden shaped his materials is also somewhat

---

13 Ibid., pp. 725-1003.

14 Frances Fuller Victor, "The American Fur Trade in the Far West," *Oregon Historical Quarterly* 3 (1902): 260-70; HMC, "Diary," November 3, 1901, CPHS; "The Beginnings of the Great West," *Dial* 32 (1902): 412-14.

15 HMC, *Fur Trade*, 2: 590, 593, 606.

disconcerting. Reviewers and later commentators on Chittenden's writings generally overlooked its structure, but this lack of positive mention of its organization is significant, for the fivefold form of the book is one that presents difficulties. For example, it might have been better to have placed the environmental section at or near the first part of the book rather than at the last. Chittenden was certainly justified in allotting about one-half his book to the narrative, but the two remaining sections on "Contemporary Events Connected with the Fur Trade" and "Notable Incidents and Characters in the History of the Fur Trade" stand out as conspicuously isolated entities rather than as clearly integrated portions. As it is, *The Fur Trade* is somewhat disjointed for consecutive reading, although there is no superfluous information and the reader with the patience to follow the frequent cross-references among the different sections and volumes can integrate the various portions of the book himself.

The style of the book was pleasing to readers of Chittenden's time and of subsequent generations. In general Chittenden's writing is clear and interesting, containing sufficient detail to make the generalizations sound without losing the reader in a welter of detail or of unrelated facts. His relating of specific events is best seen in technical matters such as the tracing of the routes of the overland Astorians. Although not great literature in a stylistic sense, Chittenden's *Fur Trade*, through lucidity of style, served his purpose of serious edification.

Modern historians have criticized Chittenden's omissions or his lack of perspective rather than his style or organization. Chittenden implicitly conceived his field of interest as the United States fur trade in that region west of the Missouri River which became a part of the United States. For this reason he was justified in saying little about the valley of the Columbia River after John Jacob Astor's ill-fated efforts at the mouth of the river before and during the War of 1812. But there was little excuse for Chittenden to omit, as critics have noted, the area of the American Southwest where a beaver trade did flourish. Robert G. Cleland, the historian of the southwestern trade, correctly faulted Chittenden for errors of fact and of omission concerning this region.[16] Why Chittenden made these lapses is inexplicable, especially for one who devoted a large section of his book to the southwestern Santa Fe trade and who had traveled through the region in his irrigation journeys. Another moot point is the chronological scope of the book. Chittenden and Coues had disagreed over the proper terminal date for the study and Chittenden decided to conclude with 1843 only after the work had been long in progress, a choice that was not particularly happy, for John Sunder's work, *The Fur Trade on the Upper Missouri, 1840-1865*, demonstrates that there was an important commerce in the Missouri country for years after Jim Bridger constructed his fort.[17]

Modern students have also pointed out other deficiencies. Chittenden did not attempt to describe the entire North American fur trade, for which he cannot be blamed, but he might have made some gestures toward putting the fur trade of the American plains and mountains into larger perspective. He did present the background to the activities of the St. Louis and New York firms in the three introductory chapters that open the historical section of his book, but thereafter he left the subject, neglecting fruitful comparisons with the experiences of Americans and citizens of other countries operating in other regions and eras of the fur trade.[18]

Other criticisms, by implication at least, of *The Fur Trade* are that it slights the role of the liquor traffic on a continental scale, that it does not pursue fully the ramifications of the fur trade as an illustration of the effect of economic metropolis upon the hinterland, and that it neglects the full international context of the fur trade. Chittenden did touch all these topics but he did not carry them as far as possible even considering the relatively limited amount of secondary works then available. He did include a brief introductory chapter on the liquor traffic and referred to some incidents concerning it later

16 Robert Glass Cleland, *This Reckless Breed of Men: The Trappers and Fur Traders of the Southwest* (New York, 1950), pp. 7-8.

17 HMC, "Historical Work," CPHS; John E. Sunder, *The Fur Trade on the Upper Missouri, 1840-1865* (Norman, Okla., 1965).

18 Dale L. Morgan, "The Fur Trade and Its Historians," *The American West* 3 (1966): 35.

in his book. He was aware of the commercial significance of
St. Louis. Though realizing that the American fur traders
were affected by their British and Spanish rivals, he never
saw the complex interplay of international political and
economic forces affecting the trade that were made clear
subsequently in the brilliant works of Frederick Merk.[19]

Critics of the historiography of the fur trade have also
pointed out that Chittenden was even sketchier in treating
other themes. The political influence of the fur trade in the
development of American land policy, the shaping of tariffs,
and the appointment of governmental officials deserved far
more attention than Chittenden gave. The impact of the
fur trade on state, territorial, and local governmental policies
also contained many possibilities for research that Chittenden
neglected. Aside from direct influence in politics the trade
was significant for the development of conservationist sentiment
in the United States. And beyond the political realm, historians
have called for definitive studies of the businessmen financing
the traders and of the whole economic side of the trade. Studies
of small local companies and the class structure and ethnic
configurations of the traders, trappers, and capitalists are also
unworked fields for study.[20]

In assessing this lengthy list of subjects where Chittenden's
book could be improved, one must come back to his purpose
in writing it: "to promote an appreciation of its [the fur
trade's] importance by presenting a history of THE AMERICAN
FUR TRADE OF THE FAR WEST during the period of its principal
operations in that extensive region." He knew the possibilities
of other topics than those he exploited but he could not develop
them either because of space limitations or the absence of
source material (especially in the realm of business statistics).
Yet even when these extenuating circumstances are taken into

19 HMC, *Fur Trade*, 1: 75-80; Morgan, "The Fur Trade and Its Historians,"
pp. 35, 92; Frederick Merk, *The Oregon Question: Essays in Anglo-American
Diplomacy and Politics* (Cambridge, Mass., 1967); Merk, ed., *Fur Trade and
Empire: George Simpson's Journal*, rev. ed. (Cambridge, Mass., 1968); HMC,
Fur Trade, 1: 22-31, 97-112.
20 Morgan, "The Fur Trade and Its Historians," p. 35; John E. Sunder,
"Problems and Opportunities in Fur Trade Research," a paper read at a
Conference on the History of the Fur Trade at St. Paul, November 3, 1965;
Doyce B. Nunis, Jr., "Needs and Opportunities for Fur Trade Research," ibid.

account, it is also clear that Chittenden on some occasions simply failed to see certain perspectives of the trade as important, omissions that weaken the work on its own terms. Most important is the failure to treat the trade in its international context and to examine its impact upon local politics.[21] Without entire success only Paul C. Phillips attempted to delve into some of these facets of the trade neglected by Chittenden, and he was painting on an avowedly broader canvas.

So far as errors of commission are concerned, contemporary reviewers of *The Fur Trade* and later scholars have noted some derived from a careless reading of the sources, some from neglect to scan certain records, and still others from faulty judgment of available records. Most of these mistakes were minor although some were of a more serious and (for a man of Chittenden's meticulousness) surprising nature. Although this is no place for a catalog of errata, a few examples serve to illustrate the point. Chittenden committed five errors in plant names in his section on the flora of the West.[22] He had the wrong birthdate for Manuel Lisa.[23]

As Merrill J. Mattes had pointed out, Chittenden was wrong (as he had been in his earlier work on Yellowstone) in declaring that John Colter had passed through the geyser region in the future Yellowstone Park.[24] Contrary to what Chittenden wrote, Jedediah Smith was aided at Fort Vancouver to recover his furs from the Umpqua Indians by the orders of Sir George Simpson, not through the good offices of Dr. John McLoughlin.[25] The first account that was published of the Yellowstone wonders was not that of W. A. Ferris in 1834 as Chittenden believed but one that appeared in the *Philadelphia Gazette & Daily Advertiser* on September 27, 1827.[26] Chittenden slipped in copying from Irving the wrong first initial

21 HMC, *Fur Trade,* 1: xxvii.

22 HMC, *The American Fur Trade of the Far West . . .* , ed. Stallo Vinton, 2 vols. (St. Paul, Minn., 1935), 2: 798-99, n. A, F, G, H. I; hereafter cited Vinton edition.

23 Ibid., 1: 136, n. A.

24 Merrill J. Mattes, "Behind the Legend of Colter's Hell: The Early Exploration of Yellowstone National Park," *Mississippi Valley Historical Review* 36 (1949): 251-82.

25 Vinton edition, 1: 289, n. H.

26 Ibid., 1: 374, n. A; the *Gazette* article was reprinted in *Niles Weekly Register* 33 (October 6, 1827): 90-91.

of Joseph Reddeford Walker, printing it as "I" rather than "J."[27] None of these mistakes detracted significantly from the value of the work, for they did not distort the meaning of events or consciously convey false impressions under the guise of accuracy.

More serious errors did appear, however. Chittenden in particular had a good deal of trouble with William H. Ashley and his business relationships with the men who would become his successors in the Rocky Mountain fur trade. As did all other historians until Dale L. Morgan discovered the truth and published it in his definitive biography of Jedediah Smith, Chittenden confused the diary of William H. Ashley with one of William Sublette.[28] Chittenden was also confounded, as Morgan was again the first to point out, by the relationship of Etienne Provost to the French Company (Bernard Pratte and Company) at the time of the negotiations between Ashley and that company that culminated in Ashley's retirement from the mountain trade in 1827.[29] As later historians have shown, he was also incorrect in tracing the wanderings of Jedediah Smith in his great journey of 1826-1828, a point Katherine Coman raised with him personally sometime after *The Fur Trade* was published.[30] On the question of the discovery of South Pass Chittenden denied that the returning Astorians first found that key gateway in 1813, for he credited the discovery to Provost in 1823.[31] Chittenden confused the Blackfoot Indians with the Gros Ventres of the Prairies (actually Arapahos) who lived among them.[32] He failed to detect that in a letter of Colonel Leavenworth describing the Mandan attack on Andrew Henry in the Yellowstone region the Colonel dated the attack August 20, rather than September 20, when it could not possibly have occurred.[33]

In the realm of interpretation Chittenden was undoubtedly

[27] Vinton edition, 1: 430, n. A.
[28] Dale L. Morgan, *Jedediah Smith and the Opening of the West* (Indianapolis, Ind., 1953), p. 405, n. 12.
[29] Ibid., p. 420, n. 9.
[30] Katherine Coman to HMC, December 9, 1911, CPHS.
[31] Vinton edition, 1: 214–15, n. F.
[32] Richard Edward Oglesby, *Manuel Lisa and the Opening of the Missouri Fur Trade* (Norman, Okla., 1963), p. 58, n. 55.
[33] Morgan, *Jedediah Smith*, p. 385, n. 4.

too categorical in some of his judgments. He condemned Charles Larpenteur for deliberately infecting the Indians at Fort Union in 1837 with smallpox in order to murder them, while a different reading of the same account absolves Larpenteur of this charge.[34] In his general assault upon Captain Bonneville, Chittenden attacked him for failure to report his actions fully to his superiors and for not requesting an extension of his leave, but documentary evidence contradicts him on both counts.[35] Chittenden certainly went too far in ascribing the sale of Fort Astor to the Northwest Company in 1813 to the treachery and disloyalty of Astor's business associates, Duncan McDougal and Donald McKenzie.[36] Finally, Chittenden's strictures against Hubert Howe Bancroft's treatment of the Astorian enterprise were clearly in error when he fulminated against that historian for "sheer falsifications and downright slander" about Astor and his enterprise on the Pacific Coast.[37] Chittenden was particularly incensed by Bancroft's criticism of Irving's *Astoria,* which he himself regarded as sound history, although in attacking Bancroft, Chittenden was uncharacteristically no more temperate.[38]

Chittenden himself was cognizant that his work had many limitations. He was particularly aware that he must have missed many sources. "The wholly unexpected places in which material of the highest value has been found, forcibly suggest that a great deal more may have been overlooked."[39] Since the time of his research Chittenden's prophecy has been confirmed as numerous documents have come to light that have made possible the development of the history of the fur trade in several facets he merely discovered.

Chittenden was confident, however, that what he had written was accurate. In the preface to *The Fur Trade,* he noted proudly, "But if it must be admitted that much has escaped discovery in these researches, it is believed that the essential facts relating to all the events herein described have been

34 Vinton edition, 2: 620, n. A.
35 Ibid., 1: 431-34, n. E.
36 HMC, *Fur Trade,* 1: 233-38.
37 Ibid., p. 245.
38 Ibid., pp. 245-46.
39 Ibid., p. xxx.

determined."[40] As we have seen, this claim was at least over-stated, but the errors were amazingly few in a pioneering work of its scope. Fifteen years later, as he knew his life was drawing to a close, he again appraised the book:

It has been often referred to as a great work and has taken its place as a standard. I am fully conscious that in a multitude of details there are inaccuracies which will come to light upon minuter research. . . . On the whole, it is essentially accurate and it deals with broad outlines in such a way that the average reader follows it with ease and interest. I have never seen any cause to regret the course I have pursued. This work I put down as emphatically a thing well done and this view is confirmed as times goes on.[41]

Time has proved this appraisal to be valid. What Chittenden attempted he succeeded in doing. What he did not attempt to do, wisely or unwisely, has been corrected and amplified by others although the field of the fur trade remains promising for historians. Proof of his scholarly merit is quite simply that all professional and popular historians of stature in fur trade history have recorded explicitly or otherwise their dependence upon him. Dale L. Morgan in his *Jedediah Smith* acknowl-edged his debt to Chittenden "whose classic study of the American fur trade has influenced all modern scholarship."[42] Robert Glass Cleland described Chittenden as an author "who, among the hosts of students of the Western fur trade, towers like Saul head and shoulders above his brethren."[43] Frederick Jackson Turner labeled Chittenden's work as "excellent."[44] Grace Lee Nute, writing in 1954 in the most recent edition of Chittenden's book, declared, "Even today one cannot point to a work that has superseded Chittenden's pioneering ven-ture."[45] Kenneth W. Porter relied extensively upon the "shrewd and careful" Chittenden for his analysis of the western activities of John Jacob Astor, and Milo M. Quaife called

[40] Ibid.
[41] HMC, "Historical Work," CPHS.
[42] Dale L. Morgan, *Jedediah Smith*, p. 10.
[43] Robert Glass Cleland, *This Reckless Breed of Men*, p. 7.
[44] Frederick Jackson Turner, *Rise of the New West, 1819-1829* (New York, 1906), p. xviii.
[45] HMC, *Fur Trade*, 1: viii.

him "one of the ablest students of the American fur trade."[46]
David Lavender, among fur trade historians the most critical
of Chittenden in claiming him to be "both careless and
prejudiced," nevertheless described his work as "monumental."[47] Chittenden, according to Don Berry, wrote a book that,
although in need of some revision, "will certainly provide the
standard against which any new work must be measured."[48]
Paul C. Phillips and J. W. Smurr, LeRoy Hafen, and many
of the individual authors in Hafen's series, *Mountain Men and
the Fur Trade,* acknowledge in their notes their heavy in-
debtedness to Chittenden's researches.[49] The highest praise of
Chittenden, however, has come from the pen of Dale L.
Morgan, who wrote in 1966:

Very few, I suspect, would place Hiram Martin Chittenden in
the same class with Turner and Webb. . . . Yet anyone disposed
to inquire into the historiography of the past sixty years will find
that Chittenden's *The American Fur Trade of the Far West* has
influenced nearly everything written about the history of the West
in the first half of the nineteenth century—that it has, indeed, been
more largely influential than the only general work Turner himself ever published (his *Rise of the New West, 1819-1829,* which
leaned on Chittenden's history and described it as "excellent").
From the year of its publication, 1902, *The American Fur Trade
of the Far West* has not only been referred to constantly by writers
of every description, but has also powerfully shaped their ideas.
. . . The idea may affront the professional historians, but it can
be seriously maintained that neither Turner nor Webb has had an
impact on the writing of western history comparable to Chittenden's. . . .
    The point I more particularly wish to make is that Chittenden
settled the ideas of two generations of historians who, directly or
indirectly, have had to come to terms with the fur trade. His was

46 Kenneth Wiggins Porter, *John Jacob Astor: Business Man,* 2 vols. (Cambridge, Mass., 1931), 2: 711; Alexander Ross, *Adventures of the First Settlers on
the Oregon or Columbia River,* ed. Milo Milton Quaife (Chicago, 1923), p. viii.
    47 David Lavender, *The Fist in the Wilderness* (New York, 1964), p. 422.
    48 Don Berry, *A Majority of Scoundrels: An Informal History of the Rocky
Mountain Fur Company* (New York, 1961), p. 391.
    49 Paul Chrisler Phillips and J. W. Smurr, *The Fur Trade,* 2 vols. (Norman,
Okla., 1961); LeRoy R. Hafen, "A Brief History of the Fur Trade of the Far
West," in *The Mountain Men and the Fur Trade of the Far West,* ed. LeRoy
R. Hafen, 9 vols. (Glendale, Calif., 1965-1972), 1: 21-176, and passim.

a liberating influence originally, for he provided a rationale by which a diffuse and refractory history was made intelligible. Over the course of time, however, Chittenden has evolved into something of a tyrannical force, for he is still conditioning the thinking of students who should be pushing the frontiers of knowledge a good deal farther out. Pioneering is never easy, but it is time those interested in the trade should be stepping out on their own.[50]

It would be hard to quarrel with this estimate of Chittenden's work by an eminent authority. Whether or not Chittenden ranks with Turner and Webb, as Morgan indicates, is debatable. Certainly Chittenden was not an imaginative framer of large hypotheses in the sense that Webb and Turner were. That Chittenden has dominated the historiography of the fur trade, however, is clear and unequivocal.

The genesis of Chittenden's second historical work, *History of Early Steamboat Navigation on the Missouri River*, was almost as early as his interest in the fur trade; both developed during his years along the Missouri. In the summer of 1896 Chittenden decided to publish a history of steamboat wrecks on the Missouri River in an attempt to discover what types of navigational improvements were most needed. Early in his search for data he met Joseph La Barge, a retired river pilot, captain, and owner, who had a vast knowledge of river calamities. Chittenden hired La Barge (although he was willing to work for nothing) to assist him. Discovering the extent of La Barge's acquaintance with the Missouri River's history and lore, Chittenden decided to ask him to compile his memories of a lifetime in the river trade. La Barge was at first reluctant to attempt the task, but Chittenden soon persuaded him to dictate his recollections to him. Work was progressing smoothly until the Spanish-American War interrupted it in April 1898. Almost a year later, while stationed at Huntsville, Alabama, Chittenden received word from St. Louis that La Barge was dying. He at once telegraphed to the son of his old friend: "Tell Captain La Barge that I shall faithfully finish his work. It will take me a long time, but I shall not fail to do it." This message, Chittenden subsequently

50 Dale L. Morgan, "The Fur Trade and Its Historians," pp. 28-29.

learned, reached La Barge one and one half hours before he died, in time to assure the still conscious riverman that his work would be completed.[51]

When Chittenden returned to St. Louis after military service and again scanned La Barge's memories, he discovered them too truncated to be used as he had originally intended. Accordingly, he determined upon a new approach which was to use the skeleton of La Barge's personal experiences to reconstruct a history of steamboat navigation. Although it was in part a measure of expediency, Chittenden came to embrace eagerly this biographical approach: "It is not the bare narration of events that gives history its true value, but those intimate pictures of human life in other times that show what people really did and the motives by which they were actuated. To this end, biography, and even fiction, possess distinct advantages over the ordinary method of historical writing."[52] This rather romantic philosophy of history mirrored Chittenden's own experiences of reading deeply and widely in novels and biography from his earliest years and gave him a more congenial guide than he had followed in the highly institutional and descriptive *Fur Trade*.

The organization of *Steamboat Navigation* reflects the tension between the biographical and institutional aspects of the topic. The subtitle was the more accurate description of the text of the book, *Life and Adventures of Joseph La Barge,* for most of its contents embraced La Barge's career. Chittenden presented La Barge's life in chronological order interspersed with topical analyses of various themes, e.g., the types of river craft employed in the fur trade, the art of steamboat navigation, the use of the steamboat in the fur trade, a description of the Indians of the Missouri Valley, and the role of the United States Army on the Missouri. Appearing throughout both the biographical and topical chapters were a great many anecdotes about life on the Missouri, for the style of the book was more informal than that of *The Fur Trade*.

[51] *ARCE*, 1897, 6: 3870-92; HMC, *History of Early Steamboat Navigation on the Missouri River: Life and Adventures of Joseph La Barge . . . ,* 2 vols. (New York, 1903), 1: xi-xii, 2: 438; HMC, "Diary," April 3, 4, 1899, CPHS.
[52] HMC, *Steamboat Navigation,* 1: xiii-xiv.

Steamboat Navigation did not lack interpretation as Chittenden went into depth in analyzing the changing character of the steamboat commerce. After tracing the importance of the Missouri fur trade, he detailed the impact of the events of the 1840s upon the river. The Mormon migration upriver to Council Bluffs in 1845-1847, the transportation of troops for the commands of William S. Harney and Alexander W. Doniphan during the Mexican War, the vast numbers of the California gold seekers who used the Missouri route, and the government exploring parties of the West in search of railroad routes all provided a more heterogeneous commerce than before 1845. In later years these sources of traffic evaporated and Chittenden, as in his reports to the Chief of Engineers, stressed the futility of the government's attempting to make the river navigable at a time when it had lost almost all its business to the advancing railroads.[53]

As in *The Fur Trade,* Chittenden attempted to comprehend the development of Indian-white relations. He again absolved the United States government of evil motives in the design of its Indian policy. He contended that the problem was essentially insoluble without inevitable injustice. "It was the problem," he declared, "of how to commit a great wrong without doing any wrong—how to deprive the Indian of his birthright in such a way that he should feel that no injustice had been done him. It was the decree of destiny that the European should displace the native American upon his own soil. No earthly power could prevent it."[54] Chittenden, however, sharply and specifically condemned the means of the government in executing the decrees of fate. He arraigned especially the treaty method, arguing that it would have been far better for the nation to have summarily taken the land of the Indians without using the farce of the treaty system to legitimatize agreements between unequal powers.[55]

So far as La Barge himself was concerned, Chittenden saw him as a romantic, heroic figure, virtuous in his relations with other men of business and bluff and honest in his

53 Ibid., 1: 171-74; 2: 423, 448.
54 Ibid., 2: 355-57 (quotation, p. 355).
55 Ibid., 2: 356-57.

personal relations. At times he served to illustrate some larger point; for instance, La Barge's competition with his sometime employer, the American Fur Company, furnished Chittenden with the opportunity to attack Astor's monopolistic and ruthless practices. Mainly, however, Chittenden portrayed La Barge as a man interesting in himself as indicative of a familiar type in the development of the American frontier.[56] It was to the man and not the commerce that Chittenden paid most attention in the book.

Chittenden blamed the rather indifferent reception of *Steamboat Navigation* upon its prosaic title and certainly it had far fewer reviews than did *The Fur Trade*. The book was reviewed in newspapers and magazines of general circulation and was praised by Frederick Jackson Turner in the *American Historical Review* for presenting an "entertaining picture, as well as a body of useful information."[57] The critics were usually favorable or noncommittal and no hostile comment was found although the reviewer in the *St. Louis Globe Democrat* considered Chittenden's role in the work as "scarcely more than the editor," manifestly a grave misjudgment.[58] Over the years the book gained recognition as the standard authority upon the topic and faced little competition until the publication by William E. Lass in 1962 of the definitive work, *A History of Steamboating on the Upper Missouri River,* that superseded Chittenden's account.[59] As a chronicle of life on the river and as a source of illustrative materials on certain of its facets, however, it has remained quite valuable and has only recently been reissued by the publishing house of Ross and Haines.[60]

As a far less seminal work than *The Fur Trade,* parts of which Chittenden incorporated (with acknowledgment) in

---

[56] Ibid., 1: 59-72.

[57] HMC, "Historical Work," CPHS; several reviews are in the HMC Scrapbooks, CPHS; F. J. Turner, "Review of HMC, Early Steamboat Navigation," *American Historical Review* 11 (1906): 443-44.

[58] An undated copy of the review is in HMC Scrapbooks, CPHS.

[59] William E. Lass, *A History of Steamboating on the Upper Missouri River* (Lincoln, Nebr., 1962).

[60] HMC, *A History of Early Steamboat Navigation on the Missouri River: Life and Adventures of Joseph La Barge . . .* , 2 vols. in 1 (Minneapolis, Minn., 1962).

Steamboat Navigation, the book did not engender the continuing analysis that had its predecessor. The style was interesting, and Chittenden himself proclaimed it better than any of his other books.[61] It was relatively easy to interweave the details of the steamboat business with the life of La Barge, but the organization of his material gave Chittenden trouble as it did in his other books. Seldom could he carry off the division of the book into narrative and topical analysis without jarring the reader in the process. The analysis of the larger forces in *Steamboat Navigation* was better accomplished than in *The Fur Trade,* perhaps because not so many of them were at work, although the book would have had a wider impact if Chittenden had compared the problems of steamboat navigation on the Missouri with those on the Mississippi and Ohio rivers as Louis Hunter was to do many years later.[62]

The number of factual errors was smaller also, again because most of the book was a biography of La Barge and his recollections were in the main unverifiable, thus providing little opportunity for those who desired to check his (and Chittenden's) accuracy. The documentation in *Steamboat Navigation* was not extensive (although it did serve to identify many places and personages of significance) because La Barge's own memory was its principal source. However, Chittenden did conclude, by checking wherever possible against other authorities, that the riverman's memories embraced a thorough and careful compilation of the events of his time, but he did not labor overlong to document this confidence with footnotes. Probably his casualness in this type of book was justified; it was not a serious defect in any case. Chittenden, regardless of criticisms of his book, remained an indefatigable historical researcher and author. Scarcely was *Steamboat Navigation* published before he was preparing to send to the publishers a massive account of another prototypical frontiersman, the missionary to the Indian tribes.

Chittenden's final major historical work, and his third published by the firm of Francis P. Harper, was *Life, Letters and*

61 HMC, "Historical Work," CPHS.
62 Louis Hunter, *Steamboats on the Western Rivers: An Economic and Technological History* (Cambridge, Mass., 1949).

Travels of Father Pierre-Jean De Smet, S.J., 1801-1873.[63]
Chittenden selected this enterprise in the fall of 1901 before
the appearance of *The Fur Trade* and to assist him in its
preparation he obtained the services of Alfred T. Richardson,
whom Chittenden regarded as a better linguist than himself.[64]
Chittenden had first met Richardson casually in Omaha in
1890 when he was awaiting the annual appropriation for river
and harbor work. They then parted and Richardson became
the principal agent for the extensive Morton family enterprises
in Nebraska City, Nebraska. (J. Sterling Morton, the family's
leader, was Secretary of Agriculture in President Cleveland's
second administration.) Richardson was manager of the
Morton starch works, editor of the *Nebraska City Conservative,*
and participant in local politics. During the years 1900-1902
Richardson also became a serious student of the history of the
Trans-Mississippi West. In the summer of 1902 he collapsed
from overwork and indulged an old fancy to participate in the
westward movement by going to Yellowstone Park for the sake
of his health. Here he met his old acquaintance Chittenden
who employed him in a summer of vigorous exercise that
restored his health. The two men became close friends, and
at the advice of Chittenden, Richardson moved his family to
North Yakima, Washington, in January 1903 to establish an
irrigated peach orchard.[65]

The two editors made slow progress in the work which
Chittenden confessed privately was a "heavy task."[66] In late
June 1904, however, he had a conference in New York City

[63] HMC and Alfred Talbot Richardson, eds., *Life, Letters and Travels of
Father Pierre-Jean De Smet, S.J., 1801-1873* . . . , 4 vols. (New York, 1905).

[64] HMC, "Diary," October 15, 1901, CPHS.

[65] For Richardson, the sources are Anna B. Smith to author, September 20,
1968; Alfred Talbott Richardson, "Something about the Yellowstone Park,"
Out West 22 (1905): 325-31; Otis Richardson to Mary Harris, April 17, 1969, in
possession of the author; Otis Richardson to author, May 22, 1969. The exact
contributions of each editor is not clear from the work itself. However, Richardson's son, Otis Richardson, informs me that about one-third of the notes
were identified as to author by Alfred Richardson in his own copy of the book.
An examination of these notes indicates that Richardson specialized in translations of French and Indian words and in identification of individuals, locations,
and De Smet's literary sources while Chittenden, although doing some of the
same work, expressed himself more freely about the significance of events and
individuals. Otis Richardson to author, May 26, 1969.

[66] HMC, "Diary," February 10, 1904, CPHS.

Chittenden at the United States Military Academy.

Courtesy of Washington State Historical Society

The Chittenden family, St. Louis, 1899.
Courtesy of Washington State Historical Society

Working party in Yellowstone Park, Chittenden at lower
left.

Hiram M. Chittenden, in retirement in Seattle.

Courtesy of Washington State Historical Society

with Francis P. Harper shortly after taking his examination for the rank of major. At this meeting author and publisher agreed upon the final details of the plan for the De Smet project.[67] The format of the book again reflected the influence of Elliott Coues, for the contract specifically stated that it was to be modeled upon Coues's edition of the *Journals of Lewis and Clark*.[68] Published in 1905, the *Life and Letters* appeared in four large volumes, handsomely printed on fine paper and bound in green and gold.

In content the work contained a brief, 144-page description of the life of the great missionary followed by correspondence and other literary memorabilia of De Smet. Chittenden's biography was a clear narrative of the major events in De Smet's life with a rather conventional character sketch at the close. This account was accurate in detail and served to orient the reader to the material that followed, but it was not a work of major interpretation. While Chittenden faithfully recorded the early years of the missionary and described his frequent journeys across the Atlantic and his work among the Indians of the Great Plains, he did not attempt to place De Smet's labors either in the larger context of Catholic missionary efforts or, except superficially, in the context of American Indian policy and Indian-white relations. Although he did not entirely ignore the latter topic, his treatment was not exhaustive and was the chief deficiency in an otherwise admirable—if largely undocumented—brief account.

Chittenden's interest in Father De Smet was obviously an outgrowth of his interest in the history of the fur trade and what appealed to Chittenden most about the missionary was not his zeal but his humanity.[69] He singled out De Smet's desire to live rather than die for his cause. "A feature of Father De Smet's career which has strongly appealed to the author since he first became acquainted with the life-work of the great missionary is the absence of that longing for martyrdom which was so characteristic of the old Canadian missionaries." To

[67] Ibid., July 7, 1904, CPHS.
[68] The contract is in CPHS.
[69] Chittenden's estimate of his interest is contained in his "Review of E. Laveille, S.J., *The Life of Father De Smet, S.J., 1801-1873*," *Washington Historical Quarterly* 7 (1916): 247-48.

put it bluntly, Chittenden felt that martyrdom was wasted upon the Indians, for it did not advance religion.[70] Chittenden alluded on several occasions to Father De Smet's sense of humor and repeatedly praised him for his efforts on behalf of the Indians, trapped between their white enemies and the failures of government policy, whom he always treated with compassion and without condescension. To a man of Chittenden's passion for service, his admiration for the utility of De Smet's life is expected. He regarded the great achievements of the Jesuit priest to be his planting of numerous missions, his great influence among the Indian tribes of the West, and his power among the white men such as government employees and Mormon emigrants, who were all swayed by him.[71]

Although the biography of De Smet accomplished its author's limited purposes, the great bulk of the book was less successful and resulted in the *Life and Letters* being the least memorable of his scholarly works. Organized both chronologically and topically the book is divided into nine parts. Parts One through Six cover the missionary's career and provide an itinerary of his major activities in those years. Parts Seven and Eight contain letters descriptive of the life of the Indians among whom De Smet lived on his long missions in the West. Part Nine contains miscellaneous letters on a variety of topics that could not be neatly compressed into any framework.

For a collection of letters that gives the impression of being complete, the De Smet work is far from ideal. The most distinguished authority on Father De Smet wrote that only approximately 30 percent of his correspondence is contained in Chittenden and Richardson. The editors of the *Life and Letters* missed the holdings of the De Smet correspondence in foreign governmental repositories, the General Archives of the Society of Jesus in Rome, and those of the North Belgian Province in Brussels. They also never saw or knew of the De Smet family records in Ghent in De Smet's homeland of Belgium. Fortunately for the completeness of the work, the failure of Chittenden and Richardson to move abroad was softened by the fact that De Smet often wrote the same letter

---

[70] HMC, *De Smet*, 1: 112.
[71] Ibid., pp. 56-57, 61, 108-12, 115-26.

to several people so that the De Smet correspondence in the archives of St. Louis University, the main source for Chittenden, did duplicate in many cases the foreign holdings. Still there was a great deal of material that Chittenden and Richardson missed, with obvious harmful results. Whether they knew of the holdings abroad and could not spare time or money to use them, or whether they were ignorant of them, remains unclear.[72]

Another disconcerting feature of the editing of the De Smet letters was the tendency of the editors to transpose and delete paragraphs in letters without indicating these alterations to the reader. Certainly the intention in this rearrangement was innocent, for it was to provide the reflections of De Smet on various topics according to the classification scheme of the editors. But the result of this artificial arranging is hardly scholarly and in some cases flatly misleading. Even when letters are presented accurately and in their entirety, they do not always appear in chronological or logical order.[73]

The translations themselves are not always valid, especially in matters of theology and religious practice. Father Davis wrote:

A glaring example of such a failure is the passage on page 234 of CR which reads: "After this I gave them for their spiritual head a very intelligent Indian . . . [to] exhort them to virtue, and *anoint the dying, and in case of need, little children* [italics mine]." De Smet's words are: *et ondoyer les moribonds et, en case de besoin, les petits enfants.* Laymen do not annoint the dying; in Catholic terminology "to annoint the dying" means commonly to confer the Sacrament of Extreme Unction, which only priests can administer. De Smet's term *"ondoyer"* here means to baptize privately, i.e. not solemnly, or with all the rites prescribed by the Church. The reference to infants means children under seven years of age who, for one reason or another, were judged in danger of death.[74]

The actual editorial paraphenalia was handled effectively. The ample notes provided mainly identification of places and

72 William L. Davis, S.J., to author, September 18, 1968.
73 Ibid.
74 Ibid.

obscure personalities. The editors identified the source of almost all the letters and, before each of the chronological sections, provided a brief and convenient summary of De Smet's career in that aspect of his life.

Why the De Smet *Life and Letters* is not up to the standard of *The Fur Trade* and *Steamboat Navigation* is unclear. Chittenden confessed that the task was laborious and he may have hurried to finish it, allowing errors to creep in through carelessness, although it was out of character for him to turn out inferior work through haste or neglect. The flaws in the editing of the letters must have been due to ignorance of proper editing procedures and to lack of knowledge of the location of the remainder of the De Smet papers. Although never justifiable, the editorial standards of the Chittenden-Richardson project were those of a day in which the criteria for successful editing were far lower than today.[75]

Reviews were generally in a favorable vein, but the work was not widely reviewed, and its influence was limited. Historians such as William L. Davis found the letters, when they had been accurately presented in Chittenden and Richardson, convenient to cite.[76] Other authors followed Chittenden and Richardson very closely in their own popular accounts of the life of the pioneer missionary.[77] The book is useful as a guide to the amateur historian or general reader wishing to capture the flavor of Father De Smet's personality and to obtain an overview of his activities; unfortunately, it is not reliable for the scholar who must go to the originals for research.

After the publication of the De Smet *Life and Letters* in 1905, Chittenden's career as historian was over. Pressures of professional work and an active retirement did not permit him energy or leisure for his significant historical talents, except for three essays on Washington, Franklin, and Lincoln, which were uncompleted and never published. He reviewed

75 HMC, "Diary," February 10, 1904, CPHS.
76 W. L. Davis, "Peter John De Smet, The Years of Preparation, 1801-1837," *Pacific Northwest Quarterly* 32 (1941): 167-96; "Peter John De Smet, Missionary to the Potawatomi, 1837-40," *Pacific Northwest Quarterly* 33 (1942): 123-52; "Peter John De Smet, The Journey of 1840," *Pacific Northwest Quarterly* 35 (1944): 29-43.
77 John Upton Terrell, *Black Robe: The Life of Pierre-Jean De Smet, Missionary, Explorer & Pioneer* (New York, 1964).

an occasional book, corresponded with regional and local historians, and welcomed Professors Edmond Meany and Oliver Richardson of the University of Washington Department of History to his home, but his major historical work was ended.[78] Yet what he had done was monumental, and memorable not only for the achievements but also for the light it shed on a practicing historian's philosophy at a transitional stage of American historiography.

So far as his own published works were concerned, Chittenden never gave any thought whatsoever to a formal philosophy of history. It was not easy for an intellect like his, turned always to practical tasks, to publish any profundities on the nature of the discipline of history. What he was attempting, however, thus emerges from the nature of his work rather than from his explicit declarations. In a methodological sense he was certainly a scientific historian. He relied insofar as possible upon source materials. He gave credit for his information in footnotes. He weighed authorities objectively. Apparently he was careful and cautious in composition, although the only surviving manuscripts of his books are outlines of the land and sea routes and biographical sketches of the Astorians that he presented in late life to the Historical Society of South Dakota.[79] Those fragments are painstakingly thorough and extensively rewritten and if they are characteristic of all his drafts they certainly stamp him as a searcher for objective truth. Beyond the methods which Chittenden employed to gather and assess the validity of data, he was scientific in a large sense.

Chittenden was affected first of all in his historical writings by Darwinian evolution, that pervasive force that touched so many aspects of American life and thought in the last quarter of the nineteenth century. When Chittenden did make large explanations of events, he fell back on many occasions upon the theory of evolution, made so popular by contemporary

[78] Theodore P. Chittenden to author, November 1965; there are many letters to HMC requesting historical data in CP; the essays on Franklin, Lincoln, and Washington are in CP; HMC, "Review of E. Laveille, S.J., *Life of Father De Smet*"; HMC, "Review of Edmond S. Meany, ed., *Mount Rainier, A Record of Exploration*," *Washington Historical Quarterly* 8 (1917): 63-65.

[79] The originals of these manuscripts are in the possession of the South Dakota Historical Society. The author has seen Xeroxed copies.

German scholarship in the United States, Great Britain, and Western Europe. A particular offshoot of Darwinism, a belief in the capacity of certain races or nations to assert themselves at particular periods in history, was especially useful to Chittenden to explain key developments. Like many scholars of the Progressive Era he was suspicious of "non Anglo-Saxon" peoples and in his own time was alarmed over the great wave of immigration to the United States from southern and central Europe.[80] He was a full-fledged Anglo-Saxon imperialist, arguing that nations must grow and expand, and he cheered Britain's victory in the Boer War and the United States's acquisition of the Philippines and the Panama Canal Zone.[81] When he contemplated the cession of Louisiana to the United States, Chittenden described the sentiments of the inhabitants in racial terms: "The new order of things was by no means generally acceptable to the foreign element of the population, either Spanish or French. They saw in it the death knell of their peculiar customs and laws, and they knew that the enterprising spirit of the Anglo-Saxon race would crowd them out of the avenues of industry and commerce even on the very soil where they had lived and toiled from infancy."[82] This philosophy of race was also evident in Chittenden's condemnation of sentimental humanitarians who wished for a different outcome of the Indian policy of the United States. They wished to see the races share the land as equals, but their desire, according to Chittenden, was based upon a false assumption: "It ignores the operation of that evolutionary process by which a weaker race disappears before a superior in spite of all that laws or military force can do to prevent."[83]

The force of Chittenden's racism was mitigated by his desire to protect the Indians while they were being subdued by the European civilization. Although Chittenden did absolve the United States government of evil intentions in creating its Indian policy, he repeatedly condemned the key elements within it. In fact Chittenden seemed to say that if the advice

[80] HMC, *War or Peace: A Present Duty and a Future Hope* (Chicago, 1911), pp. 176-85.
[81] HMC, "Diary," February 15, 1899; June 7, 1902; November 17, 1903, CPHS.
[82] HMC, *Fur Trade,* 1: 79.
[83] Ibid., p. 11.

of men like De Smet had been followed and the Indian treated with "simple justice," then the process of displacing the Indian from his lands would have been accomplished without so many of its horrors.[84] The liquor traffic with the Indians was simply vicious and he attacked it in numerous passages of his several works.[85]

Even though his philosophy partook something of fate and evolutionary determinism, Chittenden never hesitated either to praise or to censure actions and individuals. His code was basically that of Christian optimism, soon to be called the Social Gospel, and his historical writings were imbued with this faith as deeply as were his engineering accomplishments, his views on conservation, and his reflections on current political problems. While he certainly was not naive, for he knew the power of money and influence in the worlds of business and government, he always tried to judge individuals and events by Christian progressive principles, the ones that he had held since childhood. Thus, for example, he treated the American Fur Company realistically but not neutrally in writing of it: "It knew perfectly well the power of political influence, and no railroad corporation of modern times is more assiduous in the lobby than was the American Fur Company in the Departments at Washington."[86]

Although his method was scientific Chittenden was interested mainly in the romantic aspects of history. He admired the heroic figures, the movers and shakers and adventurers, who epitomized the industry and aggressiveness of the nineteenth century, although he recoiled from those who broke moral boundaries to gain their ends. In spite of the fact that only one of his historical works is even superficially a biography, all indicate Chittenden's admiration for the romantic individualist. Chittenden praised Astor's strength and wisdom, his courage, and his business sagacity. "John Jacob Astor," he declared, "although an alien by birth, is one of America's best examples of self-made men—men of humble beginnings, who, by sheer native ability, have risen to the foremost rank

84 HMC, "Review of Laveille, *Life of De Smet.*"
85 HMC, *Fur Trade,* 1: 23; HMC, *De Smet,* 1: 185, n. 5.
86 HMC, *Fur Trade,* 1: 380.

in their respective callings."[87] He praised the business morality
and the accomplishments in field and counting house of Joseph
La Barge and Ramsay Crooks.[88] He sprinkled throughout the
Fur Trade anecdotes and brief biographical sketches of the
primitive hero: Jim Bridger, Hugh Glass, and John Colter.[89]

Romantic institutions and scenes also drew Chittenden's
attention and admiration. He wrote of the steamboat: "It
has seldom happened in history that the introduction of labor-
saving devices has not robbed society to some extent of what
was poetic and sentimental, and replaced it by something more
prosaic and matter of fact. The Missouri river steamboat was
an exception, for with all the romance that attached to the
old keelboat, its own history was more romantic still."[90] He
evoked the Oregon Trail in the same vein: "There are few
more impressive sights than portions of this old highway
today. It still lies there upon the prairie, deserted by the
traveler, an everlasting memorial of the human tide which
once filled it to overflowing. Nature herself has helped to
perpetuate this memorial, for the prairie winds, year by year,
carve the furrow more deeply, and the wild sunflower blossoms
along its course, as if in silent memory of those who sank
beneath its burdens."[91]

In the frontier era Chittenden discovered a period in which
the individual had large scope to govern his own destiny, a
power which Chittenden saw possible in his own career.
Although he saw many imperfections in the frontier period, as
in his own, Chittenden neither in past nor present ever acknowledged that the individual of character and ability was
helpless to set his own course. In the end then, despite his
Darwinian gestures, Chittenden's determinism was rather mild,
really not very fatalistic at all, and only a convenient way of
interpreting some unsavory episodes like the expulsion of the
Indian, but of little meaning for explaining most of the events
and developments that he characterized.

Chittenden's historiographical ambiguity clearly illustrates

87 Ibid., p. 163.
88 HMC, *Steamboat Navigation* and *Fur Trade,* passim.
89 HMC, *Fur Trade,* 1: 257-59; 2: 698-706, 713-23.
90 HMC, *Fur Trade,* 1: 35.
91 Ibid., p. 462.

his transitional place in American historical writing. In many ways he was a follower of the first great frontier model, the dramatic, narrative, heroic approach of Washington Irving, of Francis Parkman, and of Theodore Roosevelt. Chittenden's romanticism, his belief in a democratic society that would be guided by a talented professional elite who had come to eminence through their own talents and character, his faith in the superior virtues of the Anglo-Saxon race, his concern with the exploits of individuals, all resemble closely this original genre of frontier historical writing.

But Chittenden was not simply one who concentrated upon, as Frederick Jackson Turner somewhat derisively dubbed it, "border warfare and the chase." Although Chittenden never seemed to be influenced by Turner's more sophisticated ideas about social evolution in different physiographic regions, Chittenden like Turner did take a broad-gauged approach to his study. He consciously attempted to place the narrative against the background of the environmental setting. He showed more sympathy for the customs and fate of the Indians than did Parkman or Roosevelt. He did try to analyze business records although without complete success. While neither a Turnerian nor a practitioner of what would soon be called the "New History," he did attempt to include data from several social sciences, but he did not view history, as did Turner and the "New Historians," as being particularly applicable to the solution of current problems.

His spirit was that of the trained, contemporary historian, seeking for scientific objectivity. Although his preference was for the narrative of great deeds, his conscience, and perhaps his lifetime of experience with the competing interests that bore upon any officer of the Corps of Engineers, helped him to recognize that history was not simply the exploits of colorful men. In coming to this recognition that romantic history was not the sum of historical pursuits, Chittenden did take his place as one who helped shape the writing of the history of the West in ways that it would follow in the future, when Turner's multiple-hypothesis, multiple-discipline guidelines would stimulate a multitude of writings about the westward movement, which, while not abandoning entirely dramatic narrative and individual deeds of greatness, would increasingly hold up as significant the activities of men in the "ordinary" pursuits that the narrative, romantic historians had considered mundane.

Whatever later analysts might think of his place in historiography, Chittenden himself never claimed to be a theoretician and he certainly had no school of followers as did Turner. He was a man more akin to Parkman, Hubert Howe Bancroft, or Webb, who attempted a large subject on a grand scale without bothering ever to define profoundly the purposes of history or its cosmic implications. If Chittenden ever reflected on the objective of the historian or the meaning of history, he did not commit these thoughts to paper, perhaps because he thought they were too obvious to discuss. Or perhaps his general optimism about man's rational powers and the upward course of history was never shadowed by doubt about the value of the past or the purposes of its students. What remains of Chittenden's historical reflections is not abstract speculation but three solid histories of the West, achievements sufficient to place him among the giants of frontier historiography.

5.

Second Tour in Yellowstone
1899-1906

When Hiram Chittenden returned to duty in Yellowstone Park, circumstances had changed from the time of his first appointment to that station eight years previously when he had been selected, almost by chance, as the officer who happened to have the appropriate rank for the assignment. Now, in 1899, he had considerable national reputation and the support of powerful political figures. His matured skill as an engineer allowed him to complete by 1906 the assignment—started long before—of constructing the basic road system in the park that essentially prevails to the present, and his persuasiveness enabled him to convince influential political leaders that his work there deserved sustained congressional support. Chittenden became thus responsible for both the engineering achievements and their financial foundation, while beyond the boundaries of the park he also executed many difficult projects in these seven years.

Among the Wyoming and Montana senators and representatives, Yellowstone National Park was always of great concern. Thus it was hardly surprising for General John M. Wilson, the Chief of Engineers, to receive a request from Senator Thomas H. Carter of Montana that he give Captain Chittenden responsibility for the construction of roads in the park. This post was again available to an officer of the Corps of Engineers after an interlude of almost five years during which time the acting superintendent, an officer of another military branch under the orders of the Secretary of the Interior, had combined both the engineering and administrative supervision of the park. General Wilson was quite amenable to Carter's suggestion and wrote to Chittenden offering him the post of engineer officer and suggesting that he would try to have him appointed acting superintendent as well.[1]

Chittenden gratefully accepted half of this proposal. He would be delighted to return as engineer officer, he responded, but he declined to handle simultaneously the acting superintendency since he would probably be junior in rank to the line officer commanding the troop of cavalry soldiers charged with enforcing the regulations established by the Department of the Interior and the acting superintendent, although this was subsequently not the case. The officer who served as acting superintendent was responsible for such varied matters as tracing lost persons, dealing with the concessionaires, listening to complaints from tourists about the accommodations, the roads, and the scenery, counting the visitors, dispatching animals to the National Zoo, catching poachers, and escorting dignitaries. Chittenden's problems were sufficient as road builder and, moreover, the superintendency required full-time residency in the park which would have disqualified him from other important assignments.[2]

As it turned out Chittenden got his preference when General Wilson appointed him engineer officer on March 25, 1899. The park had earlier been an interesting assignment for him and was much on his mind in the years since his departure from it after the working season of 1892. Two years later he had described the theory and practice of his road work in an article in *Good Roads* magazine and in 1895 he had published his book on the park. He had maintained a warm correspondence with his good friend Captain George Anderson, the acting superintendent, which kept him well informed about the gossip of the park community and Anderson's progress as road builder. As an authority on the history of the park, Chittenden had published a brief letter on John Colter in the *Nation* in 1896 and had contributed a chapter on the aboriginal use of the Yellowstone region in a book edited by J. V. Brower

1 HMC, "The Yellowstone," CPHS; John M. Wilson to HMC, February 18, 1899, #29969, RG 77.
2 HMC to John M. Wilson, February 23, 1899, #29969/1, RG 77; the multiplicity of duties of the acting superintendent is clearly revealed in his correspondence and journals in YNPA.

on *The Missouri River and Its Utmost Source* published in
St. Paul in the same year.[3]

Chittenden's reassignment to the park was thus most welcome, but also, as he doubtless anticipated, not without
problems. The Sundry Civil Act of March 4, 1899, had appropriated $40,000 for the improvement of Yellowstone Park
under the direction of the Secretary of War, who had assigned
the work to the Corps.[4] This statutory provision placed
Chittenden again potentially in conflict with the acting
superintendent, an officer of the line reporting to the Secretary
of the Interior, and problems of divided authority began for
Chittenden within a month of his reappointment. For his
duties in protecting the park, Captain Wilber E. Wilder, the
acting superintendent, requested $13,250 of the $40,000 that
Congress had appropriated for the fiscal year 1899-1900 but
had not earmarked for either Wilder or Chittenden. In a
telegram and following letter to the Chief of Engineers Chittenden urgently requested that the entire appropriation for
improvement be left in his hands. The Chief concurred in
his request, the matter was taken to the secretaries of War
and Interior and finally referred to Wilder and Chittenden
for settlement. They finally agreed to let Chittenden expend
$35,500 and he labeled the arrangement as, "all things con-
sidered, a satisfactory one."[5]

In his first month in office Chittenden also drafted a report
for General Wilson which, with supporting data from other
manuscripts, gives a good introduction to his work in the
next few years in Yellowstone. Of course, Chittenden always
had to balance his park activities with those on the upper
Missouri River and its tributaries plus the other assignments
that came to him. His duties in road construction consequently

3 HMC, "Roads in the Yellowstone National Park," *Good Roads* 5 (1894):
1-23; the HMC-Anderson correspondence is in YNPA; *Nation* 62 (1896): 415;
J. V. Brower, ed., *The Missouri River and Its Utmost Source* (St. Paul, Minn.,
1896), pp. 22-24.

4 John M. Wilson to R. G. Alger, March 6, 1899, #30129/1, RG 77.

5 HMC to Chief of Engineers (telegram), April 28, 1899, #30129/5; HMC to
John M. Wilson, April 28, 1899, #30129/6; E. I. Hitchcock, Secretary of the
Interior, to Secretary of War, May 12, 1899, #30129/34; R. A. Alger, Secretary of
War, to Secretary of the Interior, May 15, 1899, #30129/41; HMC to John M.
Wilson, May 29, 1899, #30129/28, all in RG 77.

were never ones upon which he could concentrate his full attention and it was a tribute not only to his excellent mind but also to his ability to compartmentalize work, that he achieved so much in Yellowstone.

About the middle of May in ordinary years the snows in the Yellowstone region began to melt sufficiently for the wagons of the working parties to penetrate into the Yellowstone plateau that included nearly all the park south of the Fort Yellowstone headquarters at Mammoth Hot Springs. For about a month the working force cleared the snow and repaired damages to the roads and bridges caused by the winter and spring freshets. About July 1, with the coincidence of the new fiscal year and clement conditions, regular work on the roads, including the extensions and changes in the system, commenced. At this time Chittenden came from Sioux City and took up summer quarters at Fort Yellowstone in the little stone engineer office on the plateau nestling under Sepulcher Mountain with the sounds of the famous hot springs bubbling to the west. Here was Chittenden's favorite station, where he and his family spent their happiest years, for they always relished the excitement of the move to the park and its clear air, spectacular scenery, and unfamiliar quiet.

If all went well Chittenden had at least one able assistant to direct the field parties while he inspected the construction between trips on the Union Pacific to Sioux City where his subordinates were attempting to dam the Osage and to carry on the routine channel improvements of the Gasconade and Missouri. But even though his assistants were skilled and loyal, Chittenden had to make many decisions himself and had to be in constant correspondence, as military regulations required, with the Chief of Engineers over most of these matters, however trivial they might be. His activities extended far beyond drawing plans and making surveys for the several projects in the park and were so numerous that his working schedule during the short construction season was typically sixteen hours a day every day.

Chittenden had to deal with the jobbers and the railroad to see that the supplies arrived on time. He had supervision of a working force that rose as high as 1,000 men, scattered throughout the park, whose welfare and safety were his responsibility. Since the government during his second term did all its work by direct hire, except for contract hire of teams, Chittenden was responsible for securing the work force in the spring, personally paying it off monthly, and discharging it in the fall. He wrote a little pamphlet establishing the rules for working parties down to sample menus and often had to demonstrate in person the proper handling of an ax to an unskilled workman. He had to obtain civil service classification for workmen and superintendents, to discharge incompetent or drunken employees, and to correspond with the acting superintendent, the Chief of Engineers, and a host of civilians who had complaints and suggestions that even included a bizarre plan to build a complete snowshed over the park road system. The engineer officer had to be an expert on matters far from civil engineering ranging from manuring the grass at the Mammoth headquarters to knowing the nomenclature of the park. Chittenden had to expose himself to a variety of weather conditions on top of his earlier typhoid attack and he had occasional paralytic seizures during his last years in Yellowstone. By the time the final working parties were paid off in November, and Chittenden could rejoin his wife and children, who had returned in September to Iowa, only the most parsimonious legislator could deny that he deserved his meager government salary.[6]

In this remote region, plans could not always be executed, as Chittenden was reminded during his first season of his second tour. The working season opened late in the park that year, the latest in history, and the work of the engineering crews was spent largely in clearing and repairing the roads damaged by the late and heavy freshets.[7] Meanwhile, Chittenden began to agitate for a project that was to occupy him

[6] Information in the last four paragraphs is drawn mainly from Chittenden's correspondence with the Chief of Engineers, 1899-1906, RG 77, especially HMC to John M. Wilson, April 6, 1899, #30129/2; Theodore P. Chittenden to author, November 1965; HMC, *Instructions to Foremen of Working Parties* (n.p., 1902), YNPA. His salary as captain was $195.00 per month and as major, $270.83. Fuel, quarters, and forage were furnished. U.S., War Department, *Official Army Register* 1885, (Washington, D.C., 1885), p. 380.

[7] HMC to John M. Wilson, May 4, 1899, #30129/29; HMC to John M. Wilson, June 21, 1899, #30129/43, both in RG 77.

for two years. He had become convinced long ago that the piecemeal system of annual appropriations made by Congress for river and harbor improvements and for Yellowstone Park was inefficient and inadequate and, accordingly, in his annual report for the fiscal year of 1899, he had recommended that Congress appropriate $310,000 to complete in a single season the road project conceived by Captain Dan Kingman in 1883 and authorized by Congress in the same year. According to Chittenden there were several advantages to the large appropriation. It would be a hedge against inflation. It would make it possible for the engineer officer to finish the project without having to worry whether to spend the small annual appropriations for repairs or new construction. Above all, the large appropriation would be beneficial to the nation, for it would finally enable completion of the original purposes of the first national park. The park had appealed to those who came for scenic wonders and recreation, had proved to be a sanctuary for the native fauna, and was now after numerous trials ably administered and protected, and adequately served by the concessionaires. "Congress," he concluded, "may therefore rest assured that an appropriation for the completion of the approved project of improvement of Yellowstone National Park will be in every sense a judicious expenditure."

Congress, however, did not see it so clearly as did Chittenden at this time, but he had prepared a sound and eloquent argument for future use. As a further measure to facilitate completion of the project, Chittenden wrote a letter to General Wilson in July asking him to visit the park. The Yellowstone project ranked, he said, in financial importance with a large proportion of river and harbor improvements and from other points of view was "immeasurably more important." Although the Chief did not fit Yellowstone into his itinerary in this year, he did pay the desired visit in 1900 and enjoyed himself immensely, remembering the pleasures of the park in later years.[8]

During 1899 Chittenden finished the construction of a four-mile road from Mammoth Hot Springs to the top of Golden

[8] *ARCE*, 1899, 6: 3867-68; HMC to John M. Wilson, July 6, 1899, #30129/46, RG 77; John M. Wilson to Mr. and Mrs. HMC, April 20, 1915, CP.

Gate Hill through a difficult stretch of limestone rock. He was also able to start construction of a new road through the Gardner Canyon. Finally, Chittenden's accomplishments for the year culminated in his favorably impressing men whose political influence was indispensable in preserving the entire road building system in the park for the Corps of Engineers.[9]

When Congress met in the late fall of 1899 House Resolution 983 was introduced to authorize again the construction of roads in the park by the acting superintendent (responsible to the Department of the Interior) rather than by the Corps of Engineers. Alarmed at this prospect General Wilson wrote on December 18 to Senator Carter of Montana calling his attention to the measure. On the same date Carter wrote to Congressman Franklin M. Mondell of Wyoming urging that the offending section be stricken from the bill and hailing the changes brought about by the recent reinstitution of the Corps as road builder: "Captain Chittenden, placed in charge there last season, representing the engineer corps of the army, did more work for the money and furnished better roads to the extent construction was pushed, than has obtained since the engineers of the Army were relieved from the work many years ago." Mondell hastily assured Carter that he would make the change.[10]

Chittenden had made a good impression on Senator Carter in other respects. On November 11, 1899, he and Carter had conferred in Helena and the senator had suggested that Chittenden prepare a statement of the requirements for future work in the park and give particular emphasis to the fiscal needs for the coming year. Carter said that he would call upon the Secretary of War for these data and hoped that Chittenden would have them ready at the proper time for presentation through channels. In February 1900 Chittenden sent his suggestions to the Chief of Engineers and on March 12, 1900, Senator Carter piloted a resolution through the Senate request-

[9] *ARCE*, 1900, 8: 5403-6; HMC to John M. Wilson, September 25, 1899, #30129/51, RG 77.

[10] Wilson's letter to Carter is lost; its contents are revealed in the reply, Thomas H. Carter to John M. Wilson, December 20, 1899, #30129/66; Thomas H. Carter to Frank Mondell, December 10, 1899, #30129/67; F. M. Mondell to Thomas H. Carter, December 22, 1899, #30129/68, all in RG 77.

ing the Secretary of War "to transmit to the Senate copies of all communications received by the Department from Hiram M. Chittenden, engineer in charge of improvements in the Yellowstone National Park, relative to present condition and appropriate plans for the development of the system of roads in said park." This letter contained the draft of a bill for the expenditure of $100,000 that was based upon his plans submitted in the annual report of 1899 although the monetary request had been scaled down from $310,000.[11]

While Carter was making this approach in the Senate, the Corps was asking in the House for the full $310,000 that Chittenden had recommended. Major James L. Lusk of the Corps appeared before a House Subcommittee on Appropriations arguing for the project based on Chittenden's authority, but the Congress saw fit to appropriate only $60,000 for the "improvement" (a term which always grated on the nerves of Chittenden, who admired natural beauty) of the park for 1900-1901. Again Congress did not divide the appropriation into engineering and administrative sections so Chittenden had to negotiate with the acting superintendent for their respective portions, with Chittenden getting all but $7,000.[12]

Chittenden increasingly came to rue this annual ad hoc division of the funds as jurisdictional disputes between the Interior and War departments (and their military subordinates in the park) continued to occur in spite of the transfer of Colonel Wilder to the Philippine Islands on July 24. Wilder's successor, Captain George W. Goode, determined to take hold of his new duties with a firm hand, was soon at loggerheads with Chittenden. In August Goode addressed a memorandum to the Secretary of the Interior requesting in all matters directly or indirectly affecting road construction, repair, or maintenance in the park, especially in the tourist season, that the acting superintendent should be advised by the engineer officer of

11 HMC, "Diary," November 11, 1899, CPHS; HMC to John M. Wilson, February 27, 1900, #30129/76, RG 77; U.S., Congress, Senate, Committee on Military Affairs, *Roads in the Yellowstone National Park*, 56th Cong., 1st sess., 1900, S. Doc. 226.

12 U.S., Congress, House, Subcommittee on Appropriation, *Hearings on Sundry Civil Bill for 1901*, 56th Cong., 1st sess., April 17, 1900, p. 361; HMC, *The Yellowstone National Park*, 3d rev. ed. (Cincinnati, Ohio, 1917), p. 251; HMC to John M. Wilson, June 17, 1900, #30129/95, RG 77.

every step he proposed and that he should obtain the consent of the acting superintendent before executing the work. This request was concurred in by the Acting Secretary of the Interior who passed it on to Elihu Root, the Secretary of War, for his endorsement. The patrician Root replied with chilliness: "The Acting Superintendent has no official relation whatever to the work, and cannot under any circumstances exercise any powers of supervision. I have no doubt that any unofficial suggestion which Captain Goode wishes to make to the Engineer Officer in charge will be courteously received, as would the suggestion of any citizen."[13]

Chittenden and Goode subsequently squabbled in the next two years over Goode's desire to use Chittenden's men to fight forest fires and Chittenden's request that his contractors be exempted from Goode's regulation that stock be herded in the daytime and tied at night. Finally, a grudging accommodation was reached by the two men in March 1901, when Chittenden frostily wrote to Goode: "I beg to assure you of my desire to avoid all future controversy in the relations of our respective departments, but in making this statement I do not wish it to be construed as recognizing the validity of your contention in any of the matters that have been at issue between us."[14]

Much more to Chittenden's taste and interest than these bureaucratic conflicts was the planning and execution of the actual work of road construction. In the appropriations statute of June 6, 1900, Congress required a complete plan for the road system of the park. Chittenden seized this opportunity to report on his progress and to assess the work ahead. The basic plan of Captain Kingman, still in force, was designed

[13] George W. Goode to Secretary of the Interior, August 15, 1900, #30129/117; Elihu Root to Acting Secretary of the Interior, August 25, 1900, #30129/22, both in RG 77.

[14] George Goode to HMC, August 17, 1900; HMC to George Goode, August 17, 1900; George Goode to Secretary of the Interior, August 18, 1900, all in #30129/27; HMC to H. C. Corbin, Adjutant General, August 18, 1900, #30129/114; HMC to John M. Wilson, September 19, 1900, #30129/126, all in RG 77; HMC to George H. [sic] Goode, October 29, 1900, YNPA; C. B. Scott to HMC, August 30, 1900, #30129/130; HMC to G. W. Goode, August 31, 1900, #30129/140; George W. Goode to HMC, September 1, 1900, #30129/141; HMC to Secretary of War (through Chief of Engineers), December 31, 1900, #30129/137, all in RG 77; HMC to George W. Goode, March 12, 1901, YNPA.

to connect the six major tourist attractions: Mammoth Hot Springs, the Norris Geyser Basin, and the Firehole Geyser Basin on the west side of the park and Yellowstone Lake, the Grand Canyon of the Yellowstone River, and the open park country at the base of Mount Washburn near Tower Falls, on the east side. Chittenden had completed half of this work by the summer of 1900.

Most of the roads were already constructed from Mammoth Hot Springs to the Canyon Junction, with the exception of some work in the Gibbon Canyon and in the Lower Geyser Basin and the realignment of the road from the Thumb to the Outlet of Yellowstone Lake, which would shorten the distance four miles. From Canyon Junction to Mammoth Hot Springs the road was largely unlocated or unopened except for two short stretches totaling three miles in length. The main east-west crossroad connecting the belt line at the center from Norris to the Grand Canyon, although open, would require severe modification and improvement. So far as approaches were concerned, Chittenden projected four, one from each cardinal point of the compass. The road from the north was completed and that from the west opened to travel; the southern and eastern roads were both located but incomplete. Chittenden also planned for about forty-five miles of side roads, such as a road over the top of Mount Washburn and two roads down both banks of the Grand Canyon, in addition to the belt line and main lines. Side roads were Chittenden's contribution, for they had been included only unofficially before this time. Foot trails were largely built but had to be maintained.[15]

In construction work, the season of 1900 saw the building of a new concrete bridge at the Golden Gate viaduct to replace the old wooden one that was so frightening to tourists. Chittenden also supervised the beginnings of the new road to the eastern entrance of the park where the chief problem was to select a suitable pass through the Absaroka Range.[16] After

15 *ARCE*, 1900, 8: 5403-15, 5441-44; HMC to John M. Wilson, September 15, 1900, #30129/123, RG 77.

16 *ARCE*, 1901, 5: 3780-82; HMC to John M. Wilson, September 14, 15, 1900, both in #30129/123, RG 77.

the 1900 working season was over Chittenden continued to advance the Yellowstone project in the fiscal realm. In December he went to Washington for five days of conferences on the needs of the park with Assistant Secretary of the Interior Thomas Ryan, with his own Engineer Department, with George H. Maxwell, and with several important representatives and senators including Joseph G. Cannon, Franklin Mondell, Thomas Carter, Francis E. Warren, and John Spooner. After his return to St. Louis, he furthered his case for increased appropriations on December 26 in a letter to Congressman Mondell who passed the news of this conversation on to Congressman Cannon early in the next year. Cannon, to whom an Illinois contractor in 1900 had commended Chittenden's Yellowstone work, was the most felicitously placed ally Chittenden could have had. Famed for his general conservatism and financial parsimony with government funds, Cannon had as firm a stranglehold on appropriations as he obtained later upon the House of Representatives when he became Speaker. It is difficult to discern why Cannon was an enthusiast for the park, for it hardly seems in character for him to be concerned with natural beauty in so distant a region, but Chittenden's work and his persuasive powers must have impressed him greatly. The appropriation voted for roads and bridges in Yellowstone Park on March 3, 1901, to the amount of $113,000, was the largest to date, and perhaps even more important, was voted in a lump sum so that the engineer officer could expend it where needed on any of the roads in the project.[17]

When spring came, Chittenden returned to the park to find the country apprehensive over an outbreak of smallpox and the weather extremely stormy so that the start of construction was delayed until May 1. Although these developments were frustrating, they were all forgotten because of the visit of Congressman Cannon. "Uncle Joe" made a tour through the park from June 26 to July 1 using the regular conveyances as

[17] J. G. Courts to John M. Wilson (telegram), December 7, 1900, #30129/135; HMC to F. M. Mondell, December 26, 1901 (the original of this letter is not extant); F. M. Mondell to Joseph G. Cannon, January 8, 1901, #30129/167; J. D. Wallace to J. G. Cannon, February 14, 1900, #34182/167; J. D. Wallace to J. G. Cannon, February 14, 1900, #34182, all in RG 77; ARCE, 1901, 5: 3785-88; HMC, "Diary," December 11-14, 1900, CPHS.

far as possible and then going by horseback over the rugged
trail from the Falls to Yanceys in the company of Chittenden
and the new acting superintendent, the roughhewn Major
John Pitcher, who had succeeded Goode on May 9, 1901.
Cannon was immensely pleased and a month after his trip wrote
to General Gillespie: "I gave considerable attention to public
work in progress . . . I am satisfied that the best results can
be had under Captain Chittenden & I do hope he will be
continued in charge until the work is done—I am satisfied
he is the right man in the right place." The austere Chittenden was for his part greatly taken with Cannon: "He is a
most entertaining travelling companion and evidently a very
able man—," he wrote in his diary two days after Cannon's
departure, "a statesman of the old school of Lincoln's time—a
wonderful storyteller with no attempt to be choice in subjects—
a most instructive talker withal." Another positive development for Chittenden this year was the good relationship that
grew between himself and Major Pitcher.[18]

In the working season of 1901 several projects were taken in
hand. A six and one-half mile piece of road was built from
the top of the hill above Yanceys toward Soda Butte and
Tower Falls. In the canyon of the Gardner River the movement of the road from the dangerous right bank to the left
was completed, including the construction of three new steel
bridges. On the east entrance road about twelve miles of new
road were constructed. Fourteen miles of road were opened
or rebuilt along the south entrance road in the park and in
the Teton Forest Reserve. Around Mammoth Hot Springs,
the park headquarters, Chittenden cooperated with the Quartermaster Department of Dakota in planning to bring in a
reliable supply of water from Glen Creek for the post, the
engineer department, and the concessionaires. This plan,
instigated by Senator Carter, proposed a water supply to make

18 HMC to John M. Wilson, May 2, 1901, #30249/79, endorsement by Judge
Advocate General, May 27, 1901; HMC to G. L. Gillespie, August 6, 1901,
#30249/86; HMC to G. L. Gillespie, June 8, 1901, #30129/178, all in RG 77;
"Journal of the Acting Superintendent Yellowstone National Park," 1901, pp.
145, 150, 154, 155, 159, 166, 167, 170, YNPA; HMC to G. L. Gillespie, July 2,
1901, #30129/181; J. G. Cannon to G. L. Gillespie, July 26, 1901, #40218, both
in RG 77; HMC, "Diary," July 3, 1901, CPHS.

possible the irrigating and planting of a lawn at the site of the headquarters as a part of a long-contemplated beautification plan that also included the realignment of the roads and sidewalks at that point.[19]

Among his other activities Chittenden also found time to experiment with the sprinkling of the park roads. Dust was the bane of tourists and for years they had unavailingly complained of it. On the new Golden Gate road Chittenden decided to sprinkle the road by water wagon and pronounced the experiment a success in appeasing the tourists and in preserving the roadbed. Still not fully satisfied, Chittenden in the fall of the year visited Bakersfield and San Francisco, where oil was being used to lay road dust. He was impressed with the results in both places and recommended further experiments.[20]

Wyoming politicians also brought Chittenden an assignment outside the park boundaries in this year. In the immemorial custom of the American frontier Wyoming residents had agitated for years for federal construction of a wagon road from Fort Washakie in their state along the Wind River to the mouth of the Buffalo Fork of the Snake River near Jackson Lake near the southern boundary of Yellowstone Park to give them a south entrance into the park. Since the government did not build civilian wagon roads, the request for the road was justified as militarily necessary to connect the garrison at the fort with the ostensibly hostile Indians in the Jackson Hole country. In 1897 Congress had authorized the project and appropriated $10,000 for it but the war with Spain and a controversy over the legality of the appropriation delayed construction. Chittenden took up the project and in the working seasons of 1901 and 1902 made a reconnaissance of the route.

The only matter of interest for Chittenden in the project, and that unpleasant, was one arising out of the action of homesteaders in obstructing the road and changing its original location. Chittenden posted notice against these

---

[19] *ARCE*, 1902, 4: 3034-37, 3042-45.
[20] Ibid., pp. 3037-39; ibid., 3: 2561-65.

trespassers but was not sure of his authority to do so since part of the road lay in the Teton and Yellowstone Park Forest reserves. The matter was ultimately referred by the Chief of Engineers to the Secretary of War and the Attorney General and the latter finally ruled that Chittenden's actions were unnecessary but proper. The appropriate forest supervisor was instructed to post the notices thereafter. As always the conclusion of a successful working season did not free Chittenden from responsibilities to the national park and he had little time to enjoy his new son, Theodore Parker, born on September 25, 1901.[21]

Congressman Cannon called Chittenden before his appropriations committee in December 1901, and also in March 1902. Chittenden's first testimony made a most interesting session, for, drawing on Cannon's memory of his own park tour, Chittenden was able to make vivid to him the particular needs in the park. He argued for a lump sum appropriation rather than the system of specific appropriations for each portion of the project, and he asked that the appropriation be made available when voted rather than at the beginning of the fiscal year, which came about six weeks after the usual time for the commencement of road work in the park. He also asked that the Congress appropriate specific separate amounts for the acting superintendent and for the engineer officer. As in the previous years Chittenden's efforts to gain a suitable appropriation were successful, for in the Sundry Civil Act for the fiscal year 1902-1903 Congress voted a continuing appropriation sufficient for the completion of the entire project. This act, adopted June 28, 1902, appropriated $250,000 available at once and $500,000 in the future.[22]

Chittenden ever remembered Cannon fondly for his generosity to the park and at the time of his defeat by insurgent Progressives in 1910 Chittenden wrote in his diary "that not

21 *ARCE*, 1899, 6: 3881-900; *ARCE*, 1901, 5: 3823-25; *ARCE*, 1902, 4: 3075; John M. Wilson to Elihu Root, September 29, 1900, #27462/86, 89, RG 77.

22 U.S., Congress, House, Subcommittee on Appropriations, *Hearings on . . . Sundry Civil Appropriation Bill for 1902*, 56th Cong., 2d sess., December 13, 1900, pp. 169-75; F. M. Mondell to G. L. Gillespie, February 13, 1902, #30129/201; J. G. Cannon to G. L. Gillespie, March 2, 1902, #30129/212, both in RG 77.

one of those who have reaped some temporary glory in the overthrow of Mr. Cannon will ever render one tithe of the service to their country that he has done nor take a place in their country's history which can in any degree compare with his."[23] But during his March interviews in Washington, despite the favorable progress of the park appropriation bill, Chittenden confided his misgivings about his personal career to his diary: "I felt deeply distressed while in Washington, for it seemed as if I was being left far behind in the race for advancement."[24] No doubt the unusual and relatively unknown character of his park work—work that lacked the "practical" value of river and harbor improvement—made his promotions come slowly compared to his peers, but he persisted in Yellowstone without public complaint.

With ample money available Chittenden's work in the season of 1902 was substantial and much of it was in addition to the building of roads. He was in charge of the general improvement of the park headquarters at Mammoth Hot Springs where, in collaboration with the Quartermaster Department, Chittenden completed the water supply plant for the irrigation of the plateau at Mammoth, constructed an electrical lighting plant for the fort and for the engineer department, and built the sidewalks about the post. He supervised the planting of a lawn in front of the headquarters building and was able to persuade the distinguished Boston landscape architect Warren H. Manning to design a plan of the grounds free of charge. The engineer buildings had been in disrepair for a number of years and Chittenden began work upon several new structures including an office building, a house for the engineer officer, a mess house, and an entrance building at the north approach to the park.[25]

Chittenden advised the Weather Bureau in regard to the correct location of an observation post near Mammoth. He succeeded in persuading Charles S. Mellen, president of the Northern Pacific Railroad, to authorize the construction of

23 HMC, "Diary," March 20, 1910, CPHS.
24 Ibid., March 24, 1902, CPHS.
25 HMC to George E. Pond, April 5, 1902, #30129/225, RG 77; *ARCE*, 1903, 4: 2885-89.

that railroad's line from Cinnabar to Gardiner where it would be possible for tourists to transfer directly to the concessionaire's stages for the park tour. He also indulged his historical interest by preparing signs to mark the location of the route of General Oliver O. Howard across the park in 1877 in the pursuit of the Nez Perce bands under the leadership of Chief Joseph. This business gave Chittenden the occasion to mount a little holiday expedition including some of the survivors of the march, officers from the post, and a party of the civilians working in the park. All these duties, in addition to the supervision of 700 workmen and 125 teams, made 1902 the busiest year for the engineer department in the history of the park.[26]

After a usual winter of routine at Sioux City attending to the office affairs of his various projects scattered about the West, Chittenden returned to Wyoming in April to prepare for a visit by President Theodore Roosevelt, who was coming to take a two-week tour of Yellowstone Park. Before beginning his tour Roosevelt invited Chittenden to dine and breakfast with him and asked for a copy of Chittenden's book on the fur trade. After these amenities, Roosevelt, his friend John Burroughs, the naturalist, Superintendent Pitcher, and a few enlisted men plunged into the park. While in the park, Roosevelt agreed to the request of a local committee to dedicate the cornerstone of a masonry arch at the north entrance to the park at the conclusion of his tour.

Preparations for this ceremony were Chittenden's responsibility but were intruded upon by the unforeseen and unwelcome orders that soon he would be transferred to the Philippine Islands to command Company M of the Third Battalion of Engineers then fighting the insurgents. Chittenden felt that the news of this transfer "cannot mean anything good." He feared the completely different type of work awaiting him in the archipelago but promised himself to hope for the best. Perhaps in normal circumstances he might have

---

26 HMC to W. L. Moore, April 8, 1902; J. H. Brigham to Secretary of the Interior, April 11, 1902; C. S. Mellen to HMC, April 30, 1902, all in YNPA; HMC to G. L. Gillespie, May 22, 1902, #30129/241, RG 77; *ARCE*, 1902, 4: 3039-40; HMC to G. L. Gillespie, August 6, 1902, #30129/253, RG 77.

regarded the transfer as an opportunity or as a challenge, but with deteriorating health it was a burden, the prospect of which was not lightened by the news of the next day that he would soon have to stand for his promotion examination.[27]

In any case, his immediate problem was the ceremony. At 4:10 in the afternoon of April 24 the president appeared around the bend of the road one-half mile distant and galloped up to the roped-off cornerstone accompanied by a few army officers. The band played "Hail Columbia," Masonic ceremonies were conducted, and the president spoke to the assembled crowd of approximately 3,000 persons. A brief reception followed and at 6 P.M. he was on the westward bound train with Chittenden riding in his private car as far as Livingston.[28]

Roosevelt, greatly impressed by Chittenden, praised his work in the park and while on the train the president dictated a letter to the Secretary of War asking that Chittenden not be sent to the Philippines but retained in the park "in the interest of the public service," for it would be a "veritable calamity" for the park to have him removed at this time. When he heard of this order, Chittenden protested it vigorously in person to the president, knowing that the order, considering the circumstances under which it was written, could be interpreted as the result of his desire to avoid service in battle. Realizing finally that Chittenden was adamant, Roosevelt wrote to the Chief of Engineers rescinding his order and explaining that his original order was issued without Chittenden's request and against his protest.[29]

When the news of Chittenden's Philippines order first became public, several individuals who knew of his park successes, including Senator Carter, Senator William A. Clark, and Major Pitcher, wrote to the president asking him to reverse it. These requests were a tribute to Chittenden's work

27 HMC, "Diary," April 12, 19, 20, 1903, CPHS.

28 Livingston (Mont.) Enterprise, June 30, 1923; New York Evening Post, April 14, 1903; Anaconda (Mont.) Standard, April 25, 1903; New York Times, April 25, 1903, p. 1; HMC, "Diary," May 3, 1903, CPHS.

29 Theodore Roosevelt to Secretary of War, April 24, 1903; Theodore Roosevelt to George L. Gillespie, April 25, 1903, both #46947, both in RG 77; HMC, "Diary," May 3, 1903, CPHS.

and must have pleased him greatly, although they must also have gnawed at him for fear that his superiors might believe he had instigated them. Finally, in spite of his previous reversal, Roosevelt again rescinded the transfer order and the Secretary of War on June 3 issued the formal order retaining Chittenden in the park for one year. When the year had elapsed so had the insurrection in the Philippines and Chittenden was permitted to remain until the project was completed. Chittenden believed that the decisive blow to retain him in the park was struck by Mellen who had persuaded Roosevelt while in Oregon that Chittenden was indispensable.[30]

Meanwhile, Chittenden on September 1, 1903, finished the arch that President Roosevelt had dedicated. Chittenden had planned this structure to relieve the drab vista that greeted the visitor alighting from the train at the railroad station at Gardiner. The flat, dry, and unimpressive view was, to Chittenden's taste, an unworthy entrance to the park. He decided to put in a pond and lawn outside the railroad station and, at the crest of a hill on the road leading to the park, built the thirty-foot masonry arch that was inscribed above the keystone with the inscription "For the Benefit and Enjoyment of the People," words taken from the act establishing the park. Along the roadway he planted trees that he irrigated from the Gardner River.[31]

The year saw the usual repairs, the completion of the east entrance road, the further improvement of the grounds at Mammoth Hot Springs, and the expansion of the road sprinkling experiment. Of greater interest were the bridging of the Yellowstone River and the construction of the Mount Washburn road. Chittenden had been in favor of a bridge across the Yellowstone Canyon for several years but had never had the appropriation or the time to build a bridge pleasing enough to do justice to the natural location. With the invention of the Melan arch and the recent congressional

30 Thomas H. Carter to G. L. Gillespie, May 11, 1903, #46947/5, RG 77; W. A. Clark to Secretary of War, May 29, 1903; John Pitcher to Adjutant General, May 26, 1903; Secretary of War to Chief of Engineers, June 2, 1903, all in #3839-A.C.P.-1884, ACP; HMC, "Diary," June 11, 1903, CPHS.
31 ARCE, 1903, 4: 2469-70, 2889-90; ARCE, 1904, 4: 4171-72.

generosity, he felt that he was able to begin work in 1903. Instead of choosing the most feasible (narrowest) site for his arch, Chittenden selected a more aesthetic one about one-half mile above the upper falls. Because of its noncommercial nature and the worldwide attention it would receive, the owners of the Melan arch patent waived their royalties on the bridge. Their confidence was justified, for the final structure was beautiful, a fine tribute to its builder for whom it was named in 1926. The span lasted until its larger successor was built in 1962.[32]

The Washburn road project was equally exhilarating, for it was the most scenic highway in the park. This road over the summit of 10,600-foot Mount Washburn was designed to bridge the only gap in the grand loop. In the spring of 1903 snow lingered long on the mountain and the water-soaked terrain delayed the work so that little was accomplished compared to Chittenden's ambitions. Further problems were the "great proportion of rock work, the high altitude, and the lack of good camping places." Still, on the south side the road came to within two and one-half miles from the summit and on the north side reached to four miles from the summit. In 1913 the road was named for its builder.[33]

Chittenden varied his work in 1903 by publishing a revised edition of his book on the park. In this edition he made several changes, updating the section on highway construction, including new data on early park history and geographical nomenclature, and presenting a new narrative of the campaign against Chief Joseph's Nez Perce in 1877. The descriptive section was lengthened and almost all the illustrations were new. To make room for this new material Chittenden eliminated the appendixes on legislation affecting the park, annual park appropriations, a list of superintendents, and a bibliography of the park literature. He also felt apparently that the boundary was secure enough to omit the sections on

[32] HMC to G. L. Gillespie, May 14, 1902, #30129/235, RG 77; *ARCE*, 1904, 4: 4172-74; *Haynes' New Guide and Motorist's Complete Road Log of Yellowstone Park* (St. Paul, Minn., 1926), p. 99; HMC, "Reinforced Concrete Arch Bridge over the Yellowstone River, Yellowstone National Park," *Engineering News* 51 (1904): 25-27.
[33] *ARCE*, 1903, 4: 2891; *ARCE*, 1904, 4: 4173 (quotation, p. 4173).

hostility to the park and the railroad threats to the park boundary.[34]

The working seasons of 1904 and 1905 were Chittenden's last in the park although he was not relieved from duty until March 26, 1906. These years saw the completion of the project authorized in 1900 and placed on a firm financial basis in 1902. About 90 percent of the road surfacing was completed through the use of gravel, machine-crushed rock, hand-broken stone, or other material. The road from Lower Falls to Mammoth Hot Springs was finished, including the difficult high line over the summit of Mount Washburn, and the lower road through Dunraven Pass. Adequate plant for any future work was completed. The landscaping at park headquarters and at the Gardiner station had been successfully accomplished and the grass and trees were flourishing. The sprinkling system was completed.[35]

Major Chittenden, writing his annual report in July 1905, made it a satisfactory valedictory. He stated proudly that "the work which was undertaken under the continuing appropriation four years ago has been practically completed, and there has also been done considerable work not contemplated in the original estimates. All the roads which it has ever been proposed to build are now open to travel." Still he knew that the future would bring greatly increased numbers of tourists, necessitating certain improvements, and he bequeathed some suggestions to his successor. He proposed that the standard width of road surface be widened from eighteen to twenty-five feet. As traffic had increased he recommended the greater use of mortar guardrails on the steep slopes of hills. He suggested that the dead and down timber should be cleared up for a width of 100 feet on each side of the road for aesthetic reasons and for fire protection. He wanted all bridges to be of concrete or steel and all culverts to be of vitrified clay pipe. Since the Union Pacific Railroad was planning to build to the west entrance of the park it was necessary to bring the entrance road from that direction up to full standards. The greatest

34 HMC, *The Yellowstone National Park: Historical and Descriptive,* rev. ed. (Cincinnati, Ohio, 1903).
35 *ARCE,* 1904, 4: 4171-77; *ARCE,* 1905, 3: 2809-13.

problem of all was to improve the road surface so that it would stand the increasingly great demands upon it in the immediate future. The cost of all of these improvements he reckoned at \$2,023,065.[36] After the close of the 1905 season Chittenden returned as usual to Sioux City, this time never to return to Yellowstone Park, but he could take pride in his accomplishments in the nation's first national park.[37]

The most recent historian of the Yellowstone roads, Bob Randolph O'Brien, credits Chittenden with three major accomplishments as the most influential of the officers of the Corps of Engineers in the park.[38] Chittenden believed in building a minimum of roads in the park so that they would reveal only the most important features of the park; he insisted, writes O'Brien, upon high quality roads that "helped prevent extension of the road system two decades before a policy based on wilderness preservation could have the same effect"; he ceaselessly advocated the construction of "park roads."[39] Since his first tour of duty in the park Chittenden had insisted that the roads be built with aesthetic considerations paramount. He led battles against the introduction of electric railways and superfluous roads, fighting against proposals in 1905 for the building of two roads from Bozeman and Red Lodge, respectively, into the park. "It has been the policy of the officer in charge of the improvement work," he wrote, "and also of the present superintendent of the park, to discourage any material extension of the park road system. There are now roads enough."[40]

Chittenden's paramount consideration in carrying out his mandate to build the park roads was not his own personal appreciation of nature. As a loyal member of the Corps he would have done his best in any situation in which the exigencies of the service placed him. Obviously his mandate had to be interpreted flexibly and as engineer officer the mode of inter-

36 *ARCE*, 1905, 3: 2813-22 (quotation, p. 2813).

37 HMC, "Diary," December 8, 1905, CPHS.

38 Bob Randolph O'Brien, "The Yellowstone National Park Road System: Past, Present and Future" (Ph.D. diss., University of Washington, 1965), pp. 101, 102.

39 Ibid., p. 102.

40 *ARCE*, 1905, 3: 2821-22 (quotation, p. 2821).

pretation to a large extent depended upon his philosophy of proper national park use and development. Equally obvious was the fact that he had a deep love for nature and that his heart was in his program for preserving as much of wild nature as possible in the process of road construction.

What Chittenden admired most about nature—and about Yellowstone Park—was not its awesomeness nor its exotic features. Rather he preferred its gentler, pastoral, almost agricultural aspects. When describing the Rocky Mountains, Chittenden wrote of the mountain parks scattered through the forests of pine and fir: "At frequent intervals throughout these forests are open spaces, filled with luxuriant grass, forming parks of faultless beauty amid the sombre solitudes of the surrounding woods. Everywhere in these wild and sublime situations occur the always pleasing groves of the quaking aspen, a grateful relief either from the gloomy view of extensive forests or the uniform prospect of grass-covered slopes. Taken together, these varied arrangements of nature present an artistic appearance that reminds one of the cultivated sections in the mountain regions of Europe where man has contributed so much to enhance the beauty of nature."[41]

Since for Chittenden the ordinary aspects of nature were the most appealing and since he felt man could in a sense "improve" upon nature, although he disliked that word, he saw little conflict between his road building activities and the preservation of nature: "As a general policy, the extension of the system should be restricted to actual necessities. The Park should be preserved in its natural state to the fullest degree possible. While it is true that highways are least objectionable of all artificial changes in natural conditions, still they should not be unnecessarily extended, and the great body of the Park should be kept inaccessible except on foot or horseback." His philosophy of roads still continues, for it is that held currently by the National Park Service and, according to a recent poll, by a majority of visitors to the national parks.[42]

[41] HMC, *Fur Trade*, 2: 729.

[42] HMC, *The Yellowstone National Park*, 2d rev. ed. (Cincinnati, Ohio, 1915), p. 237; O'Brien, "Yellowstone National Park Road System," p. 101, n. 45; *Christian Science Monitor*, September 16, 1968.

Although Chittenden never formally defended his position about the relative harmlessness of highways, he did endeavor to make some changes in nature that were consistent with his beliefs about beauty. As one example, he developed a lawn and constructed a masonry arch at the Gardiner entrance "because the natural features of the country at this portion of the boundary are about the least interesting of any part of the Park."[43] In his final revision of the *Yellowstone* published in 1915, two years before his death, Chittenden would permit the improvement of tourist facilities, but "In all other respects the greatest service which official authority can render to posterity is to maintain and transmit this possession as it came from the hand of Nature."[44] Although he was not able always to blend his philosophy and his achievements, his engineering work did approach closely his ideal within the limitations imposed by the amount of the appropriations.

John Ise, the historian of the national parks, writes flatly that "Many of the roads in Yellowstone were built under the supervision of H. M. Chittenden, and they were of course built well. Yellowstone roads were better than those of other national parks."[45] The problems that Chittenden faced in achieving these results were formidable. He did not have to make the general decision about where the roads were to be built, but he faced severe difficulties in constructing them. Climate, terrain, and soil were all inhospitable. The country of the park was largely mountainous, 84 percent of it covered with dense and towering forests, and bearing snow throughout most of the year. The snow melts in the spring and early summer made the many streams torrential and destructive. The soil was of great variety, but mainly of a volcanic type, with only the infrequent deposits of basalt being of use for macadam. The beds of gravel were also too few to be feasible for road surfacing.

Marked as these difficulties were, Chittenden was largely able to overcome them. Although he did not complete the roads to the standard he desired, particularly in the matter of

43 *ARCE*, 1903, 4: 2889.
44 HMC, *The Yellowstone National Park,* pp. 251-52.
45 John Ise, *Our National Park Policy,* p. 30.

surfacing, he did build a system of roads suitable for safe and scenic driving in the pre-automobile era and one that could be easily improved for motor traffic after 1915 when automobiles were first admitted to the park. His roads became a standard for the parks and his services were sought in other scenic areas for highway construction.[46]

Chittenden's efforts as builder of park roads would have been impossible without his services as advocate for sufficient appropriations. During his second term of service (when he was responsible for the park engineering operations) the Congress voted $1,225,000 for administration and the road system compared to $635,934.25 in all previous years.[47] Of this amount, the major breakthroughs came in 1900 when Congress voted to adopt the project as a unified entity and in 1902 when it voted the continuing appropriation of $750,000. He could take further pride in the rise in the number of park visitors from 9,579 in the season of 1899 to 26,188 in that of 1905, his last summer.[48] But the price of his accomplishment in the park was high although he took great pride in it: "It was in the fullest sense a labor of love. . . . Sacrifice, too, there was, apart from the deep draught upon physical energy, in the relinquishment of opportunities of greater professional importance elsewhere, but the determination to see the work through prevailed over all other considerations."[49] The work itself and Yellowstone always remained a consolation as Chittenden began a black period of his life, from which he never completely emerged.

For about two years his health had been failing from overexposure and typhoid attacks and his spirits had also declined during this time of adversity. In March 1905, while making a trip to the West in company with Howard Elliott, president of the Northern Pacific Railway, he indulged in uncharacteristic self-pity about his career with the Corps. Elliott's intimate views of life on the railroad on this occasion impressed Chit-

46 *ARCE*, 1903, 4: 2446-50.

47 *ARCE*, 1905, 3: 2822.

48 J. E. Haynes, *Haynes' Guide* (Bozeman, Mont., 1964), p. 34, cited in O'Brien, "The Yellowstone National Park Road System," p. 128, fig. 16.

49 HMC, *The Yellowstone National Park*, p. iii.

tenden and he wrote enviously in his diary about the railroad business that "It all had a life and business air about it that interested me greatly and I wished that my lot had fallen in similar places." Finally in November Chittenden consulted a physician, confessing that he should have done so long before, who proclaimed him after examination to be "a physical wreck." Rest and other treatments were prescribed for his nervous exhaustion and Chittenden, granted a leave of absence, entered Richard Dewey's sanitarium in Wauwatosa, Wisconsin, in December. In the privacy of his diary Chittenden's steadfast determination temporarily flagged as he wrote: "Naturally this has been a terrible blow. To be wrecked in the prime of life when the heart is full of strength and hope and ambitions is dreadful in any case. I often ask if, in view of the hard and I judge useful work I have done, I deserve it." Self-pity again took him for a while when he reflected on the lack of sympathy he had received from his fellows for not earlier dropping his work in favor of a complete rest. He felt that such a course was impractical and that to carry on was deserving of the "respect" of others rather than their "contempt." He convinced himself that to sacrifice himself in the cause of useful work was a greater sacrifice than to die in battle where the soldier received both glory and approval.

In the sanitarium Chittenden rested principally by reading widely and the work that impressed him most was Charles H. Henderson's inspirational novel, *John Percyfield,* a "superb" work both in conception and execution, but with the fault that it painted so idealized a picture of human conduct that the ordinary mortal could not emulate it. He also drew consolation from the Bible, the great stoics Aurelius and Epictetus, and La Rochefoucauld, until finally, greatly strengthened mentally and physically, he was discharged from Dr. Dewey's care in February 1906.[50]

50 HMC, "Diary," March 16, November 12, December 8, 26, 1905; January 3, February 3, 5, 1906, CPHS.

6.

Seattle District Engineer
1906-1910

Fifteen pounds heavier and to all appearances markedly restored in body and spirits, Chittenden left the sanitarium in Wauwatosa on February 3, 1906, to return to Sioux City to discover his new assignment.[1] In quick succession, he received word of his appointment as district engineer in Seattle, closed up his affairs in Sioux City, went through a round of farewell parties with his family, and departed by train for the Northwest. The children were entertained en route by consuming pounds of candy given them by friends and by perusing the latest land office maps of the route which their father took along to give them geography lessons. At St. Paul and Helena the Chittendens stopped over to visit old friends before taking up their new station on Puget Sound. Upon arrival Major Chittenden's impressions of Seattle were highly favorable, for he admired the "spirit that animates this rising community" that he pronounced, although at present "a crude and ugly place," to be "surely a city of destiny."[2]

Settling his family into a rented flat, Major Chittenden soon confirmed his initial impression of Seattle's dynamism. Economically, the city was midway through a prosperous decade when Chittenden arrived in April of 1906. Taking advantage of the enormous boon conferred upon it by the Klondike gold rush of 1897, Seattle continued in the new century to exploit its two basic advantages as a central place for service and supply of the entire Puget Sound region and as a "transportation foci and break of bulk point" for domestic, coastal, and international commerce. Population, all types of trade and commerce, and banking facilities increased enormously in the decade although manufacturing was never of great significance.[3]

The leaders of this new prosperity, Seattle's businessmen, personified the booster spirit of the frontier and the exuberant confidence of American businessmen. In origin mainly of the middle class from other states and territories, they continued to maintain financial connections outside the region, for they were the channels through which vital outside capital poured into this underdeveloped area.[4] The chief institutional focus for this entrepreneurial group was the Chamber of Commerce, which represented the business community in Olympia, New York, Chicago, and the national capital, as well as among the people of Seattle. The Chamber, proud of its role in capturing the Alaska trade in the late 1890s through the inspired propaganda of its secretary, Erastus Brainerd, now editor of the *Post-Intelligencer,* was the epitome of the "Seattle Spirit," the unabashed boosterism that trumpeted the region's opportunities.[5]

In their leisure hours, the leading businessmen frequented the select Arctic and Rainier Clubs, took the *Post-Intelligencer* or the *Daily Times* of the choleric xenophobe, Alden J. Blethen, and frequented, according to confirmed taste or changing mood, the new baseball club, the novel cinema, the visiting opera and vaudeville shows, and the still numerous (despite recent reform efforts) houses of the red-light district. These optimistic, gregarious, and thoroughly middle-class businessmen were to be Chittenden's closest professional associates for the rest of his life, even though his personal tastes, character, and ambitions frequently differed widely from their norms and led to bitter conflicts and personal differences.[6]

[1] HMC, "Diary," February 3, 5, 1906, CPHS.

[2] Alexander Mackenzie to HMC, February 1, 1906 (telegram), #58240, RG 77; HMC, "Diary," May 6, 1906, CPHS, describes the trip and his first impressions of Seattle.

[3] HMC, "Diary," May 17, 1907, CPHS; Alexander N. MacDonald, "Seattle's Economic Development, 1880-1910" (Ph.D. diss., University of Washington, 1959), pp. 153-58, 332.

[4] Norbert MacDonald, "The Business Leaders of Seattle, 1880-1910," *Pacific Northwest Quarterly* 50 (1959): 1-13.

[5] The contemporary Seattle daily newspapers and the "Minute Books" of the Seattle Chamber of Commerce located in the Chamber offices are the main sources for the activities of that body.

[6] The daily newspapers and the weekly press, the *Argus* and the *Town-Crier,* are the sources for this paragraph.

In politics, the business group was divided, since Seattle in 1906 was experiencing the stirrings of Progressivism. In the fall of the previous year various elements coalesced to combat the entrenched, corrupt, and vice-tolerant Republican machine. This alliance of organized labor (which included only a small proportion of the working class), business, and professional people formed a political party, the Municipal Ownership party, and elected as mayor William Hickman Moore, a mild reformer. More important, in the same year, the reformers obtained a new city charter which gave the people, among other things, the right to recall elected officials. At the level of state politics, Seattle provided many of the actors in the reform struggles. The chief victory of the Progressives had been the enactment of a railroad commission in 1905 in the teeth of the opposition of the Great Northern interests and the *Seattle Times*. Unsatisfied, the reformers had pressed on, working for the enactment of a direct primary law.[7]

In the next nine years Chittenden's work was to be chiefly influenced by the struggle between those who wished to extend governmental services at all levels and those who favored the status quo and by the economic vision of the city's business elite. His own particular ambitions were bound up with the shifting outcomes of these two forces and their numerous lesser components. A dedicated, highly intelligent, inhumanly industrious man, now of great professional and political experience and, with the completion of the Yellowstone work, one of national reputation, Chittenden at the age of forty-eight, worried only by the ever-present problem of his health, fixed immediately upon the Lake Washington canal as the most important project in his district.

Plans for a canal to connect the waters of Puget Sound with fresh water Lake Washington were almost as old as the city of Seattle itself.[8] In 1854, Thomas Mercer, an original pioneer

7 Keith A. Murray, "Republican Party Politics in Washington during the Progressive Era" (Ph.D. diss., University of Washington, 1946), pp. 64-71; Wesley A. Dick, "The Genesis of City Light" (Master's thesis, University of Washington, 1965), pp. 82-83.

8 U.S., Congress, House, Committee on Rivers and Harbors, HMC, *Puget Sound-Lake Washington Waterway, Washington*, 60th Cong., 1st sess., 1908, H. Doc. 953, pp. 4-6, reviews the history of the canal in the nineteenth century.

and the city's first teamster, suggested that the small lake intermediate between the Sound and Lake Washington be christened Lake Union to symbolize the eventual marriage of the waters of lake and sound. In the frontier tradition Seattle businessmen soon sought the aid of the federal government and from 1867 forward sporadically attempted to gain endorsement from the Corps of Engineers and the Congress for the construction of a canal on either of two routes between Elliott Bay and Lake Washington: to the north via Shilshole Bay and Lake Union or to the south via the Duwamish River. In the 1880s a split occurred between private enterprise, favoring the south canal route, and the federal aid advocates, preferring the north route. In time, the north canal proponents convinced Congressman William H. Humphrey of the rightness of their cause and in congressional hearings Humphrey stoutly attacked the south canal project: "Never was there a more vicious example of the venomous serpent striking its deadly fangs into the bosom that warmed it into life. As a canal scheme it was conceived in fraud, born of false pretenses, and sustained by misrepresentations."[9] These remarks were characteristic of the acrimony of the debate and remained typical until the opposing partisans buried their differences in late 1905 and decided to advocate both the private canal scheme in the south and the government canal in the north.[10]

Seattle business gave enthusiastic response to this alliance and James A. Moore, realtor, promoter, and builder of the largest number of business blocks in the city, revived the canal scheme in the spring of 1906.[11] Moore's proposal focused upon the hope for a large steel complex on the eastern shores of Lake Washington, a project that had been tried and abandoned in the 1890s.[12] In order to serve this enterprise he proposed that King County cede to him the right-of-way between Elliott Bay

[9] U.S., Congress, House, Committee on Rivers and Harbors, "Lake Washington Canal," *Hearings, December 1903 to April 28, 1904,* 58th Cong., 2d sess., April 12, 1904, p. 9.

[10] Alan A. Hynding, "Eugene Semple's Seattle Canal Scheme," *Pacific Northwest Quarterly* 59 (1968): 77-87.

[11] *Seattle Argus,* February 20, 1909, supplement, p. 57 has a résumé of Moore's career.

[12] William R. Sherrard, "The Kirkland Steel Mill: Adventure in Western Enterprise," *Pacific Northwest Quarterly* 53 (1962): 129-37.

and Lake Washington, through which he promised to build a canal with a wooden lock, subject to the approval of the federal government.[13] Moore's plan immediately stirred public interest and the Seattle Chamber of Commerce dispatched former Governor John H. McGraw to Washington, D.C., to obtain legislation for King County to acquire the right-of-way and for Moore to build a canal which he would operate for three years and then turn over to the United States government.[14]

As the canal advocates gained strength, General Alexander A. Mackenzie, the Chief of Engineers, wrote to Chittenden, as local district engineer, asking his opinion of the Moore measure. Chittenden in reply rejected Moore's proposal. The lock in the Moore plan, he contended, was much too narrow for the traffic it would have to bear and for the flowage of water from Lake Washington into the canal. Above all the construction of a timber lock was foolish because it would probably last only five years before deterioration. The United States thus would be presented with a canal with a weak lock that soon would require replacement at great expense. Finally, the promoter had grossly underestimated the costs of the project, which would be twice the $500,000 Moore expected to expend, a financial miscalculation, wrote Chittenden, that meant the project could never be constructed for lack of capital.[15]

Chittenden recommended that the Corps try to get the plan postponed until the next session of Congress when it could be considered in greater detail.[16] The Chief followed this advice but his efforts failed; the House Committee on Rivers and Harbors unanimously endorsed the bill and it then passed the Congress and was signed by President Taft on June 11.[17] Hearing this news, Chittenden was bitterly disappointed, for he feared that his chance to build a government canal had

13 *Seattle Star*, March 31, 1906; *Seattle Post-Intelligencer*, March 31, 1906.

14 Seattle Chamber of Commerce, "Minute Book," May 11, 1906; *Seattle Star*, May 11, 14, 1906; *Seattle Post-Intelligencer*, May 12, 1906.

15 HMC to A. Mackenzie, May 26, 1906, #59604/4, RG 77.

16 Ibid.

17 U.S., Congress, House, *Congressional Record*, 59th Cong., 1st sess., 1906, 40, pt. 8: 7711; *Seattle Post-Intelligencer*, June 7, 12, 1906; U.S., Congress, *Statutes at Large*, 1907, 34, pt. 1: 231.

now vanished.[18] Members of the Seattle business community hailed it as a victory because Moore's scheme was avowedly a measure to involve indirectly the federal government in a project it had repeatedly spurned. They envisioned the completed project as generating so much commerce that the United States government inevitably would have to deepen and improve the canal.[19]

Although Chittenden had been hostile to the Moore canal from the beginning, the project now deeply involved the district engineer since it was to be built under the supervision of the United States. He had now to write the city requesting that it remove the old bridges over the canal right-of-way and substitute drawbridges in the interests of navigation.[20] He also, upon request, nominated as chief engineer of the Moore project an old friend, Archibald O. Powell, much to the distress of Eugene Semple, former governor of Washington, who believed that his longtime advocacy of the south canal qualified him for the position.[21] Chittenden also corresponded with Erastus Brainerd of the *Seattle Post-Intelligencer*, about the early history of the various canal projects for his own official report to the Chief of Engineers.[22]

Chittenden's report on the Moore canal was a seventy-nine page memorandum, dated December 18, 1906, that opened by stating the federal interest in the canal.[23] The government was, of course, concerned with its commercial features as a navigable waterway; it was indirectly interested in the power to be produced at the lock, for the sale of it would help pay the maintenance costs of the operation; finally, although not of direct interest, the government would benefit by the lowering of the waters of Lake Washington, which would facilitate the drainage of swamp lands.

[18] HMC, "Diary," July 21, 1906, CPHS.

[19] Governor McGraw admitted this to the Chamber of Commerce on June 6; Chamber of Commerce, "Minute Book," June 6, 1906; see also *Seattle Post-Intelligencer*, June 12, 1906.

[20] *Seattle Post-Intelligencer*, September 25, 1906.

[21] Eugene Semple to James A. Moore, November 20, 1906, Eugene Semple Papers (University of Washington).

[22] HMC to Erastus Brainerd, October 9, 1906, Erastus Brainerd Papers (University of Washington).

[23] HMC, "Lake Washington Canal," #59604/25, RG 77.

The most important feature of the project was the nature and site of the lock. Chittenden favored the abandonment of the large (600 feet by 72 feet) lock as proposed by Moore in favor of two smaller locks, respectively 500 feet by 60 feet and 150 feet by 30 feet in dimensions. He predicted that the smaller lock would accommodate the "mosquito fleet," the pleasure boats and tugs that would voyage between Puget Sound and Lake Washington, while the larger one would serve the freighters and log rafts. Chittenden definitely recommended that the double locks be placed at the Narrows at the foot of Salmon Bay rather than at the head.

Regarding feasibility, Chittenden had to overcome earlier hostile reports, especially that of a board of engineers in 1903. He predicted that when the canal was completed, probably in three years time, then the city would require new wharfage facilities, which could be provided along the shores of Lake Union. He said that all available space for mooring buoys along Elliott Bay was in use and that the marine life and the great depth of the bay made it difficult to preserve and sink piles for new wharves. In any case, contrary to the conditions in 1903, the price of pier timber was high, adding to the expense of making new piers. The absence of tides on Lake Union and Salmon Bay after canal construction would make unloading and loading cheaper than on Elliott Bay. Finally, the value of commerce to and from Ballard and Seattle was considerable; both exports and imports had doubled since 1903 and would do so again before the canal was completed in three years. The fresh water of Lake Washington would cleanse from the hulls of ocean vessels dangerous marine life without the expense of drydocking, and the fishing fleet would find Lake Union a placid winter refuge. Finally, Chittenden said that Moore should abandon his plan for a timber lock and instead expend that money on a deeper channel while the government assumed the expenses of a masonry lock.[24]

Chittenden maintained pressure on behalf of the canal plan during this period of political maneuvering. Even though he disagreed with certain aspects of Moore's scheme, he was

[24] Data in the preceding three paragraphs is in ibid.

obligated professionally to further it at the same time that
he worked for its modification. To hasten the consideration of
the plan, on March 11, 1907, Chittenden wrote an urgent letter
to General Mackenzie urging that the government should
make its survey as rapidly as possible because there was considerable local pressure to have the canal completed in time
for the closing of Seattle's Alaska-Yukon-Pacific exposition in
the fall of 1909. In this letter Chittenden again alluded to a
problem that plagued him throughout his connection with the
canal, a problem illustrative of the local pressures facing any
district engineer. This issue was where to place the canal lock,
at the foot or the head of Salmon Bay. If the lock were placed
at the head of the bay then it would not flood the properties of
the shingle mill owners in the Ballard region. If the lock were
placed at the foot of the bay then a larger area would be
available for deep water traffic but the millmen would be
inundated. Unfortunately, the decision could not be made
solely on engineering grounds, for local members of Congress
and the Chamber of Commerce in the past had assured the
Ballard mill owners that the lock would not be placed where
it would damage them. Chittenden tried to extricate himself
from this dilemma by recommending that the best interests of
the city required that the lock be at the foot of the bay, but
he said the question should be decided by local interests since
they were financing the digging of the canal. The Chamber
of Commerce, Chittenden wrote, was the proper body to make
the decision and its choice should be accepted by the government. Chittenden suggested that it "might be advisable to
appoint a board of Engineers to consider this matter, as such
a course would relieve the local situation somewhat on the
question of lock location. If this is done, I request that I be
not made a member of the board."[25]

While Chittenden tried to escape the unpleasant burden of
choice, plans for the canal proceeded. On March 18 a bill
passed the legislature permitting the organization of assessment
districts for "River, Lake, Canal, or Harbor Improvements."[26]

[25] HMC to A. Mackenzie, March 11, 1907, #8111/578, RG 77.
[26] Washington, Legislature, *Session Laws of Washington*, 1907 (Olympia,
1907), chapt. 236.

On the twenty-fifth the Lake Washington Canal Association (formerly the Lake Shore Owners Club) empowered Thomas Burke to make a lobbying trip to Washington to ask the War Department to permit that the money raised under the assessment district be expended under the direction of Hiram Chittenden as engineer in charge.[27] On the twenty-ninth James A. Moore announced that he would assign his rights in the Canal Association in return for the amount of money he had expended, declaring that the Association could build a better canal for its $1,500,000 raised from the assessment district than he could build for $500,000 of private capital. Moore completed the transfer to the Association on May 6, thus escaping from an untenable position with no financial loss to himself.[28] On May 28 Chittenden testified before the King County commissioners as to the relationship between the United States government and the canal project.[29]

Chittenden, anticipating his imminent appointment to the position of chief engineer, had to prepare his official engineering report on the canal which again forced him to grapple with the problem of the location of the canal lock on Salmon Bay. Politics as well as engineering requirements would determine the outcome. Chittenden wrote to Erastus Brainerd for a full page in the Sunday edition of the *Post-Intelligencer* to make a public statement on the location of the canal lock.[30] In the article, published June 30, Chittenden announced a public hearing on the lock question for early July and used the columns of the newspaper to provide background data for the electorate's decision and, implicitly, to guide thoughts on the question.

When first conceived, he wrote, the canal project had included two locks, one at Shilshole Bay and the other at the portage between Lake Union and Lake Washington. Then, to protect against the threat of enemy naval bombardment, the site of the lock was shifted to the foot of Salmon Bay, condemnation proceedings were instituted, and the mill

[27] *Seattle Post-Intelligencer*, March 26, 1907.
[28] Ibid., March 30, May 7, 1907.
[29] Ibid., May 9, 1907.
[30] HMC to Brainerd, June 25, 1907, Brainerd Papers.

owners compensated for damages to their property that would ensue when the canal was constructed. Subsequently, the value of the interests at Salmon Bay increased considerably as the shingle weaving business developed in the early years of the twentieth century. These interests wanted the site of the lock moved to the upper waters of Salmon Bay so that the bay would remain open to the rise and fall of the tides. Thus, concluded Chittenden, four possibilities existed for the lock site. The first was at Shilshole Bay, where construction costs of the lock would be most economical, but where flowage rights would have to be acquired at great cost; or the lock could be built at the foot of the bay where the total cost would be the least; or a lock could be constructed at the head of Salmon Bay and, eventually, a second at Shilshole Bay after the money to compensate the mill owners had been raised from some public or private source. The fourth possibility was to build a single lock at the head of Salmon Bay. This last possibility was the only one flatly condemned by Chittenden because it would benefit only the millmen while denying the slack water harbor to all other industries on the bay.[31]

On July 10, the Seattle Chamber of Commerce, at Chittenden's express request, considered the matter of the lock site. The Chamber passed a resolution unanimously endorsing the lower site on two conditions: that it would not cause a delay in the project and that it would be recommended by the district engineer.[32] The Chamber had handed the hot potato back to Chittenden who obtained a further sampling of public opinion at a meeting at the Chamber of Commerce over which he presided on July 17. Among others, Congressman William H. Humphrey and Wesley L. Jones stated that whatever location was chosen, there should be only one lock for fear that the government would not finance a second. The millmen fell back upon the demand for two locks but were the only ones who assumed that stance so Chittenden's choice was obvious. Public opinion had decided for him and he wrote formally to General Mackenzie on July 19 recommending that

31 *Seattle Post-Intelligencer,* June 30, 1907.
32 Seattle Chamber of Commerce, "Minute Book," July 9, 1907; *Seattle Post-Intelligencer,* July 10, 1907.

the government approve the site at the foot of the bay.[33]

Chittenden then plunged into the work of preparing his full report on the canal for transmission to the Chief of Engineers, as he was convinced that if the people voted the money in 1908, he could complete the canal by the fall of 1909. He looked forward to the project with enthusiasm; while it did not rival the grandeur of the Panama Canal, awarded to the Corps of Engineers in March, much to Chittenden's pleasure, it would memorialize him as the builder of this inland waterway that would mean so much to the city he had come to love.

He faced the future thus with keen anticipation, but his remaining years in Seattle were too often bitter largely because of President Theodore Roosevelt's order that, as a part of the annual physical examination, each officer of the army (except Infantry) must undertake a fifty-mile horseback test or face retirement. Chittenden dreaded the ride because his health was precarious, for long years of labor in a score of causes, overexposure in the cold of Yellowstone, and typhoid attacks in the Missouri Valley had engendered gradual paralysis of his legs and attacks of nervous exhaustion. Yet he had to ride or face retirement at the age of forty-nine with only the prospect of a meager pension to support his wife and three minor children. As soon as Roosevelt's order was published, Chittenden anticipated the worst but nerved himself to take some short practice rides which he survived successfully.[34]

On his birthday, October 25, 1907, Chittenden faced the examining physicians, who discovered his weakened physical condition, and two of the three officers on the board refused to let him take the ride. Aghast, Chittenden begged the board to reconsider and they referred the matter to Major General Adolphus W. Greely, the senior officer. Greely left the matter to Chittenden, who started for his horse, but the general called him back saying he would have to consult the full

[33] *Seattle Times,* July 18, 1907; HMC to A. Mackenzie, July 19, 1907, #8111/584, RG 77.

[34] U.S., War Department, General Order 79, *General Orders and Circulars,* 1908 (Washington, D.C., 1909). His monthly retirement pension would be 75 percent of $291.67. *Official Army Register,* 1885, p. 380. There was no pay increase between 1885 and 1908.

board. Then he prohibited the ride. Chittenden again made a "strenuous plea" to ride. Greely relented to say he could take part of the ride. Chittenden pleaded that it would be better to take no ride at all than only a portion. Greely refused again, but finally gave in when Chittenden promised to drop out if the ordeal became too great. He rode the entire distance and noted proudly in his diary: "Whatever my physical condition and it is certainly bad enough, I still stand before the world as a reasonably well man and that will help me to become so."[35]

No estimate proved more erroneous. After the ride Chittenden's health deteriorated immediately so that he was unable to make a note in his diary for a month. He was oppressed by the fear of permanent paralysis and most of all by the threat of penury for his family, but he was not crushed by his misfortunes. As he recorded in his diary: "My family are so brave and hopeful under the shadow of this misfortune that it makes me very proud of them, at the same time that it grieves me to the heart to think of them in this new situation. But experience only proves that being thrown [on] one's own resources by no means spells disaster and often the reverse."[36] Strengthened by their resolution, and in spite of numerous problems, Chittenden finished his annual report on the Lake Washington Canal on December 2.[37] It was his last major work for the United States.

His report opened with a careful analysis of the various past proposals for a canal from the Sound to Lake Union or to Lake Washington. Chittenden flatly asserted that the lock site must be at the foot of Salmon Bay. He examined the question of using the fall of water at the lock for electric power and decided according to his usual philosophy that it would be more practical for the government to build the power plant and lease it to private enterprise than to permit businessmen to build and operate the plant. The heart of the report was Chittenden's testimony as to the feasibility of the canal. Recognizing that the board of engineers in 1903 had feared a

35 HMC, "Diary," October 25, 1907, CPHS.
36 Ibid., November 25, December 8, 1907, CPHS.
37 HMC, *Puget Sound-Lake Washington Waterway*, pp. 3-25.

paucity of commerce on the waterway, Chittenden went to great pains to indicate that it was essential to supplement the harbor facilities at Elliott Bay. Given these advantages, and obviously fearful that the economy bloc in Congress might demand greater local contributions as its price for endorsing the canal, Chittenden pleaded for government recognition of the amount of capital and energy expended by local business-men in their long battle for the canal.

In spite of Chittenden's advocacy, the canal was not to be constructed in the immediate aftermath of his report. While he grappled with a series of personal problems and while he was preparing his report on the stream flow-forestry relation-ships, the opponents of the project took heart and made many attempts to prevent its construction. This coalition consisted of the Ballard millmen, the advocates of government aid to a canal between the Duwamish and Lake Washington, the owners of tidelands in Elliott Bay, homeowners on Lake Washington, and the Harriman Northern Pacific-Southern Pacific interests, all of whom would gain if the Lake Washing-ton canal could be prevented. Determined and well financed, they were able to persuade the courts to declare the assessment district law unconstitutional and to argue successfully against the King County Commission's floating a bond issue in lieu of the illegal bonds of the district. Throughout the year 1908 the canal issue remained a stalemate.[38]

A breakthrough was at last achieved in the spring of 1909 when the lobbyist of the Seattle Chamber of Commerce, J. W. Clise, worked out a series of agreements at Olympia which removed opposition. The Ballard millmen were satisfied and the railroads appeased. The Duwamish advocates were recon-ciled when the Chamber promised to support bills to improve that waterway. With these groups mollified, a bill to provide $250,000 for the Lake Washington canal was adopted.[39] Only in the fall did the price of the agreement with the Ballard

38 J. D. Farrell, *Is the Lake Washington Canal a General Necessity at This Time?* (n.p., 1908[?]); Ballard Manufacturers Association to W. H. Taft, Secre-tary of War, March 14, 1908, #8111/594, RG 77; *Seattle Argus*, November 7, 1908; *Seattle Post-Intelligencer*, October 25, December 11, 1908; *Seattle Argus*, July 2, 1910; *Seattle Town-Crier*, September 10, 1910.
39 Seattle Chamber of Commerce, "Minute Book," March 2, 23, 1909.

millmen become public knowledge when the Chamber of Commerce announced that it now supported the placing of the lock at the head of Salmon Bay. The Chamber felt expediency made this switch necessary, and it sought Chittenden's endorsement of the change.

Chittenden reversed his earlier position. Writing to the Chamber, he said that under present circumstances all interests must unite behind a lock site at the head of the bay.[40] Although he himself still preferred the location at the Narrows, he felt that if the other interests on the bay were willing to pacify the millmen, he would go along. Chittenden's altered stance was a serious tactical error and one that was resented by those now in the forefront of the fight for the canal.

United States Senator Samuel H. Piles and the Chamber representative in Washington both urged strongly that the lock site should not be changed. They contended that the appropriation for the canal could never be made in the teeth of a recommendation by the Chief of Engineers which would echo the last published report by Chittenden.[41] Major Charles W. Kutz, Chittenden's successor, however, in January 1910, reported to the Chief of Engineers in favor of the upper site, noting the support of the Chamber of Commerce for this decision, but Reginald H. Thomson, the famous city engineer of Seattle, and other advocates of the canal insisted upon the original site in letters to Humphrey and Piles.[42] In February Chittenden suggested to Erastus Brainerd a way out of the dilemma. He had heard that the House Committee on Rivers and Harbors still favored the construction of the lock at the Narrows. To make the best of this determination, which indeed was chiefly based upon his own earlier reports, Chittenden suggested that Congress retain the site at the Narrows but that the King County Assessment District appropriate the

40 Ibid., November 23, 1909.

41 S. H. Piles to C. B. Yandell, Secretary, Seattle Chamber of Commerce, February 16, 1910 (copy of telegram); C. J. Smith to Yandell, February 16, 1910 (copy of telegram), both in Box 63, Chamber of Commerce Subgroup, Thomas Burke Papers (University of Washington).

42 C. W. Kutz to Chief of Engineers, January 12, 1910, #8111/604, RG 77; Reginald H. Thomson to W. E. Humphrey, February 7, 1910; Thomson to Samuel H. Piles, February 8, 1910, both in Reginald H. Thomson Papers (University of Washington).

sum of $100,000 to compensate the Ballard millmen for their losses caused by the overflowage.[43]

Then in March Chittenden returned to his original position and wrote to Brainerd urging that the *Post-Intelligencer* "frown down" the opposition to the canal. He had been convinced after all that Congress would not appropriate money for the canal if the lock were put at the head of the bay. Although he never admitted it—perhaps never knew it—Chittenden's earlier change of position had been most harmful.[44] Thomson, in writing to Congressman Humphrey, placed much of the blame for the precarious nature of the project upon Chittenden's earlier "wobbling" on the location of the site, a shiftiness that he said gave the opponents a certain basis for their arguments.[45] In June the state supreme court declared unconstitutional the law permitting the King County Assessment District to levy on the property owners along the proposed canal, but at the end of the month the cause was won in Congress with the passage of a statute appropriating the sum of $2,275,000 for the canal to be built as recommended in Chittenden's report of 1907.[46]

Shortly after the completion of his final report on the canal in December 1907, Chittenden had entered the Pacific Hospital in Seattle for electric shock treatments for his persisting malady. His worry over impending retirement mounted during his stay and the treatments were unsuccessful; therefore he left the hospital on February 17, 1908, physically unprepared to begin a series of ordeals piled thick upon one another that threatened to shatter him mentally and spiritually as well as to complete the destruction of his physical health.[47]

On February 23 Chittenden's diary recorded the ironic comment: " 'Whom the Lord loveth he chasteneth.' I must stand high in Divine favor."[48] On February 18, the federal attorney in Seattle had notified Chittenden that the govern-

43 HMC to Brainerd, February 15, 1910, Brainerd Papers.
44 HMC to Brainerd, March 29, 1910, Brainerd Papers.
45 Thomson to Humphrey, April 23, 1910, Thomson Papers.
46 *Seattle Argus*, June 4, 1910; U.S., Congress, *Statutes at Large*, 1911, 36, pt. 2: 664.
47 HMC, "Diary," February 17, 1908, CPHS.
48 Ibid., February 23, 1908, CPHS.

ment was instituting both civil and criminal proceedings against him and his brother Clyde for defrauding the United States of a valuable section of coal land in Skagit County.[49] A few days later he learned that his life insurance company, to which he had made premium payments since his graduation from the Military Academy, had failed.[50] His poor health of course precluded obtaining new insurance. Two weeks later, on March 7, he discovered that the Robert Clarke Company, the publisher of his book on Yellowstone, was in the hands of the receivers.[51] Of all these misfortunes, the lawsuit was clearly his most serious problem, for if lost by the defendants, it would destroy Chittenden's chances for promotion, future service, and honorable retirement.

These legal misfortunes had grown out of Chittenden's desire to take advantage of the boom times in Seattle shortly after his arrival in 1906. Convinced of the promise of the region, he had decided to invest in land. Approaching former Governor John McGraw, with whom he was working closely in the struggle for the Lake Washington canal, Chittenden had asked him for suggestions about realty investments. After buying and selling a promising residential lot, Chittenden sought an outlet for the $3,000 he had realized in this transaction and by December 1906, he had made $18,700 in realty investments in the few months since his arrival in April.[52] In the following year he heard of two sections of timber land, Sections 12 and 13 in Township 34 located in Skagit County, Washington, and he formed a pool to secure the $30,000 to purchase them.[53]

Many facts of the case regarding the transaction were uncontested. The Chittendens purchased Section 12 outright from the government. Section 13 was timber land with coal

[49] Ibid., CPHS.
[50] Ibid., CPHS.
[51] Ibid., March 7, 1908, CPHS.
[52] Ibid., October 11, 25, December 9, 1906, CPHS.
[53] Ibid., December 9, 1906. HMC to "My dear Governor" [McGraw], February 20, 1908, Richard A. Ballinger Papers (University of Washington), hereafter cited RABP; Franklin Pierce, Acting Secretary of the Interior, to Attorney General, December 24, 1907, Correspondence Files 2-74, General Land Office Records of the Office of the Secretary of the Interior (Record Group 48, National Archives), hereafter cited CFGLO.

deposits beneath it. On August 28, 1902, the Day Creek Coal Association offered to file with the United States Land Office in Seattle a declaratory statement to buy this section. On May 25, 1906, the Register of the Land Office accepted this filing. Then on December 22 of the same year the Day Creek Association agreed to sell the land to the Chittendens before the Association had obtained the final patent to the land. This contract was filed in the office of the Auditor of Skagit County. On January 5, 1907, the officers of the Association made affidavits with the General Land Office, according to its regulations, asserting that the purchase was for their own benefit and was not, directly or indirectly, for the benefit of any other party. The Chittendens paid the General Land Office the sum of $12,800 for the land. On July 12 the final patent for the land was issued by the Land Office and on July 29, as also recorded in the Skagit County Auditor's office, the Day Creek Association deeded the land to the Chittendens. Acting on the report of Special Agent Percy F. Smith, the government decided in December 1907 to bring suit to cancel the contract of December 22, 1906, and the patent of July 12, 1907, and to bring criminal charges against the Chittendens and the Association for fraud.[54]

Faced with this serious crisis in his personal affairs, Chittenden hastily engaged an attorney and hurried off two letters protesting his innocence. The first was to McGraw asking him to intercede at the War Department if he got wind that the department was contemplating punitive action against Chittenden before the case was decided.[55] Three days later he wrote to a friend, Colonel John Donovan in St. Louis, proclaiming his innocence and asking his help.[56] Apparently, either because he recognized the name of an old friend, or acted at the behest of McGraw, Richard A. Ballinger, commissioner of the General Land Office asked the Assistant Secretary of the Department of the Interior, Frank Pierce, also a Seattle man,

54 Franklin Pierce to Attorney General, December 24, 1907, CFGLO; United States v. Clyde C. Chittenden et al., File 1646, Acc. 62A371 (Federal Records Center, Seattle).

55 HMC to "My dear Governor" [McGraw], February 20, 1908, RABP.

56 HMC to John Donovan, February 23, 1908, CFGLO.

to request that the Justice Department drop the criminal proceedings.[57] But the suit in equity to cancel the transaction, of
almost equal damage to Chittenden's reputation, remained
pending.

Fortunately for Chittenden, Major General Franklin Bell,
the Army Chief of Staff, on his own initiative wrote to their
mutual friend Colonel Donovan expressing sympathy for
Chittenden's plight and disbelief that he would be involved
in any illegal scheme. In his reply Donovan enclosed Chittenden's letter to him and stated that he was confident that he
had been "wrongfully accused." Donovan referred to a visit
he had made to Chittenden at the time of the purchase the
year before and labored his scrupulousness in the matter: "All
during his purchase of timber land he kept impressing on me
the fact that the government had been imposed on in that
section, and that he wanted me to be very careful not to be a
party to that imposition. . . . If there is any way you can get
before the proper department (the Interior Department, I
suppose) and have this matter looked into and acted upon
promptly, it would be a great thing for Chittenden."[58]

On March 2 McGraw wrote to Ballinger asking that the suit
against Chittenden be dismissed immediately as Chittenden
could not possibly be "knowingly guilty of even a technical
violation of the laws of his country."[59] Shortly thereafter Bell
wrote to Secretary of the Interior James A. Garfield asking
him to take a personal interest in the case to see that justice
was done.[60] On March 24 Garfield wired the Register and
Receiver of the Land Office in Seattle asking them to report
fully on their dealings with Chittenden in the case. The replies
of these two officials completely vindicated Chittenden's statements in his letters to Donovan and McGraw. The Receiver
summed it up: "In fact, I have no recollection of any person
who, having business to transact with this office, was uniformly
so extraordinarily cautious and punctilious in his efforts to

57 Richard A. Ballinger to Frank Pierce, February 29, 1908, RABP.

58 Franklin Bell to John Donovan, March 2, 1908; Donovan to Bell, March
10, 1908, both in CFGLO.

59 John H. McGraw to Richard A. Ballinger, March 2, 1908, RABP.

60 J. F. Bell to James R. Garfield, March 14, 1908, CFGLO.

keep wholly within the letter, spirit and intent of the law."[61] Garfield asked the Attorney General to drop all charges; he complied, and Judge Cornelius H. Hanford of the District Court on May 15 quashed the case with prejudice to the government.[62]

Chittenden escaped his ordeal of four months with his reputation unblemished. He never discovered the genesis of the case and the records are silent on it, but in a grateful letter to General Bell after the matter was well on the way to happy conclusion, Chittenden stated that the matter was commenced, as far as he could ascertain, by enemies of the owners of the Day Creek Association "to even up old scores."[63] Agent Smith's original report is not found in the National Archives and the origin of the case remains mysterious. What is clear is that Chittenden's friends in high places, by intervening on his behalf, saw that he obtained justice with speed and without the strain and expense of a public trial that would blot his reputation by publicity even if he were vindicated. Equally evident is the fact that Chittenden was guiltless. The open record of the proceedings in the case, his lifetime reputation, and the opinion of men of unimpeachable veracity such as Secretary Garfield proved his innocence.

While the Lake Washington canal and his personal problems burdened Chittenden, they did not completely preclude other activities. Every district engineer contends with a myriad of problems, some challenging, some dull, but all placing him in the center of contesting public and private interests. While Chittenden was in reasonably good health, he spent the bulk of three years, 1906-1908, in vigorous service in the district. Perhaps the most interesting work outside of the canal was the tourist road into Mount Rainier National Park, a project reminiscent of his labors in Yellowstone.

61 James R. Garfield to Register and Receiver, U.S. Land Office, Seattle, March 24, 1908 (telegram); J. Henry Smith, Register, to Secretary of the Interior, March 25, 1908; F. A. Twichell, Receiver, to Secretary of the Interior, March 25, 1908, all in CFGLO.

62 James R. Garfield to Attorney General, April 9, 1908; M. D. Purdy, Acting Attorney General to Secretary of the Interior, April 11, 1908, both in CFGLO; United States v. Clyde C. Chittenden et al., File 1646, Acc. G2A371 (Federal Records Center, Seattle).

63 HMC to J. F. Bell, April 16, 1908, #67220/4, RG 77.

The park had been founded in 1902 and the Corps had assumed road building duties one year later. In the three working seasons of the years 1906-1908, Chittenden presented a plan for the construction of a road twenty-five miles in length from the western boundary of the park to its terminus at Camp of the Clouds on the mountain and actually built fourteen miles of this road through his usual method of direct hire of labor rather than through contracting. Although he did not have the satisfaction of completing the project, its planning and partial execution under his own authority gave him needed relief from the political infighting of the canal venture.[64] In addition to planning the canal and supervising the building of the Mount Rainier road, Chittenden was also concerned with a variety of lesser projects of a routine nature during his years in Seattle.

In November 1906 a great flood occurred on the plain south of the city of Seattle through which the White River flowed to the sea through King and Pierce counties. Landowners in both counties appealed to district engineer Chittenden to make a survey for a permanent channel. Chittenden, however, had no funds to make the survey so he suggested that a solution could be worked out if local business raised the money privately. The two counties and four railroads provided the sum of $4,000 to finance the expenses of a nine-member board of engineers including Chittenden. The board met and deliberated and reached a solution publicized in a report written by him.[65]

More satisfying undoubtedly, because they were under his direct control, were Chittenden's projects around the Puget Sound area that were financed directly by the United States. In the fiscal year 1906-1907, for example, he was engaged in supervising a total of fourteen projects that included improving the harbor at Olympia, removing the sunken schooner

[64] *ARCE*, 1908, 3: 2553-54.

[65] *Report of an Investigation by a Board of Engineers of the Means of Controlling Floods in the Duwamish-Puyallup Valleys and Their Tributaries in the State of Washington* (Seattle, 1907); C. L. Henden's summaries of the work in *Transactions of the International Engineering Congress, 1915. Waterways and Irrigation* (San Francisco, 1916), pp. 186-87; H. H. Wolff, "Design of a Drift Barrier across White River, Near Auburn, Washington," *Transactions of the American Society of Civil Engineers* 80 (1916): 2061-85.

Challenger from the harbor at South Bend, Washington, and inspecting fish traps on Puget Sound to ensure that they were not navigational impediments.[66] He inherited from his predecessor the task of constructing fire control towers for the coast artillery batteries at Forts Flagler, Casey, and Worden that made up the defenses of the city of Seattle and its harbor at Elliott Bay.[67]

As always, local boosters favored improvement of rivers and harbors that they hoped would be of commercial importance, and, when their representative was able to get money appropriated for surveys, this work fell to the local engineer. Chittenden made two such surveys, a canal from Grays Harbor to Puget Sound and the improvement of Blaine Harbor, Washington. Contrary to the stereotype of the district engineer as one always working hand-in-glove with local interests to draw upon the federal pork barrel, Chittenden was reluctant to endorse both of these projects.[68] What Chittenden's feelings about these minor matters were is not known; probably he rather enjoyed dispatching them crisply and efficiently in his usual manner provided that they did not interfere with his great work on the canal. However onerous and tedious they were, they were infinitely desirable compared to ruined health and forced retirement that increasingly threatened him from the middle of 1908 until his official retirement as a brigadier general in 1910.

As early as December 1907 rumors floated about Seattle that he would be retired. Seattle friends contacted Richard Ballinger, former mayor and now commissioner of the General Land Office, and Ballinger promised his aid and that of Senator Francis E. Warren, Chittenden's old ally from the reservoir survey and chairman of the Senate Committee on Miliary Affairs, to prevent Chittenden's retirement.[69] In January—on behalf of Warren—Ballinger spoke to Secretary

66 *ARCE*, 1906, 2: 2021-48.

67 Office of Chief of Artillery, "Memorandum to Major Abbott," August 14, 1906, #35522/305, RG 77.

68 U.S., Congress, House, Committee on Rivers and Harbors, *Blaine Harbor, Washington*, 60th Cong., 1st sess., 1907, H. Doc. 69; U.S., Congress, House, Committee on Rivers and Harbors, *Canal Connecting Puget Sound with Grays Harbor*, 60th Cong., 1st sess., 1907, H. Doc. 70.

69 Richard A. Ballinger to HMC, December 13, 1907, RABP.

of War Taft and gained the impression that Taft wanted to keep able officers of the Corps in service regardless of their physical condition rather than retiring them.[70] In July 1908 Chittenden received a four-months leave of absence, in the hope that respite from official duties would give him the needed time to recover; realistically, however, he was prepared to face retirement and recommended that he be assigned an assistant who could learn the work before succeeding him.[71] Unfortunately there was no successor available and he carried on his duties in spite of his leave.

Even before the fateful horsemanship test Chittenden was in low spirits because of declining health that shadowed the future and dimmed his characteristic optimism. "It is easy enough to believe in God," he wrote later in his diary, "when everything is coming one's way. The test comes when everything is going the other way."[72] Then the day of the ride and its disastrous consequences determined that it was inevitable that he must face an early retirement. As he now lacked any life insurance, the brightest prospect for a steady income in time of retirement would be his government pension; furthermore, if he could be promoted before retirement his pension would increase significantly. If his real estate investments proved profitable, and if he could do some engineering consulting on the side, then his family might look forward to some security.

The year 1909 was a year of waiting for Chittenden. He had received a second sick leave, this one of six months duration, in the previous December, and in his enforced leisure he revised his stream flow paper, answered his critics' comments, and noted that the paper was debated in Congress in the discussions over the Weeks bill.[73] He prepared his annual report for the Chief, dictated a memorandum for Senator Piles on the Duwamish waterway improvement, and published his plan for a Cascade Mountains tunnel.

[70] Richard A. Ballinger to HMC, January 4, 1908, RABP.
[71] HMC to Adjutant General, July 1, 1908; U.S., War Department, Special Order 165, July 15, 1908, both in #3839-A.C.P.-1884, ACP; HMC to Smith S. [name unclear], #13640/2, RG 77.
[72] HMC, "Diary," September 9, 1908, CPHS.
[73] HMC, "Diary," March 7, 1909, CPHS.

One evening Chittenden came to the meeting of the Pacific Northwest Society of Civil Engineers with an imaginatively titled paper that must have intrigued the members. None of them had ever heard of the railroad "The Puget Sound and Inland Empire Railway" that was the subject of the essay, nor of its author, Itothe Phucher, the line's chief engineer. Chittenden's whimsical approach was to deliver a report about a nonexistent railroad sixteen years after its completion as it might be seen from the perspective of October 1925. But his paper was completely serious once the preliminary material was surmounted.

The basis of the paper was the reminder that Seattle and Puget Sound, though deriving advantages from the hand of nature, suffered some physiographic disadvantages. In contrast to her great rival, Portland, a city that enjoyed the water level route to the interior along the banks of the Columbia River, Seattle was walled off from the rich hinterland of the Inland Empire by the towering Cascade Mountains that were over-topped by three railroads with a minimum vertical ascent of 3,520 feet for westbound traffic between Seattle and Spokane. For eastbound freight the minimum ascent of the three lines was 5,400 feet. By contrast, on the Columbia Valley route the westbound climb was a mere 375 feet, all at Spokane, and the eastbound was 2,238.

From his mythical vantage point of 1925, Chittenden recalled what the Seattleites had done in the early days of the century to surmount these challenges. What these progressive (if fictional) men did was to construct a tunnel, the longest railroad tunnel in the world, between Leavenworth in the Wenatchee Valley and Skykomish in the valley of that stream, a distance of 32.25 miles. This tunnel connected the metropolis of the Inland Empire, Spokane, with Seattle, the throat through which the ports of Puget Sound would be served. Hence the name for the new railroad, the Puget Sound and Inland Empire Railway.

To finance such a railroad, Chittenden argued that the sum of $75 million sufficed, including the cost of electrification. This enormous sum, beyond the resources of a single railroad or a consortium, was derived from government. The state of

Washington and its counties made a contribution of $15 million for the benefit of opening up state timberland for sale and, more important, for its general economic welfare that was enhanced by linking the regions east and west of the Cascades. Furthermore, Chittenden reported that the United States had resumed its long abandoned policy of aiding railroad construction directly. The same principles that had motivated the government to develop the Columbia River by river and harbor improvements were also significant in persuading the United States government to contribute another $15 million and to give the railroad company the free use of timber for construction and liberal water power concessions for the electrification of the line. The remaining amount was contributed by the existing railroads who jointly financed the new line: the Great Northern, Northern Pacific, Burlington, Canadian Pacific, Milwaukee, Union Pacific, and North Coast. All these lines were thus relieved of a heavy mountain climb because much of their freight and their investment was returned rapidly enough to make the tunnel and the railroad a paying proposition.

So far as construction features were concerned, the project had been completed by the company itself rather than by working through contractors (a feature resulting probably from some of Chittenden's own bitter experiences) and this method of hiring had resulted in the completion of the tunnel in six years. A final interesting aspect was that the tunnel was used for highway communication for wagons, trucks, and automobiles. At each end of the tunnel was a ramp leading to a train equipped with a light locomotive and ten cars to transport the vehicles. This novel feature was one inducement that had persuaded the state and counties to contribute to the cost of construction.

If his project were actually carried out, Chittenden argued, the two sections of Washington would be economically united to take advantage of the publicity given to the region by the Seattle World's Fair and the opening of the Isthmian Canal. Furthermore, the salutary lessons of cooperation learned by the railroads in this project would benefit them in other aspects of their business in the future.

Chittenden's vision of the glorious future of the state made possible by the Cascade tunnel route was shared by few. The plan was discussed favorably by a speaker at the Seattle Rotary Club over a year later, but that seemed to be the extent of its positive reception. The *Seattle Town Crier* derided the plan and the *Portland Oregon Sunday Journal* noted with self-satisfaction that the Rose City did not have the problems of Seattle. The *Portland Morning Oregonian* likened the practicality of the Cascade tunnel to that of raising bananas in Greenland. Undeterred, Chittenden let it gestate and then revived it a few years later after he had retired from active service.[74]

These various projects kept Chittenden active for a time in spite of failing health, but in June he surrendered to his declining physical condition and wrote to General Marshall that he would have to retire. Facing neural surgery in July, he felt that he could no longer earn his pay.[75] In his reply Marshall wrote that there was a plan projected to appoint Chittenden brigadier general and that he should apply for a leave of absence until early November when there would be the next opening for a general officer.[76]

On the Fourth of July, 1909, Chittenden entered a hospital in Chicago for neural surgery on the following day. The results of the operation were not successful and its cost of $1,000 further added to his financial worries and required him to mortgage his family farmstead in New York State. His state of mind was hardly improved by the news in August that the Robert Clarke Company had again gone into receivership; the publisher offered Chittenden a cash settlement of thirty-five cents on the dollar for his royalties from *The Yellowstone National Park*.[77]

In the middle of September Judge Burke and Judge Hanford called on Chittenden, now confined to his home, and assured

74 Itothe Phucher [HMC], *The Puget Sound and Inland Empire Railway,* "*Cascade Tunnel Route,*" (Seattle, [1909]); *Portland Oregon Sunday Journal,* February 19, 1911; *Portland Morning Oregonian,* February 20, 1911; *Seattle Town Crier,* December 10, 1910: HMC, "Diary," June 13, 1909, CPHS.
75 HMC, "Diary," June 13, 1909, CPHS.
76 Ibid., CPHS.
77 HMC, "Diary," August 6, 25, 1909, CPHS, summarizes his life since July 4.

him that they would aid him in his hopes for staving off retirement.[78] On the thirtieth of September, R. H. Thomson wrote to Secretary of the Interior Ballinger urging Chittenden's promotion and Ballinger in turn advocated this step to his cabinet colleague, Secretary of War Jacob M. Dickinson, who referred the matter to General Bell.[79]

Others persisted in Chittenden's cause. A group of influential Seattle citizens telegraphed Senator Piles; Judge Hanford wrote to President Taft; Joseph G. Cannon, the Speaker of the House, also wrote a personal note to the president; Judge Burke and C. S. Mellen, who had known Chittenden in Yellowstone when Mellen was president of the Northern Pacific Railroad, wrote to Dickinson; Senator Wesley Jones wired the Secretary of War advocating the promotion; Senator Warren telegraphed the president reviewing Chittenden's service to the nation in Yellowstone Park and in the cause of reclamation and irrigation.[80]

On the twenty-ninth of November the good news came from General Marshall, as Chittenden wrote to Ballinger, that the president would promote him when General John G. D. Knight retired on January 24, 1910.[81] This news was most welcome, for the time of retirement was at hand. On December 1, 1909, Chittenden wrote to the Adjutant General stating that he did "not feel justified in asking for a further extension of my leave and I therefore await such action as may be deemed necessary in the premises."[82]

On December 18 the six members of the retiring board met in Chittenden's home because he was unable to leave his house for the original meeting place of Ft. Vancouver. The proceedings, which Chittenden described as having "all the formality of a court martial" moved rapidly and satisfactorily.[83] Brigadier General Marion P. Maus called the court to order

78 Ibid., September 15, 1909, CPHS.
79 R. H. Thomson to Richard A. Ballinger, September 30, 1909, Thomson Papers; R. A. Ballinger to J. M. Dickinson, October 4, 1909; Secretary of War to J. Franklin Bell, October 11, 1909, both in ACP.
80 These communications are all in ACP.
81 HMC to Richard A. Ballinger, November 29, 1909, RABP.
82 HMC to Adjutant General, December 1, 1909, ACP.
83 HMC, "Diary," December 18, 1909, CPHS.

at 5:15 P.M., Chittenden waived counsel, and asserted that he was ready to accept retirement. Upon oath Chittenden stated that his illness was locomotor ataxia—of at least six years duration—a condition greatly aggravated by his disastrous ride in October 1908. The medical officers of the board both testified that Chittenden's disability was caused by this disease, that it was permanent, and that it incapacitated him for further service. The board then read a summary of Chittenden's annual efficiency reports, his military history, and his medical record. Accordingly, the board retired for deliberations and recommended that Chittenden should be retired for disability incurred as incident to the national service. At 6:50 it adjourned, bringing to a close thirty-six years of service.[84]

By New Year's Day, 1910, Chittenden could look ahead with some security and, without self-pity, look back on "Another quick year—but all years are quick—and that, in spite of my imprisonment, is no exception."[85] All that remained of his army career was to await the news of promotion to brigadier general which came on February 5 (retroactive to January 24) followed by retirement five days later.[86] With these bittersweet formalities dispensed with, Chittenden plunged into a period of retirement that was especially taxing because he was so very seriously crippled that he was rarely able to move unassisted from his chair.

[84] "Proceedings of an Army Retiring Board . . . ," ACP.

[85] HMC, "Diary," January 1, 1910, CPHS.

[86] HMC, "Diary," February 5, 21, 1910, CPHS. Chittenden's retirement promotion to brigadier general, in bypassing the rank of colonel, gave him a retirement pay of $375 per month compared to that of $281.25 per month for a lieutenant colonel. U.S., War Department, *Official Army Register,* 1909 (Washington, D.C., 1908), p. 580.

7.

The Conservation Controversy 1908-1917

Among the numerous factors contributing to the rise of the organized conservation movement in the United States, historians have long recognized the importance of scientific theories and scientific evidence.[1] One important component of forest conservation theory was the hypothesis that deforestation had radically affected runoff and stream flow. More specifically, conservationists argued that clearing of timber had increased the height and frequency of floods, accelerated soil erosion, and retarded precipitation—all results disastrous for water power, commerce, irrigation, agriculture, and natural beauty. They made predictions that the United States, because of its mistreatment of the forest, would follow many ancient civilizations down the irretraceable path of desiccation and destruction. This thesis was widely publicized in manuals of forestry, in popular and technical conservation journals, and in the general press, and was further disseminated by forestry organizations and sympathetic politicians.[2]

Although the conservationists were undoubtedly effective in stressing the impact of forests upon stream flow at the turn of the century, several observers and theorists disparaged the idea. These critics, some objective and some self-interested, concentrated their attacks upon the qualitative and deductive nature of the conservationists' evidence, evidence drawn from limited personal experience, "common sense," and historical analogy. They delighted in pointing out that no experiments had ever been conducted in which stream flow and runoff from two similar watersheds, one deforested, one timbered, were measured accurately. Even William B. Greeley and Gifford

Pinchot, later leaders of the United States Forest Service, were temperate in their claims for forest influences as late as the year 1905.[3]

In spite of doubters the forest-stream flow hypothesis gained additional support with the passage of the Newlands Act and the creation of the Reclamation Service in 1902. Thereafter it was argued with increasing certitude that afforestation was valuable to protect irrigation reservoirs as well as navigation, timber, and power interests.[4] By 1905, Gifford Pinchot not only had acquired the national forests for the Department of Agriculture, but also had assumed the leadership of the hitherto disparate forces that were advocating separate Southern Appalachian and White Mountain national forests. He now became the chief advocate of a single Appalachian Forest and staked the prestige of his new Forest Service upon obtaining it.[5] By 1907 conservationists, through the application of some nineteenth-century forestry theorems and a few observations in Illinois, Texas, and the Appalachians, had produced a consensus regarding the influence of forests on stream flow and runoff. Their three major propositions were: forests retain rainfall and melting snow in their beds of humus and expend it gradually to equalize the runoff; forests retard the melting of snow in the spring and prolong the runoff from snow; forests prevent erosion. Foresters who had once been judiciously

[1] The role of science in the conservation movement is traced in A. Hunter Dupree, *Science in the Federal Government: A History of Policies and Activities to 1940* (Cambridge, Mass., 1957), and in Samuel P. Hays, *Conservation and the Gospel of Efficiency: The Progressive Conservation Movement, 1890-1920* (Cambridge, Mass., 1959).

[2] The literature is ample and most of it is traceable to George P. Marsh's classic, *Man and Nature*, ed. David Lowenthal (Cambridge, Mass., 1965). An excellent bibliography is contained in Raphael Zon, "Forests and Water in Light of Scientific Investigation," U.S., Congress, Senate, *Final Report of the National Waterways Commission*, 62d Cong., 2d sess., 1912, S. Doc. 469, pp. 274-302.

[3] See, for example, R. S. Fulton, "How Nature Regulates the Rains," *Science* n.s. 3 (1896): 546-52; John Minto, *A Paper on Forestry Interests* (Salem, Ore., 1898), pp. 4-5; W. B. Greeley, "The Effect of Forest Cover upon Stream Flow," *Forestry and Irrigation* 11 (1905): 163; Gifford Pinchot, *A Primer of Forestry*, pt. 2, *Practical Forestry* (Washington, D.C., 1905), pp. 68-69.

[4] Theodore Roosevelt, "The Importance of Practical Forestry," *Forestry and Irrigation* 9 (1903): 170; Gifford Pinchot, "Relation of Forests to Irrigation," *Forestry and Irrigation* 10 (1904): 551-52; U.S., Department of Agriculture, *Report of the Secretary of Agriculture, 1904* (Washington, D.C., 1904), p. LVI.

[5] Charles D. Smith, "The Movement for Eastern National Forests, 1899-1911" (Ph.D. diss., Harvard University, 1956), p. 213.

tentative about the role of the forests became more dogmatic with each triumph of their cause until they came to assert it unqualifiedly. Pinchot was once asked at a congressional hearing: "Are the conditions such that those floods [on the Southern Appalachian rivers] were, as a demonstration, traceable to the denuding of the forests?" He replied: "Directly; directly. . . . It is a perfectly clear cut proposition."[6]

A series of events in 1907 and 1908 brought the conservationist arguments for the power of the forest as regulator of stream flow into national prominence. The great floods on the Ohio River in 1907 seemed to document the case. Typical of this position was an editorial in *Forestry and Irrigation* which asserted: "The simple fact is that, if we will permit the deforestation of slopes controlling stream flow, we must prepare for floods."[7] Vastly more important for the conservation crusade than the Ohio disaster was the fact that in 1907 W J McGee, Marshall O. Leighton, and Gifford Pinchot drew together various strands of conservationist thought into the seminal doctrine of multiple-purpose river development. A river system, they argued, should be treated as a unit from source to mouth. This imaginative concept benefited from the limitless enthusiasm of President Roosevelt, who appointed an Inland Waterways Commission to gather data to support the principle. The Commission's preliminary findings on stream flow supported the forestry theory.[8]

Multiple-purpose resource use also found a spokesman in

6 William L. Bray, *The Timber of the Edwards Plateau of Texas: Its Relation to Climate, Water Supply, and Soil*, U.S., Department of Agriculture, Bureau of Forestry, Bulletin 49 (Washington, D.C., 1904); HMC, "Forests and Reservoirs in Their Relation to Stream Flow, with Particular Reference to Navigable Rivers," *Transactions of the American Society of Civil Engineers* 62 (1909): 246; U.S., Congress, Senate, Committee on Forest Reservations and the Protection of Game, *Message of the President of the United States, Transmitting a Report of the Secretary of Agriculture in Relation to the Forests, Rivers, and Mountains of the Southern Appalachian Region*, 57th Cong., 1st sess., 1902, S. Doc. 84; G. Frederick Schwarz, *The Diminished Flow of the Rock River in Wisconsin and Illinois, and Its Relation to the Surrounding Forests*, U.S., Department of Agriculture, Bureau of Forestry, Bulletin 44 (Washington, D.C., 1903); U.S., Congress, House, Committee on Expenditures in the Department of Agriculture, *Hearings January 5 to February 20, 1907*, 59th Cong., 2d sess., February 2, 1907, p. 806.

7 "The Upper Ohio Flood," *Forestry and Irrigation* 13 (1907): 169.

8 U.S., Congress, Senate, Committee on Commerce, *Preliminary Report of the Inland Waterways Commission*, 60th Cong., 1st sess., 1908, S. Doc. 325, p. 21.

Senator Francis G. Newlands of Nevada, who in December 1907 introduced a bill to create a new federal department to plan river works and to coordinate all efforts in this direction among existing agencies, whether they had been previously concerned with flood control, navigation, reclamation, water power, or forestry. In advocating such a radical departure from past departmental independence, it was highly desirable for the proponents of the Newlands bill to stress the direct relationship of deforestation and floods to support their claim of the unity of a watershed.[9]

The Weeks bill for the establishment of an Appalachian National Forest benefited from the same specific reasoning; indeed, the forestry-stream flow theory had now become indispensable for its success. Reports of the Geological Survey and the Forest Service, proposals by the Secretary of Agriculture, and recommendations from the White House had all emphasized the connection between denudation of the Appalachian and White Mountain slopes and increased floods.[10] So enthusiastic were the partisans of the measure that their public remarks became increasingly unguarded. Testifying before a congressional hearing, Pinchot displayed an unidentified photograph of a denuded and eroded hillside as proof of deforestation's evil effects everywhere and poured water upon the photograph and upon a sheet of blotting paper to illustrate the respective effects of cleared land and forests upon runoff. One lecturer for an Appalachian National Forest even poured water upon the bald pate of a spectator as a surrogate for deforested ground.[11]

9 Hays, *Conservation*, pp. 109-10; Smith, "Movement for Eastern National Forests," p. 292.

10 E.g., U.S., Congress, Senate, Committee on Agriculture and Forestry, *Report of the Secretary of Agriculture on the Southern Appalachian and White Mountain Watersheds*, 60th Cong., 1st sess., 1908, S. Doc. 91, pp. 19, 37-39; M. O. Leighton and A. H. Horton, *The Relation of the Southern Appalachian Mountains to Inland Water Navigation*, U.S., Department of Agriculture, Forest Service, Circular 143 (Washington, D.C., 1908); M. O. Leighton, M. R. Hall, and R. H. Bolster, *The Relation of the Southern Appalachian Mountains to the Development of Water Power*, U.S., Department of Agriculture, Forest Service, Circular 144 (Washington, D.C., 1908).

11 U.S., Congress, House, Committee on the Judiciary, *Hearing on H.R. 208*, 60th Cong., 1st sess., February 27, 1908, pp. 17-18; Smith, "Movement for Eastern National Forests," p. 138.

Zeal and qualitative judgments were not enough to pass the measure, however, for a roadblock in the form of the House Committee on the Judiciary impeded its progress. There was real danger as the year 1908 opened that the Committee would report against the bill on the constitutional ground that the federal government had no power to acquire land for national forests. The Weeks bill was accordingly amended on the floor of the Senate by adding the words "for the purpose of preserving the navigability of navigable streams" to include the measure beneath the sheltering arms of the commerce clause.[12] This amendment sufficed to win a report from the Judiciary Committee certifying that it was constitutional for the federal government to purchase forested land if that land "has a direct and substantial connection with the conservation and improvement of the navigability of a river actually navigable in whole or in part, and any appropriation made therefor is limited to that purpose."[13] This amendment was accepted: "By the end of 1908," writes Charles E. Smith, "friends of eastern national forests were much encouraged as to their prospects for success in the new year. Yet acceptance of the decision of the Judiciary Committee left only a small front along which they could attack."[14]

The enemies of conservation moved to roll back this front. The leader of those forces was the Corps of Engineers of the United States Army whose members looked suspiciously at the theoretical innovations of the multiple-purpose conservationists and upon the proposed redistribution of federal responsibility over natural resources. Especially did the military men resent the foresters' emphasis upon the woodlands as regulators of stream flow so they brought all their strength to bear upon this hypothesis.

The Corps of Engineers, however, was in a weak position to defend its traditional prerogatives against the new onslaught of organized conservationists. Under attack for several years, the Corps had been originally denied the great work of the

[12] Smith, "Movement for Eastern National Forests," p. 285; U.S., Congress, Senate, *Congressional Record*, 60th Cong., 1st sess., 1908, 13, pt. 5: 4663.

[13] Cited in Smith, "Movement for Eastern National Forests," p. 286.

[14] Ibid., p. 298.

Panama Canal and only after some difficulty had it obtained this prize in 1907.[15] Its members, the proudest defenders of the tradition of honor of the United States Military Academy, of which institution all its officers were graduates, had been shaken by an enormous scandal at the end of the century. Oberlin M. Carter, an officer of the Corps, had been convicted by court martial of defrauding the United States of thousands of dollars while in charge of the harbor works at Savannah. During his trial, likened to an "American Dreyfus Case," by his supporters, there had been well-publicized insinuations that the Corps had tried to shield Carter from punishment to protect its reputation for probity hitherto unblemished.[16]

More serious as a threat to the Corps than the peculations of Captain Carter were charges that it was incompetent to carry on the river and harbor works so ardently demanded by publicists, businessmen, and politicians who assumed that the railroads could not handle the burgeoning commerce of the nation and that water transport must fill the gap. Early in 1908 a committee of the Board of Trade and Transportation of New York City reported that the Corps was too small in numbers for the task of developing water-borne commerce since many of its 169 officers were occupied with other duties in addition to their civil works responsibilities. It urged the establishment of a federal Department of Public Works.[17] The influential *Engineering News* reprinted this criticism and suggested that the president's Inland Waterways Commission should, in its forthcoming report, make a definite proposal about future control of waterways projects.[18] Its implications were that the Corps might have to stand aside. Later the editors of the same journal argued ominously: "We reveal no secrets when we say that there is a strong feeling among many influential men who are active in the present movement for increased waterway facilities, that the government's civil engineering work should be removed entirely from the jurisdiction

---

[15] Miles P. DuVal, Jr., *And the Mountains Will Move: The Story of the Building of the Panama Canal* (Stanford, Calif., 1947), pp. 243-72.

[16] *New York Times,* December 12, 1897, p. 3; August 19, 1899, p. 6; September 1, 1899, p. 12; April 25, 1900, p. 3; November 28, 1903, p. 1.

[17] Untitled editorial in *Engineering News* 59 (1908): 125.

[18] Ibid.

of the Corps of Engineers.''[19] The National Rivers and
Harbors Congress took a slightly different tack by formally
resolving late in 1908 that Congress should double the size
of the Corps and authorize it to plan all river and harbor
works, pending the creation of its preferred solution, a
permanent waterways commission.[20]

Convinced that it was fighting for its life, the Corps struck
back against its multiple-purpose adversaries by focusing upon
one of their gravest weaknesses: a lack of reliable quantitative
data in their theory about the relationship of forests and stream
flow. In the summer of 1908, at the request of the commanding
officer of the Corps, Major Henry C. Newcomer prepared a
sixteen-page report in which he concluded that rainfall and
temperature, not the degree of forestation, are the main controlling factors in producing high and low waters, but his
records were drawn from such a variety of times and places,
and were so uncontrolled, that they were as quantitatively
unconvincing as those of the conservationists.[21] Chittenden, in
semi-retirement in Seattle, voluntarily plunged into the
struggle on behalf of the embattled Corps on July 4, 1908,
when he began an extended essay dealing with this controversy.[22]

Chittenden was certainly not an uncritical devotee of the
Corps and its conservative waterways policies. He feared that
the reluctance of the Corps to recommend expenditures for
public works would cause it to lose control of public works
to another agency, for the public demanded vigorous action
in the waterways area.[23] In December 1908, along with the
other officers of the Corps, Chittenden was asked by the Chief
of Engineers to comment on two bills prepared by his office to
alleviate the critical shortage of army engineers. The Chief's
two alternatives were bills either to increase the size of the
Corps or to form a separate nonofficer Corps of United States

[19] "A Proposed Increase in the Corps of Engineers," *Engineering News* 60
(1908): 591.
[20] "Resolutions Adopted by the National Rivers and Harbors Congress,"
Engineering News 60 (1908): 730.
[21] Henry C. Newcomer, "The Relation of Forests to Stream Flow on Navigable
Rivers," July 20, 1908, #68551/931, RG 77.
[22] HMC, "Diary," July 4, 1908, CPHS.
[23] HMC, "Diary," December 7, 1908, CPHS.

Civil Engineers to be selected from the civil engineers now connected with river and harbor work. Chittenden thought little of these options, for he considered them palliatives. Instead, he recommended that the Corps admit into its ranks highly qualified civil engineers who would not be second-class members of the Corps. He granted that most officers of the Corps would resent this idea, "But the Corps is facing a crisis in its history. The movement now gaining such headway has been gradually gathering strength since the creation of the Reclamation Service, and even for several years before. The public cares little for tradition and its demands in regard to river and harbor works are becoming imperative. We cannot close our eyes to the fact that there is some justice in these demands." If the Corps did not make a radical change, he concluded, it would lose its civil works.[24]

While originally an advocate of the forestry-stream flow thesis, Chittenden's observations in Yellowstone Park had changed his mind long before the inland waterways and forestry campaigns began. In the first edition of his Yellowstone book published in 1895 Chittenden had accepted the forestry theory, but by 1897 he had serious misgivings about its validity, and he expressed these reservations in a private letter to his friend George Anderson, acting superintendent of Yellowstone Park, who did accept the theory.[25] His subsequent desire to prepare a solidly documented attack upon the conservationist theory did not meet with approval by all members of the Corps and one senior officer suggested that he drop the project, Chittenden later wrote, for fear of antagonizing members of Congress and of the executive branch. But Chittenden was not intimidated, for in the stream flow controversy he saw the interests of public policy, objective science, and the Corps as identical and, so motivated, he completed his influential paper on "Forests and Reservoirs in Their Relation to Stream Flow with Particular Reference to Navigable Rivers,"

24 "Circular Letter to All Officers of the Corps," December 16, 1908, #70025; HMC to W. L. Marshall, December 26, 1908, #70025/26, both RG 77.
25 HMC to George S. Anderson, June 11, 1897, YNPA; George S. Anderson, "A Plan to Save the Forests: Forest Preservation by Military Control," *Century* n.s. 27 (1895): 633-34.

in time for publication in September 1908 in the *Proceedings* of the American Society of Civil Engineers.[26]

Chittenden's arguments in this influential work were based on abstract theory, his own experience, and the reports of other observers. He opened his paper by a general affirmation of his conservationist faith, a faith that his career had proved unquestionably sincere although it did not always appear so to his opponents: "[The author's] sympathies are wholly on the side of the present movement for the conservation of natural resources, and, so far as this paper takes issue with certain tendencies of that movement, it is only for the purpose of inquiring whether such tendencies are not really inimical to the cause to which they pertain." More specifically, and perhaps more convincingly, he openly endorsed the principles of the Weeks bill as sound.[27]

Chittenden followed these avowals by stating as his basic proposition that the forestry advocates erred in resting their stream flow theory upon a single fact and a single assumption based thereon: a large portion of the forests in the eastern part of the United States had been cut down and hence floods and low water had occurred more frequently than before lumbering and agricultural operations had begun. He continued by arguing that humus was not always effective in equalizing rainfall; it failed "in those periods of long-continued, widespread and heavy precipitation, which alone cause great floods in the large rivers." Under such conditions, the forested watershed contributes to flooding more than cleared ground because its litter has already accumulated water from normal precipitation and is hence impervious.[28]

Colonel Chittenden also contended that forests have a deleterious effect on runoff because they "distribute the snow in an even blanket over the ground" and retain it longer than the drifts in the open country.[29] In the open, he argued,

26 HMC, "Notes on Forestry Paper," CPHS; *Proceedings of the American Society of Civil Engineers* 34 (1908): 924-97; the original paper with discussion and Chittenden's rebuttal is reprinted in *Transactions of the American Society of Civil Engineers* 62 (1909): 245-546, hereafter cited, "Forests and Reservoirs."
27 "Forests and Reservoirs," pp. 246, 316-18, 505.
28 Ibid., pp. 247-51 (quotation, p. 249).
29 Ibid., p. 251.

snow runs off gradually because it freezes nightly and melts in the daytime. In the shaded forests, by contrast, snow vanishes rapidly when the heat and warm rains of spring and summer disperse it in a rush of flooding.[30] Regarding the causes of erosion, Chittenden attributed it not to deforestation but to agricultural operations: breaking the soil and building roads and trails. When forests were removed, he argued, a second growth quickly sprang up if the farmer permitted it to do so. Soil wash, he said, was minimal even from agricultural operations, for in the areas where it chiefly occurred, as in the Missouri River watersheds, there was little cultivation but much natural erosion.[31]

In attempting to prove these contentions, Chittenden employed all the published records of river stages for the Mississippi, Ohio, Tennessee, Missouri, and Connecticut rivers. Although he criticized those who had used the same data because the longest records only ran back eighty years, he himself tried to prove that they indicated no impact of deforestation on river flow. He drew the same conclusions from the researches of Ernst Lauda, chief of the Hydrographic Bureau of the Austrian government, who had examined the records of Danubian floods for the past 800 years. But Chittenden could furnish no accurate information on the amount of land logged off any of the watersheds he studied nor did he seem aware of any other possible variables in the watersheds.[32]

After disposing of a few minor points in the forestry argument, Chittenden summed up in seven propositions his conclusions about the effects of forestry on stream flow: 1) The bed of humus and litter in forests retains precipitation during dry seasons better than "soil and crops of deforested areas similarly situated." 2) "The above action fails altogether in periods of prolonged and heavy precipitation, which alone produce great general floods." 3) In "extreme summer heat" forests reduce runoff better than open areas because "they absorb almost completely and give off in evaporation ordinary

30 Ibid., pp. 252-62.
31 Ibid., pp. 270-77.
32 Ibid., pp. 258-65.

showers." 4) "The effect of forests upon the run-off resulting from snow melting is to concentrate it into brief periods and thereby increase the severity of freshets." 5) "Soil erosion does not result from forest cutting in itself, but from cultivation, using that term in a broad sense. . . . The natural growth which always follows the destruction of a forest is fully as effective in preventing erosion, and even in retaining run-off, as the natural forest." 6) Climate, especially precipitation, has "not been appreciably modified by the progress of settlement and the consequent clearing of the land." 7) "The percentage of annual run-off to rainfall has been slightly increased by deforestation and cultivation."[33] Chittenden concluded that the truth of the above propositions demonstrated that "no aid is to be expected in the control or utilization of our rivers, either for flood prevention, navigation or water power, by any practicable application of forestry" and that "forestry will be left to work out its own salvation without any reference to the rivers."[34] The path to this salvation lay in arguing for forestry on its merits. His own support of the Weeks bill to purchase land for national forests was not based upon the proposition that it would aid navigation by preventing floods.[35]

Recognized almost at once as a penetrating and provocative analysis, Chittenden's essay was vigorously scrutinized by conservationists and engineers. It was originally read—in the absence of Chittenden—by Charles W. Hunt, the secretary of the American Society of Civil Engineers at the November 4, 1908, meeting of the Society in New York City. A large crowd of over 100 members and guests was in attendance and Pinchot and Leighton, among others who discussed it, attacked it from the floor.[36] In its editorial columns the influential *Engineering News* agreed with Chittenden's key proposition that forests do not prevent floods, but disagreed with his beliefs that forests do not favorably affect stream flow on smaller streams, that snowfall melts more slowly in the open than on forested ground, and that second growth springs up quickly when the virgin

33 Ibid., pp. 280-81.
34 Ibid., pp. 281, 282.
35 Ibid., pp. 316-18, 505.
36 HMC, "Notes on Forestry Paper," CPHS; *Proceedings of the American Society of Civil Engineers* 34 (1908): 460.

forest is cut. The same periodical took Chittenden to task for saying that deforestation neither injures reservoirs nor causes erosion.[37] These editorials were followed by vigorous discussion in the letters column of the periodical.[38]

Chittenden was attacked by more powerful men than hydraulic engineers. President Roosevelt, in his message to Congress in December 1908 referred to the devastation and decline of civilization in China allegedly caused by deforestation and demanded that Congress yield inland waterways projects to the care of men who took the multiple-purpose approach. He condemned the lack of knowledge and the short-sightedness of the military engineers and he thrust directly at Chittenden and his colleagues by saying: "Prominent officers of the Engineer Corps have recently even gone so far as to assert in print that waterways are not dependent upon the conservation of the forests about their headwaters. This position is opposed to all the recent work of the scientific bureaus of the Government and to the general experience of mankind."[39] In a similar vein, Herbert Quick, the popular literary figure and advocate of inland waterways and reforestation, advised the layman confused by the controversy engendered by Chittenden's essay: "Common sense teaches that the influences which have ruined Northern China will ruin any region similarly situated and treated in like manner. Science, if one not too fully instructed may presume to judge, speaks the same judgment. Science cannot really be permanently at variance with educated common sense—nay, science is only educated common sense."[40]

From date of publication well into 1909 the Chittenden

[37] *Engineering News* 60 (1908): 478, 561.

[38] Ibid., pp. 564, 619, 720-21.

[39] *A Compilation of the Messages and Papers of the Presidents, 1789-1908*, James D. Richardson, comp., 12 vols. (Washington, D.C., 1909), 11: 1376-81 (quotation, p. 1381). When this address was published separately it contained ten photographs of devastation in China attributed to deforestation. *Message of the President of the United States . . . at the Beginning of the Second Session of the Sixtieth Congress* (Washington, D.C., 1908). Roosevelt's speech was later cited by Congressman Weeks in support of his Appalachian forest bill, U.S., Congress, House, *Congressional Record*, 61st Cong., 2d sess., 1910, 45, pt. 8: 8976.

[40] Herbert Quick, *American Inland Waterways: Their Relation to Railway Transportation and to the National Welfare; Their Creation, Restoration, and Maintenance* (New York, 1909), pp. 209-10.

paper continued to have a wide hearing and gained great influence. The most prestigious of his commentators, favorable and hostile, published their remarks with Chittenden's rebuttal and the original paper in the *Transactions* of the American Society of Civil Engineers in March 1909. While his supporters mainly endorsed his ideas without adding documentary support, the critics were more pointed in this symposium.[41]

Stephen Child, a lobbyist for the American Civic Association on behalf of the Weeks bill, revealed the political impact of the paper. "Certainly his arguments are strong and most interesting," he wrote, "and the writer frankly admits that he is entirely unable to meet them."[42] He feared that they would impede the progress of the Weeks bill through Congress.[43] On more scientific grounds, George O. Smith, Director of the United States Geological Survey, claimed that Chittenden had overstated conservationist support of forest humus as a storage unit for rainfall and had neglected its function in filtering rainfall into the ground.[44] Another critic, George F. Swain, by admitting the difficulty of employing quantitative methods in measuring the impact of forests on runoff, implied that the conservationists had been justified in neglecting their use.[45] Swain also asserted that it was more important "to diminish the frequency of great floods than the height of extreme floods which occur only at long intervals."[46]

Marshall O. Leighton's major criticism was that Chittenden had "revealed a fundamental misconception" in claiming that conservationists had previously asserted that the bed of forest humus absorbed a great deal of precipitation.[47] Rather, said Leighton, "The common understanding is that the forest mulch

---

[41] Its influence as one of the best statements of the critics of conservation was widely recognized in and out of Congress. U.S., Congress, Senate, *Congressional Record*, 61st Cong., 3d sess., 1911, 46, pt. 3: 2582; Quick, *American Inland Waterways*, pp. 181-211; Smith, "Movement for Eastern National Forests," p. 299. "Forests and Reservoirs," p. 386.

[42] "Forests and Reservoirs," p. 328.

[43] Ibid., p. 329.

[44] Ibid., pp. 361-65.

[45] Ibid., pp. 365-66.

[46] Ibid., p. 367.

[47] Ibid., pp. 394-95.

is not the storage agent in any except a merely nominal sense. Its whole function is to protect the ground."[48] Leighton argued further that forests do not distribute snow in an even blanket on the ground, as Chittenden had charged the conservationists with believing, and that American rainfall records, which he presented in great profusion for quinquennial and decennial periods, were sufficient to reach conclusions about the influence of forests on stream flow, although he did concede that an extremely high or low water might be reached in one decade that was not attained in another. He justified his admission by stating, "These extreme conditions are mere sports, due to unusual occurrences."[49]

Gifford Pinchot summarized his objections to the Chittenden paper under four headings, maintaining that the engineer was erroneous in stating that conservationists had claimed that humus stored water rather than letting it filter into the ground beneath it, in arguing that river records do not show an increase over the years in frequency of flood and low waters, in asserting that the critical point to be considered is flood heights rather than flood frequency, and in "his conception of forestry in general."[50]

In all the criticisms, as in the original paper, there was a dearth of quantitative data gained from actual experiment. One critic, Bailey Willis, conceded that "Statistics of comparative run-off from bare and forested slopes, which are observed in such a way as to yield data for close comparison, are not known to the writer. It is probably safe to say that they have not been observed in the United States."[51] Although Leighton had included many tables of rainfall data in his remarks, they were not coordinated with any quantitative information on the amount of deforestation in the watersheds or other variables, and criticisms of other commentators suffered from similar methodological weaknesses.

Chittenden's own lengthy rejoinder to his adversaries restated his seven propositions and evaluated the assaults upon

[48] Ibid., p. 395.
[49] Ibid., p. 402.
[50] Ibid., p. 466.
[51] Ibid., p. 386.

them.[52] His major contribution in this rebuttal was to show that his paper had already forced the conservationists to reverse their own previous theses in several respects. He expressed surprise that Leighton now denied that the forest humus absorbed water to pay it out later in even stream flow. He quoted Leighton and Horton in a forestry publication of the year before wherein they had stated: "The Southern Appalachian forests act as a great storage reservoir, and this is done largely through the medium of its humus, the litter of decomposing vegetable matter which forms the forest floor * * * [citation of foreign authorities] * * The function of the forest and of the humus beneath as a storage reservoir is of high importance."[53]

Chittenden also rejoiced that, again using Leighton's earlier words to prove his change of heart, the conservationists now admitted that flood heights were no greater because of deforestation than they had been in a state of nature.[54] Also significant was his proof of the "complete change of base" of Leighton, Pinchot, and Swain in now asserting that the average high waters rather than the extremes are of the chief importance in flood control work. Chittenden demonstrated the absurdity of the contention that forests could control "great floods" but not "extreme floods" and hence that "extreme floods" could be overlooked in calculating the benefits of forestry.[55]

Chittenden showed convincingly that Leighton's tables were inadequate and he also exposed many of Pinchot's watershed data as unreliable. Finally, he rejected conclusively the conservationist claim that deforestation had caused the downfall of ancient civilizations by showing that many of these civilizations had never possessed extensive forested land, or if they had, that they had undergone so many other changes besides deforestation that to single it out as the ultimate cause of decline was preposterous.[56]

[52] Ibid., pp. 466-546.

[53] Ibid., pp. 470-71; the paper cited by Chittenden was Leighton, Hall and Bolster, *Relation of the Southern Appalachian Mountains to the Development of Water Power.*

[54] "Forest and Reservoirs," p. 472.

[55] Ibid., p. 473.   [56] Ibid., pp. 475-84, 530-33, 518-25.

Led by Chittenden's vigorous essay, the Corps gained some useful allies in 1909 and 1910 while continuing its own efforts to defend its traditional positions. Charles F. Scott, the chairman of the House Committee on Agriculture and an opponent of the Weeks bill, asked the Chief of Engineers for a copy of the Newcomer report on January 21, 1909, so that he could use it in studying the various bills to purchase forested land.[57] Major William W. Harts examined in 1909 the rainfall records and river stages at three places on the Cumberland and Tennessee rivers and concluded that floods were no greater and navigability no more hazardous than at any period in the past.[58] Another officer of the Corps, Colonel Edward Burr, prepared an elaborate study of the stream flow conditions on the Merrimac River between Haverhill and Lowell and published it in 1911. He analyzed rainfall and river gauge records and concluded: "The facts brought out by this study covering a period of 60 years do not show that reforestation to the extent of 25 per cent of the Merrimac Basin has exerted any beneficial effect upon the flow of that river or that the later part of the period of deforestation had any adverse effect thereon. On the contrary there are a number of indications that this reforestation has been coincident with adverse effects on the regimen of the river in some of its aspects." Burr sent a prepublication copy of his report to Congressman Scott.[59]

Willis Moore, the controversial head of the United States Weather Bureau, at the behest of Scott, prepared a paper summarizing his views on stream flow for the Committee on Agriculture. Moore's opinions on the question had first come to the attention of the Committee at a public hearing in December 1908, when he admitted that Chittenden's essay on stream flow had caused him to change his views about the alleged effects of forests on rivers and to admit, "I must say that I have been considerably influenced by the discussion of Lieutenant-Colonel Chittenden of the Army. He differs from

57 Charles F. Scott to Chief of Engineers, January 21, 1909, #68551/533, RG 77.
58 William W. Harts, "The Relation of Forests to Stream Flow," U.S., Army, Engineer Bureau, *Professional Memoirs* 1 (October-December 1909): 397-404.
59 U.S., Congress, House, Committee on Rivers and Harbors, *Merrimac River, Mass., between Haverhill and Lowell*, 62d Cong., 1st sess., 1911, H. Doc. 9, pp. 31-32; Edward Burr to Charles F. Scott, March 2, 1910, #68551/940, RG 77.

me."[60] The Chittenden influence ultimately and specifically prevailed in Moore's report, published by the Committee on Agriculture in early 1910. His conclusions echoed those of Chittenden in arguing that the floods are caused by excessive precipitation, that runoff is not materially caused by any other factor, and that "the high waters are not higher, and the low waters are not lower than formerly." The marked similarity between the Moore paper and that of Chittenden was noted by William L. Hall of the Forest Service who prepared a confidential memorandum on it for Pinchot: "In fact, it seems that the only points made with real force in this discussion are those in which the argument of Col. Chittenden is reiterated." Moore himself acknowledged Chittenden's pioneering work.[61]

The counterattack mounted by the Corps, the Weather Bureau, and independent critics of the forestry theory had mixed results. The proponents of the Weeks bill had an uncomfortable time at the hearing on the measure in 1910: "For their part," declares Charles E. Smith, "those speaking for the Weeks bill found themselves on the defensive. Pinchot spent the bulk of his time pointing out the fallacies he saw in the Chittenden thesis and in insisting that the presence of forests aids rivers in maintaining a continuous flow of water for a greater mean depth over a given length of time."[62] Although its opponents scored some points in this hearing and in the minority report of the committee, the Weeks bill passed the Senate overwhelmingly on February 15 and was signed by the president on March 1, 1911.[63] In final form, however, this bill contained provisions establishing a National Forest

[60] U.S., Congress, House, Committee on Agriculture, *Hearing on the Estimates of Appropriations for . . . 1910 . . . ,* 60th Cong., 2d sess., December 15, 1908, p. 33; U.S., Congress, House, Committee on Agriculture, *A Report on "The Influences of Forests on Climate and on Floods," by Willis L. Moore* (Washington, D.C., 1910).

[61] William L. Hall, "Notes of Comment on Prof. Willis L. Moore's Report on Stream Flow," February 21, 1910, Box 1906, Gifford Pinchot Papers; Moore to HMC, February 12, 1910, #LR 954-1910, Weather Bureau General Correspondence (1870-1912), Records of the Weather Bureau, Record Group 27 (National Archives), hereafter cited WBGC.

[62] Smith, "Movement for Eastern National Forests," p. 323.

[63] U.S., Congress, Senate, *Congressional Record,* 61st Cong., 3d sess., 1915, 46, pt. 3: 2602; ibid., pt. 4: 3958.

Reservation Commission, composed of the secretaries of Agriculture, Interior, and War plus two senators and two representatives, to determine what land was to be purchased and at what price. Before the Commission could buy any piece of land, it had to have the certification of the Geological Survey that the purchase of the land in question "will promote or protect the navigation of streams on whose watersheds they lie."[64] It is significant that the quantitative test, long desired by the foes of the forestry theory, was finally to be put in action, although after qualitative appeals had sufficed to pass the bill.

The difficulties in furnishing quantitative proof were aptly described in a memorandum from John C. Holt, the Geological Survey's engineer in charge of surface water investigations, to the director of the Survey on May 15, 1911. He wrote, in part: "The effect of vegetation on stage of flow from any area depends in a large degree upon the other controlling factors. Therefore, any study to determine its magnitude is very difficult, and conclusions based thereon may have only local application. . . . In order to obtain data from which any hope of showing effect on runoff could be had, an exceedingly refined series of investigations, extending over a series of years, will be required and even then it is questionable whether such records would prove anything."[65]

In spite of Holt's advice, a Survey team made a brief study of a few months' duration in 1912 of two small watersheds in New Hampshire, Burnt Brook and Shoal Pond Brook, respectively 5.165 and 4.75 square miles in extent. On June 4, 1912, a preliminary report was issued based on investigations of these watersheds by a geologist, a hydrographer, and an engineer. The report answered the question, "Does a storm of known depth produce different run-off characteristics on a forested basin from those occurring on a similar basin deforested?" by stating that in general the flow of streams is influenced by many factors, but in this important case:

64 U.S., Congress, *Statutes at Large*, 1911, 36, pt. 1: 962.
65 "Memorandum to the Director," May 15, 1911, #1793, Water Resources Branch, Records of the Geological Survey, Record Group 57 (National Archives), hereafter cited RUSGS.

The comparison between two adjacent basins during critical periods is presented in this preliminary statement as a sufficient showing for the purposes of the National Forest Reservation Commission. While data covering larger periods for both these and other basins in the White Mountains have been collected and will be available for the more complete report, the particular case of the Burnt Brook and Shoal Pond basins is typical for the region and establishes the general conclusion that a direct relation exists between forest cover and stream regulation.

The results of the Burnt Brook-Shoal Pond Brook studies are held to show that throughout the White Mountains the removal of forest growth must be expected to decrease the natural steadiness of dependent streams during the spring months at least.[66]

Although this investigation was, to say the least, limited, "The fact remains that upon this inconclusive study rests the full weight of vast areas of national timberland in the White Mountains."[67] Scientifically dubious, the report did accomplish the vital conservationist purpose of justifying the Weeks Act, but it also marked the high point of uncritical use of the forestry-stream flow theory, for increasingly both friends and enemies of conservation called for broader and more thoroughly gathered quantitative data by which to test it.

The first truly scientific attempt to obtain these data began in 1910 under the joint supervision of the Forest Service and the Weather Bureau at Wagon Wheel Gap in Colorado. The experiment was started in February 1910, when two watersheds of similar character in Colorado were selected for study. After a decade of measurements of stream flow, runoff, and precipitation, one of the watersheds was completely denuded in 1920.[68] The Forest Service justified this type of study, and implicitly condemned its earlier "research," in the words of District Forester Carlos Bates in a public speech: "The experiment which I have described to you is the only one of its

---

[66] George O. Smith, "U.S. Geological Survey Report No. 13, Preliminary Statement on White Mountains, N.H.," #1793, RUSGS.

[67] Smith, "Movement for Eastern National Forests," p. 354, n. 1.

[68] C. G. Bates and A. J. Henry, "Forest and Stream-Flow Experiment at Wagon Wheel Gap, Colo. Final Report on Completion of the Second Phase of the Experiment," U.S., Weather Bureau, *Monthly Weather Review*, Supplement no. 30 (Washington, D.C., 1928), p. 2. This report is an excellent summary of the work at Wagon Wheel Gap.

kind which has ever been instituted, except the Emmenthal experiments in Switzerland, near Zurich. It must, as I believe, always act as an example of the scientific thoroughness in the solution of forestry problems, which can only be obtained by concentrating the efforts of experts at permanent experiment stations *on the ground.*"[69]

Opponents of the stream flow thesis also made some gains on the state level. Clarence T. Johnston, the able state engineer of Wyoming, commended both Chittenden and Moore in their attacks upon the forestry theories.[70] In Wisconsin, the essay stimulated and reinforced opposition to the movement to reforest the northern portion of that state. Professor Daniel Webster Mead of the University of Wisconsin College of Engineering led the attack under "the influence of Chittenden's paper," and it became "clear that such attacks had a retarding effect upon the forestry program."[71]

In general, the forestry-stream flow theory declined in influence after the Moore-Chittenden efforts. The great Seine inundations of 1910 which flooded Paris were not attributed to deforestation.[72] The Mississippi River floods of 1912 staggered the entire valley but produced no call for reforestation as a remedy.[73] In 1916 a committee of the American Society of Civil Engineers prepared an elaborate report on flood control. In the section on reforestation, the committee stated that the past few years had seen many discussions of the forestry influence on stream flow and that "in these discussions the

69 "Influence of Forests on Stream Flow, the Stream-Flow Experiment. By Carlos G. Bates. Read before the Society of American Foresters. November 17, 1910," Box 1906, Gifford Pinchot Papers, LC. It is significant that of 340 references in a recent work on forest influences, only seventeen were published before 1908. E. A. Colman, *Vegetation and Watershed Management: An Appraisal of Vegetation Management in Relation to Water Supply, Flood Control, and Soil Erosion* (New York, 1953), pp. 373-91.

70 Clarence T. Johnston to Willis Moore, February 15, 1910, #954/1910, WBGC; U.S., Congress, Senate, *Congressional Record*, 61st Cong., 2d sess., 1910, 45, pt. 8: 8527.

71 Vernon Carstensen, *Farms or Forests; Evolution of a State Land Policy for Northern Wisconsin, 1850-1932* (Madison, Wis., 1958), pp. 52, 53.

72 "The Engineering Features of the Recent Floods in Paris," *Engineering News* 63 (1910): 327-31; "The Floods in the Seine," *Engineering* 89 (1910): 149-51.

73 E.g., "What Is the Remedy for the Mississippi Floods," *Engineering News* 67 (1912): 997-99.

greatest diversity of opinion has been expressed, and even the advocates of reforestation as a means of flood control fail to give any quantitative determination of the effects of forests upon floods." Although neither Leighton nor Chittenden was satisfied by the report, it may stand as the consensus of the profession at the time of its writing.[74]

A final result of the attacks on the forestry-stream flow theory was to reshape the Newlands bill. In April 1915 an interdepartmental committee (Agriculture, Commerce, Interior, and War) reported on the measure. The War Department representatives, all officers of the Corps of Engineers, refused to sign the report endorsing the bill. Although the bill was passed in 1917, continued opposition to it resulted in the repeal of the waterways commission feature in the Water Power Act of 1920.[75]

In the second and less significant portion of his paper, Chittenden grappled with the effect of reservoirs on flood control.[76] Insofar as the Ohio River was concerned, the distinguished engineer Charles W. Ellet had provided a plan as early as 1852 whereby a series of reservoirs would be built on the headwaters of the Ohio River to provide flood control and to insure an ample supply of water for navigational purposes in the dry seasons. Ellet's plan was at once assailed by an engineer of equal reputation, Milnor Roberts, who denounced the scheme as impossible because of its great cost. Since the middle of the nineteenth century other engineers had debated the plan, but their arguments had led to no results of a concrete nature.[77]

After the year 1895, however, the old interest in controlling navigation and flood problems returned with the expression of hope that improved waterways would reduce increasing freight rates and that reservoirs might be one means for reaching this objective. A general movement for better water-

[74] "Final Report of the Special Committee on Floods and Flood Prevention," *Transactions of the American Society of Civil Engineers* 81 (1917): 1218-310.

[75] Hays, *Conservation*, pp. 230-40, has an excellent discussion of the later legislative history of the Newlands Act.

[76] HMC, "Forests and Reservoirs," pp. 287-318.

[77] Gene D. Lewis, *Charles Ellet, Jr.: The Engineer as Individualist, 1810-1862* (Urbana, Ill., 1968), pp. 133-51.

ways transportation that included several regional schemes developed with most attention focused on an Atlantic-Gulf of Mexico intercoastal waterway and a Lakes-to-the-Gulf Deep Waterway. Projects for reviving the commerce of the Ohio River and for protecting its cities from floods were also widely broached. Hydroelectric power came to the forefront.[78]

In an appendix to the report of the Inland Waterways Commission Marshall O. Leighton of the Geological Survey revived and modified the Ellet scheme for the taming of the Ohio River. It appeared in abridged form more accessibly in the *Engineering News* of May 7, 1908. Frankly labeling his project as a statement of possibilities and not a finished project, Leighton advanced the thesis that it was possible to control readily almost all the rivers in the United States by the employment of reservoirs. Hence in the "majority of cases" it was "improper and illogical" to control floods by carrying them between "high and expensive levees." He cited as proof the Chittenden board report of 1905 on the Upper Mississippi reservoirs, a system built for navigational improvements but almost as useful for flood control. To make his plan more specific, Leighton stated that on the Ohio River he had calculated that the stream could be controlled absolutely by the construction of 100 headwaters reservoirs at a cost of $125 million. Much of the cost he planned to recoup for the government by leasing the water power facilities to private interests at the annual rate of twenty dollars per horsepower.[79]

Leighton's plan gained a mixed reception. The *Engineering News* in an editorial accompanying the original article stated that it had seldom presented a more important paper. Although it questioned the low cost of the project, the journal declared that it might be worth executing ultimately even at two or three times the cost Leighton had estimated. Members of the Corps of Engineers were no more friendly to this plan than they were to the stream flow theory of the forestry advocates.

[78] Hays, *Conservation*, pp. 91-121.

[79] "Relation of Water Conservation to Flood Prevention and Control in Ohio River," U.S., Congress, Senate, Committee on Commerce, *Preliminary Report of the Inland Waterways Commission*, 60th Cong., 1st sess., 1908, S. Doc. 325, pp. 451-90; citations here are to the summary in M. O. Leighton, "The Relation of Water Conservation to Flood Prevention and Navigation in the Ohio River," *Engineering News* 59 (1908): 498-504 (quotations, p. 498).

The Corps had of course, by necessity, followed the constitutional interpretation that Congress could regulate interstate waters solely for the purpose of navigational control, although in practice, as everybody knew, much flood control work was carried on as navigational improvements. It can be hazarded that the Corps posed two other objections to Leighton's plan, one political and one technical. The Corps might well oppose the plan because it feared that it would be carried out by some other agency and it might objectively claim that it was unsound in an engineering or financial sense. As in the forestry fight, the two objections could be intermixed and the scientific objections could be used to accomplish the (publicly unstated) political goals.[80]

Captain William D. Connor, a correspondent of Chittenden and a fellow officer, led the assault in an article in the *Engineering News* on June 11, 1908. He branded Leighton's data as inadequate and his plan as accordingly unfeasible and impracticable. Leighton rejoined that the paper he had written was only a statement of possibilities and that his reservoirs were to supplement rather than supplant navigational improvements such as channel rectification.[81] Chittenden's views followed up this early skirmishing and were included in his forests and reservoirs essay following the section on forestry.

Chittenden began with some general propositions and with the historical background. He opened by stating that artificial reservoirs could be built for flood control, and that he himself had recognized this point in his report on the arid lands in 1897, for there was no theoretical objection to the plan. But in practice, as he had done for the Wyoming and Colorado sites, engineers had rejected reservoirs built exclusively for flood control because of their great cost. Leighton's scheme embraced water power also, but this multi-purpose approach still did not save his proposal for Chittenden, who refused to recognize that, as revealed in Leighton's plan, power and flood control benefits could be combined.[82]

In practice, regardless of theory, the Leighton plan failed

---

[80] *Engineering News* 59 (1908): 511-12, 638-39.
[81] William D. Connor, "The Application of the Reservoir System to the Improvement of the Ohio River," *Engineering News* 59 (1908): 621-24.
[82] HMC, "Forests and Reservoirs," pp. 287-96.

for reasons of cost. Chittenden's critique was devastating on quantitative grounds, although perhaps it was unfair to judge Leighton's scheme as more than a "statement of possibilities." He centered upon Leighton's data for determining the unit of cost, showing, for example, that it was unwise to compare the Upper Mississippi sites, which were lakes, to the dry (and hence vastly more expensive) Ohio sites. He concluded his financial analysis by arguing that a true unit of cost would show that the whole scheme would cost $500 million, four times Leighton's estimate. Moreover, Leighton's plan, according to Chittenden, would take from the community the use of land with an annual product worth $7.5 million while the return from water power leases (at five not twenty dollars per horsepower) would be only $6.4 million. Thus both the expensive construction costs and the limited annual income would make the Leighton project impossible.[83]

Chittenden did not conclude his reservoir comments on this negative note, but characteristically took a larger and more charitable view by attempting to salvage something from Leighton's efforts. He argued that no reservoir system could be justified on its benefits to flood control or navigation. Neither could pay the price, separately or together. It took an industrial (by which he meant manufacturing or irrigation) use to pay for the cost of a reservoir. He went so far as to praise reservoirs and power produced by them as the most important parts of conservation: "The writer thoroughly believes in developing this power through public agencies and preserving it from private ownership and control. His present criticism is directed not at all at the principle involved, but at the extravagant expectations now being fostered as to the possible revenue which the Government may derive from such development." But Chittenden felt in this case that the government could not obtain the twenty dollars per horsepower fee and cited the example of a recent contract made by the Forest Service for a site in the Cascade Mountains where the maximum rent for a forty-year period would be four dollars per horsepower.[84]

83 Ibid., pp. 296-305.
84 Ibid., pp. 305-9 (quotation, p. 306).

Since the possible fees could never build the power plants that would finance the reservoir dams, Chittenden called for a radical solution, government construction of the power plants, although he "admitted that this suggestion will grate harshly on many ears because of its newness and its departure from the established ideas." In urging this principle Chittenden argued the many virtues of federal construction. Complications arising from competing ownership of water and power would be avoided. The government was the only institution that could put an entire interstate river to several uses: flood control, navigation, and power production. Finally, the government could afford to build a structure to stand for all time, thus foregoing immediate profit, while a private corporation could only afford to build for the present and the immediate future. Although this idea of government construction seemed advanced at the time, Chittenden maintained that the nation would soon accept it, arguing by analogy that when he presented his report on reservoirs in the arid regions in the last years of the nineteenth century public opinion opposed government construction of irrigation works in any form. He himself at that time had only advocated that the government build the dams. In the Newlands Act, however, the government had, with popular approval, been designated not only the builder of the dams and the irrigation works but also the distributor of the water.[85]

In conclusion Chittenden argued for a modified multiple-purpose approach. He believed that the United States should control the waters of a river valley as a single unit, but he did not advocate that a single department have this responsibility. What he did was to break down the water users into two classifications, each with a different federal agency to sponsor it. He contended that water power and navigation were related as both were connected with transportation. Irrigation, erosion control, and forestry, all connected with vegetable resources and hence agriculture, should be in another separate department. For the moment then, he declared, it was still necessary to rely most heavily upon the traditional devices of levees, revetments, locks and dams, dikes, and

85 Ibid., pp. 306-13 (quotation, pp. 309-10).

dredging for river and flood control. Reservoirs remained in the background for insurance purposes. Whether they would ever attain the results that Leighton envisioned could be determined only in the future, presumably after they had become economically feasible. Of one thing Chittenden was certain: the absurdity of the constitutional objection that the United States could not build dams for water power. If there were doubt, he said, the constitution could be amended easily to accomplish this conservation principle since public opinion was overwhelmingly in favor of such an amendment.[86]

Chittenden's reflections on reservoirs stirred less of a reaction than his remarks on stream flow and forests. The focus of Leighton's plan was regional, not national; it lacked the emotional fervor of the crusade to save the forests; and by the time Leighton got around to replying to Chittenden in the *Transactions* of the American Society of Civil Engineers, he had expended most of his counterarguments upon Captain Connor and Major Henry C. Newcomer, with whom he contended in the *Engineering News* in June and November 1908. In his formal rebuttal to Chittenden, Leighton repeated his arguments made earlier, although he now admitted that his scheme might cost the $500 million Chittenden predicted but maintained that it would still be worth this vast expenditure.[87]

There the issue remained, clarified but unresolved. Chittenden and Leighton and their respective interests each gained something and each lost something in the struggle over the Ohio reservoir plan. Chittenden's voice was one of many raised successfully against the plan, a plan which was never adopted as Leighton had envisioned it. Chittenden did realize correctly that a reservoir could be used for many purposes and his prediction that this multiple use would occur when it could be financed by industrial interests came true in the case of the great pioneering projects of the 1920s and 1930s: Boulder, TVA, and Grand Coulee. But Chittenden never

[86] Ibid., pp. 314-18.

[87] William D. Connor, "The Application of the Reservoir System to the Improvement of the Ohio River," pp. 624-25; M. O. Leighton, "The Proposed Reservoir System in the Ohio River Basin," *Engineering News* 60 (1908): 504-7; "Discussion" of HMC, "Forests and Reservoirs," pp. 420-22.

knew or admitted that a single agency could handle the administration of one of these great projects. Leighton too was both gainer and loser. He successfully prophesied the great multiple-use project of the future although it did not occur in the Ohio basin. He lived to see the TVA a reality under the control of a single agency. Although his data on the Ohio project was unclear, he at least pointed the way to future efforts of a more objective nature. As in the case of forestry the reservoir controversy illuminated the painful birth pangs of the modern conservation era.

In summing up his essay's impact in an autobiographical fragment dictated in 1916, Chittenden claimed that the forestry section of the paper had—in conjunction with the construction of the Panama Canal—rehabilitated the reputation of the Corps of Engineers and that "in the eight years that have elapsed since the publication of the full paper its principles have come to be generally accepted except among a small group of irreconcilables and I can honestly feel that the whole result has been a work well done."[88]

This estimate was overgenerous. In spite of the experiment made at Wagon Wheel Gap, the Forest Service never relied upon its results, for they did not prove its theory about forests and stream flow. However, by 1927, the Service began to mute its propaganda about forest retardation of stream flow and began to promote the more generally accepted influence of vegetation on erosion; the idea that forest litter soaked up great amounts of precipitation was also abandoned at this time. The Geological Survey also dropped its alliance with the Forest Service on the stream flow question after the disastrous floods on the Mississippi in 1927. After this date, the Service still continued to advance its old stream flow arguments, but came to insist instead (or simultaneously) upon the beneficial effect of vegetation upon erosion. In the interagency struggles of the New Deal era, the Forest Service, supported by a combination of its old qualitative arguments on stream flow and its new experiments, fought on against the Corps and the Soil Conservation Service and not until 1949 did it

[88] HMC, "Notes on Forestry Paper," CPHS.

turn fully toward a quantitative approach, but by this time it had yielded leadership in flood control in the Department of Agriculture to the Soil Conservation Service.[89]

The stream flow controversy illustrates not only the emotionalism of the conservation movement and its misrepresentations of science, but also reveals much about the contemporary concepts of the nature of science itself. There is no doubt that the Progressives were sincere in their trust in science, a belief exemplified by Theodore Roosevelt: "Social and economic problems, Roosevelt believed, should be solved, not through power politics, but by experts who would undertake scientific investigations and devise workable solutions. He had an almost unlimited faith in applied science."[90]

It was quite natural for Americans to have these great expectations, for science, particularly biological science, always had been intimately connected with immediate human problems of health and welfare. Americans of the Progressive generation were familiar with the numerous ramifications of the evolution controversy and were excited by the seminal researches of Pasteur in microbiology. Since the Civil War, taxpayers had been accustomed to supporting government scientists and to witnessing intellectual and bureaucratic struggles among them, and it was thus equally natural for the public to expect that conservation measures would be undertaken by agencies of federal and state governments.[91] Almost inevitably then, both because of its nature and its source of support, the field of forest influences was one in which discoveries would be widely publicized and heatedly discussed. For these reasons alone it would be difficult for scientists in this discipline to maintain a spirit of dispassionate objectivity.

Furthermore, scholars interested in ecological investigations, even if committed solely to the pursuit of objective truth, were handicapped in their quest because of their view of the scientific method. Historically, biologists had mainly depended upon observation rather than experimentation, nowhere more

[89] Ashley L. Schiff, *Fire and Water: Scientific Heresy in the Forest Service* (Cambridge, Mass., 1962), pp. 133-63.

[90] Hays, *Conservation*, p. 267.

[91] Dupree, *Science in the Federal Government*, especially pp. 120-301.

so than in America where almost any observation advanced at least the descriptive knowledge of the subject.[92] Although Pasteur's controlled experiments were well known, most American biologists remained mere amateur observers. Observation then, frequently labeled "common sense," "common experience," and "general knowledge," were what most conservationists meant when they discussed scientific method and scientific truth.

As their opponents were always ready to point out, however, evidence gained by observation alone is always suspect to the scientist, for it cannot be accurately quantified. Pressed by their critics who were proposing the new quantitative methodology, the forestry advocates, some of whom were privately aware of their own methodological weaknesses, fell back upon enthusiasm and, on occasion, duplicity. Their commitment was to a cause, not to scientific evidence, if the evidence contravened the cause. Nor was the stream flow struggle an isolated case of dogmatism, as is indicated by a conflict within the Forest Service over the value of fire prevention to protect longleaf pine and the difficulty of proving quantitatively the possibility of an impending "timber famine."[93] Although their evidence for the forestry-stream flow theory was dubious, the conservationists, as Progressives were wont to do, framed their arguments in moralistic terms by stigmatizing their enemies as militarists, monopolists, traditionalists, and other opprobrious creatures. Toward the close of Chittenden's life, Bernhard Fernow, Pinchot's old superior in the Bureau of Forestry, wrote a letter to Chittenden in which he acknowledged the political approach in Pinchot's use of dubious photographs: "In the case of Mr. Pinchot before a Congressional Committee it is to be understood that at such meetings considerable buncombe needs to be performed, if you want to handle the half-informed legislators. It is sad that it is still the expert's position in court & legislative committees to have to accentuate one side to the detriment of the exact truth, but that seems

[92] Daniel J. Boorstin, *The Americans: The Colonial Experience* (New York, 1958), pp. 164-68.

[93] Schiff, *Fire and Water*, pp. 15-115; Smith, "Movement for Eastern National Forests," pp. 98-99, 324.

needful in this mundas qui vult decipi!"[94] As has been noted elsewhere, there was considerable contempt within the Progressive ideology for politics and politicians.[95]

At this transitional period in the development of American science, however, arguments based upon observational "buncombe" were inadequate to convince the majority of biologists, engineers, meteorologists, and members of the informed public of the truth of the forestry-stream flow theory. Their opponents skillfully exploited the methodological weaknesses of the conservationists by demanding quantitative evidence drawn from controlled experiments. This request had to be answered, but the response, in the form of hastily constructed investigations like the Burnt Brook-Shoal Pond Brook study, were scientifically unconvincing. In the field of forest influences, where scientists even today are drawing only tentative conclusions from their experimental work, the conservationists were extremely slow to attempt controlled experiments and did so only in the crudest manner.[96] Yet they argued for their cause as though its truth were irrefutable.

Their adversaries such as Chittenden were in many ways similar to these conservationists. They, too, were practical men who wanted concrete results from the application of scientific theories rather than investigations of basic scientific problems. They, too, were ignorant of the multitude of observables, let alone possible variables, in any ecological investigation on the scale of a large watershed. Hence they, too, oversimplified their case. But the critics differed from the Pinchotites in that they called publicly for objective, controlled experiments that would lead to a quantitative evaluation of the truth of the forestry-stream flow theory. They were successful in forcing this test upon the reluctant conservationists and in so doing showed that they understood the trend of modern biological investigation. They were much more forward-looking than their foes who branded them as reactionary.

94 Fernow to Chittenden, ca. September 1, 1916, Bernhard Fernow Papers (Cornell University).

95 Hays, *Conservation*, pp. 1-4.

96 Joseph Kittredge, *Forest Influences: The Effects of Woody Vegetation on Climate, Water, and Soil, with Applications to the Conservation of Water and the Control of Floods and Erosion* (New York, 1948), p. v; Colman, *Vegetation and Watershed Management*, pp. 355-63.

Regardless of his essay's future significance, in his time of trials from 1908 to 1910 it sufficed for Chittenden to know that he faced retirement from the Corps with his major final service to it successfully completed, knowledge that would make his career as a civilian easier to bear. He also could take satisfaction in that his opposition to Pinchot, Leighton, Newell, and the others did not sour him, for he remained friends with Newell and Leighton throughout his life and he could write dispassionately in his diary at the time of Pinchot's downfall in 1910: "Politically there is considerable excitement over Mr. Pinchot's removal from office a few days ago."[97]

[97] HMC to R. B. Marshall, November 8, 1918, MP; HMC, "Diary," January 10, 1910, CPHS; Chittenden gave a luncheon for Leighton in his home on October 12, 1912. HMC, "Diary," October 12, 1912, CPHS.

8.

Final Labors
1911-1917

After General Chittenden's retirement he had more leisure for his family than a military career had ever permitted. He handled the parental tasks of discipline and encouragement, helped Hiram with his algebra, played cards with Eleanor and Teddy, and opened his home to his children's friends. His brother Clyde moved to Seattle in 1906 and the families of the two brothers often gathered for spontaneous visits as well as for planned occasions such as Thanksgiving Day. His parents came for a long stay in 1909 from their home in Lansing, Michigan, and the purchase of an automobile in 1911 afforded Chittenden, in spite of his paralysis, a greater opportunity to call upon his friends and acquaintances than at any time in the past three years.

Numerous visitors from the world beyond Seattle, along with a heavy correspondence, kept Chittenden's intellectual interests *au courant*. David Starr Jordan, president of Stanford University, renowned ichthyologist, and student and writer on international peace, visited at Chittenden's new home (purchased in 1914) at 2010 North Broadway. From the world of letters his visitors included J. B. Lippincott the publisher and Ellery Sedgwick of the *Atlantic Monthly*. Arthur E. Morgan was an honored guest at a luncheon for twenty-five people in Chittenden's home. The Progressive economist John R. Commons was a visitor as were many others including George Bird Grinnell and classmates from West Point, Colonel Harry Taylor and Major Hugh J. Gallagher. Ominously, during the last two years the most frequent caller of all, often two or three times weekly, sometimes twice a day, was Henrietta

Crofton, his physician, for Chittenden suffered constantly in his last two years. The only antidote for his pain, besides family and visitors, was work, and in the last six years of his life he took on a variety of tasks that enabled him to continue to employ his unimpaired intellectual powers.[1]

His first opportunity for regular activity came late in July 1911, as his diary records it: "I have decided to accept a nomination for commissioner of the new Port of Seattle. Election comes off Sept. 5th. I may be running some risk but I think I will chance it."[2] Chittenden's new venture was rooted in the interest of Seattle businessmen in the commercial opportunities that they anticipated would arise from the construction of the Panama Canal. As early as February 1907, proponents of developing the port facilities of the city had introduced a bill into the legislature to create a public port that would open Seattle's door to the prospective isthmian commerce. Governed by a popularly elected three-man commission, this agency would have the authority to levy bond issues for the construction of public docks, warehouses, and all other necessary commercial appurtenances. After lengthy discussions and debate the bill finally passed the legislature and was signed by the governor on March 14, 1911. Robert E. Bridges, a Populist politician, realtor, and former state land commissioner, Charles E. Remsberg, owner of a small suburban bank, and Chittenden were the first three commissioners chosen.[3]

The first official meeting of the Seattle Port Commission was held on September 12, 1911, in the rooms of the Pacific Northwest Society of Engineers in the Central Building. Chit-

[1] The sources for these two paragraphs are entries for the years 1911-1917, in HMC, "Diary," CPHS.

[2] HMC, "Diary," July 30, 1911, CPHS.

[3] Norman F. Tjaden, "Populists and Progressives of Washington: A Comparative Study" (Master's thesis, University of Washington, 1960), pp. 2-4; Clarence B. Bagley, *History of King County, Washington*, 3 vols. (Chicago, 1929), 2: 876-80; *Seattle Star*, December 4, 1913; *Tacoma Daily Ledger*, August 17, 1896; Bridges to John McCulloch, March 28, 1912, Robert Bridges Papers (University of Washington Library); Robert C. Nesbit, *"He Built Seattle": A Biography of Judge Thomas Burke* (Seattle, Wash., 1961), pp. 291-352; Arthur S. Beardsley, "The Codes and Code Makers of Washington, 1889-1937," *Pacific Northwest Quarterly* 30 (1939): 35; William F. Prosser, *A History of the Puget Sound Country . . .* , 2 vols. (New York, 1903), 1: 409-10; HMC, "Port Commission Personal Observations," CPHS.

tenden was elected president and Bridges secretary. These two officers, along with Remsberg, filled positions that, although honorific and unpaid, were hardly sinecures, for they had supervision over a large executive engineering staff and clerical and technical aides. Once organized the principal task before the Commission was to develop a comprehensive scheme of projects and plans for financing it in time for the impending election of March 5, 1912, when they would be presented to the voters.[4]

The fundamental guideline of the first port commissioners was to concentrate upon projects that would accommodate the four principal exports of Seattle and its hinterland: lumber, grain, fish, and fruit. To provide the proper facilities for these products the Commission planned piers, grain elevators, cold storage plants, and a winter haven for the local fishing fleet in various parts of the city's harbor on Elliott Bay. The commissioners first outlined their comprehensive plan in a full-page article in the *Seattle Times* on January 21, 1912, and their campaign seemed well launched until there burst almost simultaneously upon the public consciousness the sensational plan thereafter known as the Harbor Island scheme, which almost destroyed the public port and which furnished Chittenden the greatest opportunity of his retirement years for public service.[5]

Harbor Island was a man-made development created in the early years of the century through the dredging of the Duwamish River by the South Canal Company headed by a former governor, Eugene Semple. It was a substantial, flat island, seemingly ideally suited for the development of manufacturing if port facilities were supplied. The island's property owners were hopeful that the comprehensive plan of the Port Commission would include the purchase of their speculative holdings but were disappointed in their wish. Still, they remained undaunted.[6]

On Christmas Eve, 1911, Chittenden was summoned to the

4 Seattle, Port Commission, *First Annual Report,* 1912 (Seattle, Wash., 1912), unpaged.

5 *Seattle Times,* January 21, 1912.

6 Alan A. Hynding, "Eugene Semple's Seattle Canal Scheme," *Pacific Northwest Quarterly* 59 (1968): 77-87.

telephone to answer a call from Scott Calhoun, the counsel of the Commission. Calhoun sought permission to make a trip to New York City to continue private and secret negotiations with the financial interests of the metropolis regarding a plan to use Harbor Island. Because of the press of business before the Commission Chittenden refused the request, but Calhoun called again on the next day and Chittenden agreed to meet him and Alden J. Blethen, publisher and editor of the *Seattle Times*, to discuss the matter further. At this meeting, Calhoun again urged that he be allowed to go, Chittenden's resistance was worn down, and the attorney soon departed for New York at his own expense and in an unofficial capacity.[7]

Once in the East Calhoun and his financial associates concocted a proposal, thereafter known in Seattle's history as the Harbor Island plan (or "scheme" or "swindle") that threatened the comprehensive program of the Port commissioners and indeed the very existence of a public port in the city. Calhoun, the agents of the Seattle Chamber of Commerce, and eastern capitalists conceived a "tentative agreement" to construct all the Port Commission facilities on Harbor Island where a new terminal complex would arise modeled on the successful private developments of Irving T. Bush in Manhattan, although no engineering plans were ever presented by the syndicate for a single structure.[8]

This plan was complex. Private business groups (unspecified in the agreement) would form a terminal company. The Port of Seattle would bond itself to raise the money (ultimately set at five million dollars) to buy 147 acres of land on Harbor Island from its present owners. The Port would lease this land to the company at a deferred rental for thirty years with the company having the option to renew the lease for another thirty years. The company agreed to provide $2,575,000 for buildings and equipment that would become the possession of the Port at the end of thirty years, or sixty years, or as soon as constructed, all at the option of the company. The company further promised to build six piers and then turn them over

7 HMC, "Harbor Island Episode," CPHS.
8 Ibid.

to the Port at cost of construction plus 10 percent. The Port would then lease the piers for either thirty or sixty years as the company desired.[9]

Under a great barrage of publicity led by the city's two major newspapers, the *Times* and the *Post-Intelligencer,* Seattle's businessmen hailed the Harbor Island plan as the panacea that would ensure the city a glorious economic future even more attractive than the prosperity engendered by the Klondike gold rush at the close of the nineteenth century that had made Seattle the metropolis of the Northwest. Mass meetings, newspaper editorials and news articles, and letters to the editor trumpeted the scheme whose supporters wished the Port Commission to abandon its carefully drawn, comprehensive plans in favor of their program. Under heavy pressure from almost all articulate sentiment in the community, the commissioners decided upon a compromise whereby at the March election the voters would have the option of voting for the original Commission plans, the Harbor Island project, both, or neither. Although distrustful of the financial soundness of the Harbor Island venture and of its engineering feasibility, the commissioners decided that it would be prudent to have the electorate decide upon the merits of the proposal rather than for them to refuse to place it upon the ballot. In this decision, Chittenden at least was heavily influenced by the advice of Irving T. Bush, the New York terminal magnate, who was not himself interested in the Seattle plan despite the contrary insinuation by the Harbor Island advocates including R. F. Ayers, a former publicity man in the Bush organization.[10]

At the election both the projects of the Commission and the Harbor Island proposal carried handily leaving the commissioners with the pressing problem of making a lease with

9 The "tentative agreement" is in Seattle, Port Commission, *Bulletin Number One* (Seattle, Wash., 1912), pp. 46-52.

10 *Seattle Times,* January 28, 1912; *Seattle Post-Intelligencer,* January 28, 1912; *Seattle Star,* January 29, 1912; C. B. Yandell to Thomas Burke, February 1, 1912 (telegram), Thomas Burke Papers, Chamber of Commerce Subgroup (University of Washington Library); Irving T. Bush to Port Commission of Seattle, February 6, 1912, Seattle Port Commission Papers (University of Washington Library), hereafter cited SPCP; "Minutes," February 6, 1912, SPCP.

the Harbor Island syndicate that would protect the public in the unlikely possibility that the syndicate ever did attempt to build its promised facilities. From March to August the commissioners and the syndicate, now headed by Ayers and officially incorporated as the Pacific Terminal Company, wrangled over the terms of the lease that was finally signed on August 23, 1912.[11] The lease was far more beneficial to the people of the Port District than had been the "tentative agreement." The amount of land was reduced from 147 to 25 acres; the Port District became a full partner in the plan rather than simply a lender of credit; the size of the financial investment was scaled down; and the Port Commission became the supervisor of the terms of the project.[12]

It soon became evident, even to the most mesmerized original supporters of the syndicate, that Ayers's group was never going to be able to meet the terms of the carefully drawn lease. Its only hope had been in the "tentative agreement" with all its possibilities redolent of a get-rich-quick scheme in the classic manner of frenzied finance. After obtaining delay after delay, the syndicate's schemes evaporated, to the relief of the public, on April 16, 1913, when the Commission canceled its lease. But the heritage of the Harbor Island syndicate was not one of unmixed gratitude to the commissioners because many in the city, led by the Chamber of Commerce, argued that the Commission had drawn up too stringent a list of conditions in the lease and thus had deprived the Ayers group of its opportunity to build a great complex for the economic well-being of Seattle. An opportunity had been missed, they argued, by the excessive caution and the bureaucratic legalisms of the commissioners.[13]

The firstfruit of this hostility was an attempt led by the Chamber to obtain state legislation to enlarge the membership of the Port Commission by two or four members (the plans

[11] The correspondence is in Hiram Martin Chittenden Papers (University of Washington Library). *Seattle Municipal News,* July 6, 1912, pp. 1-2; "Certificate of Incorporation of Pacific Terminal Company," August 8, 1912, SPCP.

[12] Seattle, Port Commission, *First Annual Report,* 1912, unpaged.

[13] *Seattle Times,* April 15, 16, 17, 1913; Seattle, Port Commission, *Second Annual Report,* 1912 (Seattle, Wash., n.d.), pp. 5-6; *Seattle Municipal News,* April 26, 1913; *Seattle Post-Intelligencer,* June 18, 1913.

changed over the years) who would be appointed by the governor or who would assume their positions ex officio as holders of other local offices such as the mayoralty of Seattle. From 1913 through Chittenden's retirement two years later the Commission had to resist this enlargement scheme designed to remove popular control of the Port of Seattle from the voters and place authority in the hands of elected or appointed officials who were more receptive to the plans of private enterprise as interpreted and supported by the Chamber of Commerce.[14]

While these matters of great public interest were being raised and resolved, the Commission under Chittenden's leadership pressed ahead with the comprehensive scheme that had been supported by the voters in that first election of March 1912. Bonds were marketed, a capable engineering staff led by Reginald Heber Thomson was engaged, and work was begun on a variety of construction projects from the north end of the Seattle harbor on Salmon Bay to the mouth of the Duwamish River at the south. In spite of the political pressures and alarms of the Harbor Island and Commission-enlargement proposals, construction progressed so rapidly that on December 31, 1913, the Commission made its first major lease of a Port facility, an agreement with the American-Hawaiian Steamship Company to occupy the entire East Waterway project at Stacy and Lander streets at the south end of the harbor.[15]

The year 1914 was a busy one for Chittenden although not so dramatic as the two preceding ones. Two elections were held. On March 3 the voters approved a transfer of funds of $525,000 from the East Waterway to the Central Waterfront and Salmon Bay projects at the suggestion of the Commission.[16] In November Chittenden ran again for commissioner and won handily in his central district. Significantly in this campaign both his editorial supporters and enemies depicted Chit-

[14] *Seattle Argus,* February 8, March 8, 1913; *Seattle Municipal News,* January 25, 1913; Seattle Chamber of Commerce, "Minute Book," February 18, 1913.

[15] Seattle, Port Commission, *Annual Reports,* 1912-1915 (Seattle, Wash., 1912-1915), passim.

[16] Seattle, Port Commission, *Third Annual Report,* 1914, p. 17.

tenden as the Commission's real force, the man whose ideas became those of the Commission and the one who should receive credit or blame for the manner of their execution.[17] He had no opponent on the ballot and polled 7,342 votes to 417 write-in ballots for other candidates.[18]

In June Chittenden was the leader in calling the first Conference of Port Authorities of the Pacific Coast, held in Seattle, June 23-25, 1914. He was also elected president of the convention, a remarkable tribute to a man who, until the last three years, had no experience whatsoever in port development, public or private.[19] July 31 was a great day for the commissioners when the American-Hawaiian vessel *Nebraska* left the Port Commission wharf in Seattle for the Atlantic seaboard, the first ship outward bound from Seattle to pass through the Panama Canal.[20] In this year construction engineer Paul Whitham resigned from the Commission in October and R. H. Thomson took a long vacation, because the construction projects were rapidly being completed.[21] Another personnel matter signified the coming phase of the Port's history and led to a serious breach between Chittenden and his fellow commissioners. Now that the building projects were being completed it seemed wise to create the position of traffic manager for the Port's increasing commerce, and in August the Commission chose F. R. Hanlon, formerly of the Oregon and Washington Railway and Navigation Company, to fill the new position. Hanlon was Chittenden's candidate, a well-qualified individual, whose appointment was hailed by the shippers' journal, *The Railway and Marine News*.[22]

The appointment of Hanlon, although supported by Bridges

17 Ibid.; *Seattle Municipal News,* November 7, 1914; *Seattle Sunday Times,* December 6, 1914.

18 Seattle, Port Commission, *Third Annual Report,* 1914, p. 17.

19 *Seattle Municipal News,* July 4, 1914; HMC, "Purpose of Conference," *Proceedings of the Conference of Port Authorities of the Pacific Coast* (Seattle, Wash., n.d.), pp. 7-8 and passim.

20 Seattle, Port Commission, *Third Annual Report,* 1914, p. 36.

21 *Railway and Marine News,* October 1914, p. 25; "Engineers Report," August 25, 1914, in Seattle Port Commission, "Progress Reports 1914" (Seattle, Wash., 1914), pp. 1-2, in Seattle Public Library.

22 *Seattle Municipal News,* July 11, 1914; *Railway and Marine News,* August 1914, p. 9.

and Chittenden, was bitterly opposed by Charles E. Remsberg who had his own candidate, E. J. Foreman, his close friend and former business partner. When Foreman was not chosen, Remsberg retaliated with a vigorous campaign against Hanlon. Bridges, soon realizing that Hanlon was not confining his plans to those suggested by Bridges, also turned against him. The crisis came at the Commission meeting on January 16, 1915, when Remsberg charged Hanlon with various inefficiencies and moved that he be dismissed. Chittenden first tried to postpone indefinitely action on the motion, and when this effort failed, he sought to delay Remsberg's motion until Hanlon had a chance to answer the charges against him. When this tactic also was defeated, Chittenden, seeing that he could not save the traffic manager, then delivered a bitter attack upon Remsberg and accused him of opposition to Hanlon solely because the Commission had passed over his own choice for the position. Hanlon's dismissal dismayed not only Chittenden but also the *Municipal News,* the voice of the Seattle Municipal League, which predicted that all the Port Commission staff positions would now fall victims to the spoils system. Four weeks after the Hanlon dismissal, Remsberg called upon Chittenden and offered to forgive him for his public rebuke and to cooperate with him in the future, but Chittenden had no more use for him and contemptuously rebuffed the offer of reconciliation.[23]

The serious division within the ranks of the Commission over the traffic manager was simply the first public indication of what had been beneath the surface for at least two years. Chittenden had condemned the integrity of both Remsberg and Bridges since early 1913, when Remsberg and J. M. Clapp had sold a docksite on Lake Union to King County. Clapp was also connected with Bridges, for he was formerly chief engineer of the Duwamish Waterway project which Bridges had headed; Bridges was in the realty business with the chairman of the Board of County Commissioners, the governmental

23 HMC, "Port Commission Personal Observations," CPHS; *Seattle Municipal News,* January 16, 1915; Seattle, Port Commission, *Fourth Annual Report,* 1915, p. 22.

agency that had bought the property. Chittenden at the time felt that the deal was legal although immoral and regretted having supported Remsberg in his successful campaign for reelection the previous fall, the outcome of which he had then pronounced "much to my satisfaction."[24]

By the autumn of 1915 Chittenden decided that he could contribute no more to the Port of Seattle and resigned on October 1 effective in two weeks time. The rupture with Bridges and Remsberg and the continued attacks upon the Commission in the legislature were contributing factors in his decision, but his chief reason was a simple one. The Commission's engineering work that Chittenden was so suitably qualified to guide was almost over. All the projects in the original comprehensive scheme from Salmon Bay to the East Waterway were finished except for a fish cold storage plant and a fruit warehouse, both on Spokane Street and due to be finished in November.[25] Chittenden's decision to let the Port Commission post go to a man more experienced in business operations and with greater physical strength for political maneuvering was wise, for there was little he could now add to his record as a commissioner.

Chittenden's work on the Port Commission did not require all his intellectual energies in these years, and he wrote a book and several articles that further revealed him to be a true progressive, hopeful and optimistic about the future of humanity, in spite of his own personal reverses. The most ambitious of his efforts was a book on international affairs entitled *War or Peace: A Present Duty and a Future Hope,* published in 1911.[26] Ironically, in these years just before the First World War, the organized peace movement was at flood tide when numerous proposals for international accord flourished and the "peace book" became a popular literary genre. In 1910 William James published *The Moral Equivalent of War* and Norman Angell wrote *The Great Illusion,*

24 HMC, "Port Commission Personal Observations," CPHS; HMC, "Diary," December 2, 1912, CPHS; *Seattle Municipal News,* February 15, 1913; *Seattle Town Crier,* February 15, 1913.

25 Seattle, Port Commission, *Fourth Annual Report,* 1915, pp. 22, 27, 56-57.

26 HMC, *War or Peace: A Present Duty and a Future Hope* (Chicago, 1911).

and in the following year, besides Chittenden's book, appeared J. Novicow's *War and Its Alleged Benefits*.[27]

Chittenden's book contained some surprising affirmations for a man who had served as a military officer for thirty-six years. His plan of organization was first to assail the arguments for military preparations and war as productive of the survival of the fittest among men and nations, of material progress, and of artistic masterpieces. He could not accept war as a greater producer of patriotism, heroic virtues, or a more virile or strenuous life than peacetime. After refuting the arguments for war, Chittenden then turned to its condemnation. He listed the moral, material, and intellectual losses of war, writing, "The pathway of war is the trail of the serpent, and wherever it passes it is as clearly marked by its moral wreckage as by the material ruin which strews the track of its destroying armies."[28]

War or Peace is Chittenden's least successful work. Although it was widely reviewed in the United States and Britain, there was little agreement on the part of the reviewers, as one might expect from a work on such an emotional topic, except to praise Chittenden's sincerity and his lucid powers of style and argumentation.[29] In any case the book was unsuccessful, for it suffered from a vagueness and idealism, almost utopianism, that robbed it of specific guideposts for individual or national action. Chittenden did not specify what steps would be taken to obtain a world court or parliament, how it would be organized (with the exception of an allusion to the United States House of Representatives and Senate), or how its decrees would be enforced.[30]

Still, the limited influence of his book did not cause him to abandon the cause of international peace. He joined the

[27] Robert Endicott Osgood, *Ideals and Self-Interest in America's Foreign Relations: The Great Transformation of the Twentieth Century* (Chicago, 1953), pp. 86-102; William James, *The Moral Equivalent of War* (New York, 1910); J. Novicow, *War and Its Alleged Benefits*, trans. Thomas Seltzer (New York, 1911); Norman Angell, *The Great Illusion: A Study of the Relation of Military Power in Nations to Their Economic and Social Advantage* (New York, 1910).

[28] HMC, *War or Peace*, p. 63.

[29] Chittenden's scrapbooks in CPHS contain seventy-two reviews of the book.

[30] Ibid., pp. 248-60.

American Society of International Law in 1911, and though poor health prevented his attending, he was an invited guest when William Howard Taft and other prominent public figures gathered in Independence Hall in Philadelphia in 1915 to form the League of Peace that was one of the antecedents of Wilson's League of Nations. In a review article he derided Homer Lea's militaristic jeremiad, *The Valor of Ignorance*, which was directed against the rising power of imperial Japan. He published three articles in national magazines on the problems of world peace in the years 1912-1915, a period during which, as the powers first approached and then plunged into world war, he became less confident about the strength of enlightened international opinion working through a world parliament or world court to arbitrate points of international tension.[31]

All these articles still left room for other themes as Chittenden wrote essays on the crossing of the East Waterway in Seattle, designed a plan for the ideal northern railroad entrance to that city, and drafted a plan with A. O. Powell for the Spring Valley Water Company in San Francisco.[32] In 1915 he made his final revision of *The Yellowstone National Park* which brought the tour of the park up-to-date and included some minor rearrangements of existing data. In the preface to this revision, Chittenden realistically recognized that the old days of largely untrammeled freedom were over and he mourned this condition without condemning the present; for example, he never opposed the introduction of automobiles into the park, although he had once predicted

---

[31] James B. Scott to HMC, July 14, 1911, CPHS; H. C. Phillips to HMC, February 24, 1913, CPHS; HMC's copy of the invitation is in CPHS; HMC to Wesley L. Jones, May 23, 1911, CPHS; HMC, "Government by Fright," *Pacific Monthly* 25 (1911): 489-99; HMC, "Over-generous Concessions," *Outlook* 98 (July 8, 1911): 554; HMC, "Peace and Heroism," *Forum* 47 (February 1912): 185-93; HMC, "Does Human Nature Change?" *Atlantic Monthly* 109 (1912): 777-82.

[32] HMC, "The Crossing of East Waterway, Seattle, Wash.," *Proceedings of the Pacific Northwest Society of Engineers* 11 (1912): 10-16; HMC, "A Northern Railroad Entrance to Seattle," *Proceedings of the Pacific Northwest Society of Engineers* 13 (1914): 3-7; HMC and A. O. Powell, *Report on the Water Supply System of the Spring Valley Water Company, San Francisco, Cal.* (San Francisco, 1912).

they would never appear for fear of frightening the freight teams.[33] Although these literary projects revealed Chittenden's personal faith in man's rationality and humanity, his significant accomplishments of these years were those connected with the building of the Port of Seattle. After resigning from the Port Commission, although no longer officially connected with public service, Chittenden continued to deal with civic problems in spite of sinking health and growing discouragement at the premature collapse of his physical powers.

Henry Suzzalo, the president of the University of Washington, was the first to seek Chittenden's counsel in his second retirement when he asked him to serve as a member of the Advisory Board of the Department of Civil Engineering at the University. Retirement also gave Chittenden the opportunity to revive his Cascade tunnel project in an article in the *Engineering News* on November 16, 1916. Although widely discussed in the United States and abroad, no immediate action followed its second unveiling, for it was too expensive for the state and too daring for the railroads to finance, either singly or in combination.[34]

Beyond his home region, Chittenden's engineering imagination was captured by one of the significant flood control works of American history, a project that helped reshape his views of water resources. The roots of this change were the great floods in the Miami Valley of Ohio in late March 1913, a tragedy that caused the death of at least 361 persons and property damage estimated in the amount of $66,765,574. In the aftermath of this catastrophe, the citizens of the valley employed the Morgan Engineering Company, headed by the

33 HMC, *The Yellowstone National Park: Historical and Descriptive*, 2d ed. (Cincinnati, Ohio, 1915), p. iv. This edition, Chittenden's second revision, was described as "new and enlarged."

34 HMC to Henry Suzzalo, April 8, 1916, June 13, 1917; Henry Suzzalo to HMC, April 10, 1916, all in Henry Suzzalo Papers (University of Washington); HMC, "Diary," May 18, 1916, May 23, 1917, CPHS; HMC, "A 30-Mile Railway Tunnel under the Cascade Mountains," *Engineering News* 76 (1916): 928-35; HMC, "Diary," May 18, 1916, May 23, 1917, CPHS; Seattle Chamber of Commerce, "Minute Book," January 23, 1917, pp. 2699-700; *New York Times*, November 19, 1916, Section V, p. 13; *Seattle Post-Intelligencer*, November 16, 1916; [Charles Warren Hunt], "Memoir of HMC," *Transactions of the American Society of Civil Engineers* 82 (1918): 1676.

distinguished engineer Arthur E. Morgan, to investigate the floods, and in February 1914 the legislature of Ohio adopted a pioneering statute that permitted counties to form conservancy districts for flood control ruled by their own courts. A month after the law was passed, the Morgan Company formed a special board of consulting engineers to aid it in reporting to the city government of Dayton. Chittenden agreed to serve as a member of this board, although the reasons for his selection were unusual.[35]

Arthur Morgan later wrote that Chittenden had been chosen for the board to play the devil's advocate, for he was known throughout the country for opposition to the use of storage reservoirs for flood control purposes, a view he had advanced as early as his report on the arid lands in 1897. In that document, as subsequently, he had maintained that the only way to make reservoirs valuable for floods would be to finance them by industrial and agricultural uses.[36]

In March 1914 Chittenden began his work on the project by spending twelve days in Dayton and revisited the Miami Valley in September 1915, when he and his wife came by way of Lansing, Michigan, to visit his parents and sister. Confined to a Dayton hotel room by his crippling illness, he spent a month on the project. With his wife to care for his needs, Chittenden worked steadily for eight to twelve hours a day every day in the week, keeping busy a group of six to twelve assistants gathering data. He also summoned large numbers of men to his room for oral interviews. After digesting the mass of data, Chittenden became an enthusiast for the plan drawn up by Morgan and the board.[37]

In order to adopt this positive position, Chittenden had to

[35] Arthur E. Morgan, *The Miami Valley and the 1913 Flood*, Miami Conservancy District, *Technical Reports*, pt. 1 (Dayton, Ohio, 1917), pp. 117-18; HMC, "The Battle over the Miami Flood-Prevention Plans," *Engineering News* 76 (1916): 906-10; C. A. Bock, *History of the Miami Flood Control Project*, Miami Conservancy District, *Technical Reports*, pt. 2 (Dayton, Ohio, 1918), pp. 46-54.

[36] Comment by Arthur E. Morgan on HMC, "Detention Reservoirs with Spillway Outlets as an Agency in Flood Control," *Transactions of the American Society of Civil Engineers* 82 (1918): 1493.

[37] Ibid., pp. 2009-10; HMC, "Diary," March 15-27, 1914; September, October 1915, passim, CPHS.

be willing to change his earlier views, for the board proposed that five reservoirs should be constructed solely for the purposes of flood control. The Miami Conservancy Court held public hearings on this plan, and Chittenden was summoned as a witness before the court in September 1916. His support was forthright and enthusiastic; he defended the reservoir plan as being the most careful and thorough engineering plan he had ever known, and he specifically did not except the Panama Canal from that encomium. On the twenty-fourth of November the conservancy court upheld the official plan and construction began shortly thereafter. "It was really a great victory," Chittenden wrote in his diary, "and is a source of much satisfaction to me." The plan, and the arguments that underlay it, demonstrated Chittenden's flexibility of mind and proved to be outstandingly successful. There were great floods on the Miami in 1922, 1924, 1929, 1933, 1937, and 1943, but the plan proved to be so successful in restraining these inundations that a historian of water resources summarized the Miami project as "a prominent and handsome mark in the history of flood control."[38]

Chittenden was not so complacent as simply to advocate his newly conceived positions on reservoirs. He kept expanding his views and his last published work on engineering problems was a lucid attempt to keep open the minds of others to the possibilities of reservoirs. Fearful that the single-purpose reservoir of the Miami basin might, by the very enthusiasm of its reception, cut off speculation about other uses, he published an article in the *Proceedings* of the American Society of Civil Engineers in November 1917. Chittenden opened his essay by restating the general belief that it was impractical to employ a reservoir for both flood control and industrial use. But he also stated that engineers felt that ideally such a complementary use could be effected. The purpose of the paper was to try to resolve the apparent contradiction in these two beliefs. He noted that in his report on the arid lands he

[38] Bock, *History of the Miami Flood Control Project*, pp. 131, 184; HMC, "Battle over the Miami Flood-Prevention Plans," HMC, "Diary," September 21-30, 1916, passim, CPHS; George R. Schneider, "History and Future of Flood Control," *Transactions of the American Society of Civil Engineers*, Centennial volume (1953): 1079 (quotation, p. 1080).

had stated that theoretically, if industrial uses could pay the costs, reservoirs could serve both flood control and industrial objectives. He noted also that, in a significant change of heart from the time of his duel with Leighton in 1908 and 1909: "If reservoirs alone can never solve the flood problem on all our streams—and they certainly cannot—they may probably do more than most of us in recent years have believed to be possible."[39]

What Chittenden proposed was a confessedly familiar idea. He suggested that at a single site, two reservoirs be built, one upon the other, each with a different purpose. The bottom one would have sluiceways and gates and would be controlled for the purpose of power production. The upper reservoir superimposed upon the lower would be automatic with permanently open sluiceways to carry off the crest of floods for flood control. He added, of course, that levees would be needed on the lower rivers even if the headwaters were equipped with these dams. The commentators on Chittenden's paper, including Arthur Morgan, correctly showed that his purposes in publishing it were not to reveal any startling engineering feature, but to indicate that the engineer should keep a flexible mind about the future use of reservoirs.[40]

Chittenden's flexibility of mind on river control was also demonstrated in other ways in the last three years of his life. When the International Engineering Congress met at San Francisco in 1915, Chittenden prepared a major paper for the meeting in which he praised the Miami flood control plan and also advocated the project drawn up by the flood control commission established by the city of Pittsburgh after the Ohio flood of 1907.[41] This plan recommended a seventeen-reservoir project and an increase in the height of the levee at Pittsburgh. In this unusual case only the reduction of the flood height would completely prevent the floods, so Chittenden admitted that reservoirs could be relied upon chiefly,

39 HMC, "Detention Reservoirs," pp. 1473-82 (quotation, p. 1482).

40 Ibid., pp. 1485-92; comment by Arthur E. Morgan on HMC, "Detention Reservoirs," pp. 1493-94; comment by Morris Knowles on ibid., p. 1536.

41 HMC, "Flood Control: With Particular Reference to Conditions in the United States," *Transactions of the International Engineering Congress*, 1915. *Waterways and Irrigation* (San Francisco, Calif., 1916), pp. 110-253.

but "there are few flood problems to which it is so directly applicable." Besides benefiting the citizens of Pittsburgh, there were other reasons for trying the plan. "It is greatly to be desired," he wrote, "that the scheme be fully tried out. Not only would it give Pittsburgh a large measure of relief, but the effect of the example, in settling many disputed theories, would be of great value to the engineering profession and the country at large." The commentators again praised Chittenden's mastery of the technical details of his subject, the pluralism of his thought, and his ordered presentation, Arthur Morgan especially singling out Chittenden's statement that "The flood engineer must be bound to no system, but, with judicious insight, determine the treatment which best suits the particular case."[42]

In terms of practical politics Chittenden's solution for national flood control policy in his last two years of life was his endorsement of the Ransdell-Humphreys bill for federal aid for levee construction on the Mississippi and Sacramento rivers, a plan that had been first broached in 1912. Partisans of the multiple-purpose Newlands measure looked askance at this single-purpose plan and from November 1913 until well into 1916 there were attempts to reconcile the views of these two groups in a single measure.[43] In late June 1916 Chittenden wrote a letter to the editor of the *New York Times* in which he praised the House of Representatives for passing the Ransdell-Humphreys bill by a four-to-one margin. He criticized those who wanted a reservoir plan by stating that only the largest (and hence too expensive) reservoirs could control floods, and he rebuked those who advocated the Newlands approach of a single federal multiple-purpose agency by saying that this plan was theoretically attractive but in practice impossible. He said that the regulation of streams was too complex a task for a single agency and that it was better to keep separate the Corps, Weather Bureau, and Forest Service, and their respective functions in resources work.[44]

On international relations, Chittenden also was changing

42 Ibid., pp. 169, 247.
43 Hays, *Conservation*, pp. 234-40.
44 *New York Times*, June 29, 1916, p. 10.

in his last years toward a more nationalistic position than he had espoused in his book *War or Peace*. In a letter to the editor of the *New York Times* Chittenden reasserted some points he had made earlier in his book. Rejecting the belief that war preparations worked to prevent war—and now he had the outbreak of the World War to prove his case—Chittenden again argued that the United States should have a "rational program for defense" because it was forced to it by other nations, but by June of 1916 he felt that no plan of peace could halt the war and it must rage on until it decided the issues. "Then there may be real peace." In the same month he hailed a military preparedness parade in Seattle.[45] By autumn Chittenden argued that one rational way to prevent future wars was for the United States to enter this one. He held no hope for continued American neutrality and no virtue in it. He condemned in his diary President Wilson's famous "Peace without Victory" speech to the Senate on January 22, 1917, but after Germany resumed unrestricted submarine warfare on January 31 he wrote that the United States would now be drawn into the war, concluding: "I hope so. We must do our share."[46] By April, his long labors for preparedness and his support of the Allied cause seemed to him to be validated by American entry into the war; his only regret was that he was too crippled to serve himself, although his eldest son, Hiram, Jr., served in an artillery regiment.[47]

The support that he gave to American preparedness and intervention was Chittenden's last public cause, and in the final year of his life, conscious of his impending death, he calmly prepared for it. As for so many years, his tasks were lightened by the faith and cooperation of his family. His daughter was a close companion, and in 1915 Chittenden approved her engagement to Lieutenant James B. Cress of the Corps of Engineers, the son of a fellow officer whom Chittenden had met in Yellowstone Park. In his diary the General recorded that bride and groom made a fine couple and that the wedding on September 14, 1916, went off in good spirit and

[45] Ibid., December 21, 1915, p. 12; HMC, "Diary," June 6, 10, 1916, CPHS.
[46] HMC, "Diary," January 23, February 2, 1917, CPHS.
[47] Theodore P. Chittenden to author, November 1965.

without a hitch. Perhaps he was aware of death's approach, which would explain the additional poignancy of his daughter's departure. As he confided to his diary: "It seems impossible that she is really gone, and that I shall now listen in vain for her sprightly step, her meadow-lark laugh, and her always sympathetic touch on the piano. We have always been confidential companions and I shall miss her so much." But Eleanor and James were able to pay visits and they all had a happy reunion in early June 1917.[48]

One of the great moments of Chittenden's last year was the official opening of the Lake Washington Canal. On the Fourth of July 1917 the canal was officially inaugurated before so very large a crowd, one half the population of the city, that it had to be accommodated in two ceremonies. Judge Burke presided at the daytime exercises and read an address prepared by Chittenden tracing the history of the canal, but the man most responsible for the planning of the project was too ill to participate and sat blanketed in a wheelchair on the porch of his home.[49] He remained silent while the long line of boats passed out of sight toward Lake Washington and only then, in a voice trembling with emotion did he whisper, "It is done, it is done."[50]

Late in the month Jim and Eleanor came to visit again. "I presume it is my final goodbye to Jim," he wrote in his diary, "for I shall probably not be here when he returns. He leaves next Wednesday. Events like these certainly show up the tragic side of war." On August 1 his final diary entry appeared on the date of the departure of James's regiment for the fighting front in France. His consolation was that Eleanor would remain in her father's house while her husband was in service. By September he could not write at all and his daughter was taking the last of his dictation for the autobiographical fragments that are indispensable for his biographer. Clear, straightforward, objective, they indicate that his mental powers were unimpaired to the end. Outwardly,

48 HMC, "Diary," July 22, 1915; August 23, September 14, 1916; June 1, 2, 1917, CPHS.
49 *Seattle Times,* July 5, 1917; "Background Material on General H. M. Chittenden and U.S. Government Locks & Canal at Ballard," CPHS.
50 "Background Material," CPHS.

in spite of being cut down prematurely, he remained serene and in his final agonies mentioned to a visiting clergyman that he was fully prepared for death and that he only regretted that he had not accomplished more and left a greater financial heritage for his family. On October 9 he died at the age of fifty-eight at home at twenty minutes after midnight.[51]

Two days later the funeral services were held in his Plymouth Congregational Church with the Reverend Mark Matthews conducting the service. Because the nation was at war, a military funeral was not held and the traditional notes of taps went unsounded. In keeping with the general's wishes the service was simple with a prayer and two hymns; Matthews spoke, recalling Chittenden's services to the city and to the nation. The pallbearers, honorary and active, were his friends from business, his profession, and the university, including Brigadier General Henry L. Styer from the Corps of Engineers, Judge Burke, Professors Oliver H. Richardson and Edmond S. Meany, Reginald H. Thomson, and O. B. Thorgrimson.[52]

Obituary writers from the *New York Times,* the engineering societies, the army, and the Seattle press all attempted to assess the man and all agreed upon certain aspects of his career.[53] They dealt only with Chittenden's easily measurable accomplishments and made little effort to probe Chittenden's character and personality except in conventional ways. Beyond listing his specific public services, they spoke only of his integrity and sense of duty.

In later surveying Chittenden's career, one is struck repeatedly by the energy that enabled him to extract so many achievements from his prematurely shortened life. First goaded by personal ambition that later fused with the passion for public service which stamped his manifold careers, Chittenden's zeal for work was astounding, and the range of his achievements and their generally high quality is equally impressive.

[51] HMC, "Diary," July 29, 1917, CPHS; interview with Mrs. Eleanor C. Cress, August 3, 1968; "Certified Copy of Death Certificate of HMC" (Seattle-King County Department of Public Health), #2063; *Seattle Post-Intelligencer,* October 12, 1917.

[52] *Seattle Post-Intelligencer,* October 12, 1917.

[53] *New York Times,* October 10, 1917, p. 11; Hunt, "Memoir of HMC," pp. 1675-78; *Seattle Town Crier,* October 13, 1917; *Seattle Post-Intelligencer,* October 10, 1917.

Willingness to work never left him, although in the discouraging years of the late 1880s and early 1890s his career was unspectacular and certainly promised little of fame or material reward. In Yellowstone Park, he was busy sixteen hours a day every day during the construction season, while simultaneously he had to keep an eye on his assignments on the Upper Missouri and to handle the multitude of other tasks, assigned or voluntarily assumed, that marked his most productive years from 1899 to 1906.

One means that Chittenden employed to maintain his vigorous pace of labor was to indulge his appreciation of nature and the outdoors. He loved not only the exotic geysers and spectacular canyons but also the common wildflowers and pastoral scenes. In Yellowstone, and also in Yosemite, he was ever vigilant to confront those who would use the parks for transportation or mining purposes in a manner abusive of the aesthetic purposes of the national park ideal.

From boyhood, although the record is not full, he softened his ambition and leavened his energetic zeal with a saving sense of humor. At the Ten Broeck Academy Hiram penned humorous letters and poetry to his friends and even the gloomy verse of later years was relieved by occasional poems of humor and satire. Within his family he joked and teased and wrote limericks, and his younger son vividly recalls his peals of laughter while reading Mark Twain. This sense of humor, another means of self-appraisal, enabled him to retain the friendship and respect of many men whom he opposed in controversies.

Chittenden's sense of humor did not conceal a strong religious feeling that remained throughout his life. He was not a narrow sectarian, for what he learned of Protestant Christianity at home, from the great debates over religion at Cornell, and from his early readings all led him to a rather catholic and progressive faith. Theology disinterested him; what he espoused was a religion of service, a belief that undoubtedly accounted for his lifelong admiration for Benjamin Franklin. He had always admired the Philadelphia sage from college days and in his last year wrote an unpublished tribute to him that likened him in stature to Washington and Lincoln.

Chittenden thus combined the traditional Christian view of personal morals and morality as taught by the evangelical churches with the new religion of service that came to be called the Social Gospel in the twentieth century. Personal integrity, a sense of decency, and respect for the dignity of others were lifelong attributes. An independent mind himself, he respected the independence and personality of those with whom he walked.

Chittenden's independence, although he appeared aloof or shy to many, was not that of a hermit or misanthrope. He enjoyed many close friends, particularly in his last years in Seattle after his retirement from the Corps of Engineers released him somewhat from the bondage of governmental correspondence and red tape. These friends were drawn from many businesses and professions and they frequently gathered in his home, for example, for the meeting of the University of Washington chapter of Phi Beta Kappa in April 1915, when he held a dinner for the members. From the university he numbered friends from the Department of History, among them the popular lecturer and bibliographer Edmond S. Meany, and Oliver H. Richardson, professor of European history. Reginald H. Thomson, the city engineer of Seattle, was a close friend as was big, genial, Archibald O. Powell, who was with Chittenden in the days of the Spanish-American War and later became his associate on the canal and Port Commission projects. Lawyers in his circle of acquaintances included Judge Thomas Burke, James J. Hill's representative in Seattle, the Progressive attorney Harold Preston, Federal Judge Cornelius Hanford, and James Haight, who wrote Chittenden's obituary notice for the *Post-Intelligencer*. Even in earlier days, as hunter, fisherman, and tennis player, he participated in many areas of life besides the office and study, and his many-sidedness enabled him to number among his acquaintances men from all walks of life.[54]

His warmth and humor were best revealed among the members of his family where his austere public countenance, emphasized by his formidable whiskers, disappeared except for

[54] Data in this paragraph are drawn from HMC, "Diary," 1911-1917, passim, CPHS.

the purpose of disciplining small boys for neglect of duty. He read to the children and saw that the house was amply stocked with quality books and periodicals including *Harper's, Atlantic,* and the daily and weekly Seattle papers. He played chess and double-solitaire with the children, wrote them humorous letters when they were away at school, composed limericks for them, and helped them with their school assignments, one time reminding Eleanor that the French *je ne sais pas* translated phonetically "Jenny, say pa." He took his obligations as a parent seriously, recording in his diary the triumphs and troubles of his family. Once his daughter's class was asked to name the five most famous men and women in the nation; at the dinner table that evening nine-year-old Teddy suggested his father, a comment that prompted Chittenden to muse: "But not every one can be prominent before the world. A parent may, however, set an example to his children in his particular walk of life which shall be a guide and even an inspiration. He does not have to have worldly prominence to do that."[55]

Although his religious faith, his distinguished position among his professional peers, and the security of his family's love gave Chittenden courage and confidence, he was not a man who passed through life untroubled or unreflecting. Pessimism was always lurking, pessimism that most frequently took the form of worry over his health. This concern was not hypochondria or self-pity, for Chittenden had serious health problems from the eve of his professional career. He never publicly alibied for his ill health or complained of his physical misfortune, nor did his worries ever limit his effectiveness so far as can be detected by the documentary evidence of his career.

Although his life was one largely of vigorous exercise, frequent travels, and rugged survey work, Chittenden also enjoyed the library and the study as well as the office and the field. He was a scholar by temperament but never a serious abstract thinker. This intellectual strain was evident in his wide reading of a great variety of material, in his authorship

[55] Interview with Mrs. Eleanor C. Cress, August 3, 1968; HMC, "Diary," January 16, 1910, CPHS.

of distinguished books, and in his style of mind. He had a scholar's passion for ascertaining factual data, a spirit of objectivity, and an unwillingness to accept the conventional belief simply because of its antiquity or the strength of emotions of those who held it. As a thinker he was not always innovative, but he did make some contributions that demonstrated that he was capable of original insights. Chittenden was one of the first to conceive the project of federal aid to irrigation improvements; he came earlier than better-publicized people to the belief that the river basin was a unit from source to mouth; he saw the magnificent scope of a history of the American fur trade.

He was willing to alter his views on the basis of new evidence. Originally a supporter of the theory that forests control floods, he later repudiated it on the basis of his own observations in Yellowstone Park. He changed his mind on the lock site in Seattle when the Lake Washington Canal was projected. Although originally an opponent, he was convinced after studying the facts that the Miami Conservancy District flood control plans were meritorious. He came to accept the use of reservoirs to control floods, at least to protect the city of Pittsburgh, after originally opposing the plan.

Willingness to change and grow is coupled with Chittenden's independence of mind and personal courage. Chittenden was a nonconformist when his convictions drove him in that direction. Not a dissenter for the sake of dissent, hardly a maladjusted complainer who felt himself mistreated by peers and superiors, Chittenden took his positions on the basis of his beliefs, always admitting their tentative nature, and always willing to be convinced of their invalidity. He defied the sentiment of the time in advocating federal aid for the construction of irrigation dams in the arid regions. In his report of 1903 he penned the heretical idea that the Corps should drop the fiction of controlling floods to advance commerce. In the preparation of his epochal report on forests and reservoirs he rejected timorous counsels from his superiors and assailed the popular crusade for conservation led personally by the president of the United States.

Many of his personal traits of character merged into his

philosophy of life and of human nature. He was an optimist and a devotee of the life of reason. Chittenden believed, like so many of his fellow progressives, that skilled, professionally trained intelligence, could provide solutions for the quandaries and dilemmas of the times. His training as an engineer gave him confidence in the use of educated reason that appeared in practically all his projects from building Yellowstone roads to writing a book on the prevention of war. But in spite of his faith in trained intelligence, Chittenden was no elitist who felt that the state should be guided by a coterie of intellectuals. He believed in democratic education, that the average man could see reason, and that the open society was preferable to the closed.

Chittenden from youth was given to self-assessment. Whether he took stock or not in the fall of 1917 is unknown, but to the dispassionate observer his life's record was as he might well have planned it. His desire was for hard work in the service of the public. He fulfilled this goal and was honored for it in his own time and by posterity.

Bibliographical Essay

The materials included in this bibliographical essay are intended to serve two purposes: to illustrate the principal materials I have employed in the preparation of this biography and to suggest the wealth of sources available to scholars who might be interested in pursuing several fruitful, if neglected, topics in the history of the American West, particularly in the realms of the use and conservation of natural resources and the development of civil public works.

Manuscripts. There are two major deposits of Chittenden materials. The most important is his correspondence with the Office of the Chief of Engineers contained in the Records of the Chief of Engineers (Record Group 77), the National Archives. These letters, which are both incoming and outgoing, cover an enormous range of matter from the significant to the trivial. In the same record group are included a great number of reports of individual officers, civilian employees, boards, and other agencies of government and private groups that supplement the thousands of letters to and from the Office of the Chief. Record Group 77 also includes data of every conceivable sort drawn from the local districts of the Corps. It is indispensable for the biographer of any officer of the Corps. The second chief source of Chittenden material is the Chittenden Papers held by the Washington State Historical Society. In this collection are scrapbooks, diaries, autobiographical fragments, photographs, a few letters, and mementos: certificates, diplomas, licenses, and reprints of his official reports. Bruce Le Roy has ably edited several of Chittenden's unpublished writings in his *H. M. Chittenden: A Western Epic* (Tacoma, Wash., 1961). Some of the autobiographical essays are also contained in the Chittenden Papers at the University of Washington Library as is some of his correspondence from the era of his service on the Seattle Port Commission. Chittenden's letters to his mother from his years at West Point are held in the library of the United States Military Academy. Valuable records for Chittenden's military progress are in his ACP file in the Records of the Adjutant General (Record Group 94), the National Archives. Unfortunately, in none of these collections are there more than thirty letters that would in any way reveal much about the inner workings of Chittenden's mind or his personal feelings about most matters unconnected with his official duties.

Manuscript data on certain aspects of Chittenden's career are widely scattered. For his work on the reservoir sites in Wyoming and Colorado the Francis E. Warren Papers at the University of Wyoming and the Elwood Mead Papers at the Wyoming State Archives and Historical Department contain helpful materials. For Chittenden's career in Yellowstone Park the Yellowstone Park Archives contain his correspondence with the acting superintendent of the park and miscellaneous material. In regard to Chittenden's role as an opponent of the forest-stream flow theory there is information in the Records of the Weather Bureau (Record Group 27), the Forest Service (Record Group 95), and the Geological Survey (Record Group 57), all in the National Archives. There is a small amount of correspondence concerning the work of the Yosemite Park boundary commission in the Patents and Miscellaneous section of the Records of the National Park Service (Record Group 79), National Archives. The last phases of Chittenden's career—his years in the city of Seattle—are documented in the following collections at the University of Washington Library which furnish, in composite, an excellent groundwork for the historian of the city in the Progressive era: Richard A. Ballinger Papers, Erastus Brainerd Papers, Thomas Burke Papers, Seattle Port Commission Papers, Eugene Semple Papers, Joe Smith Papers, Henry Suzzalo Papers, and the R. H. Thomson Papers. Contributing to a full picture of this era are the minute books and other records of the Seattle Commercial Club and the Seattle Chamber of Commerce, both now contained in the offices of the Chamber.

Published Writings of Hiram M. Chittenden. Chittenden published a great variety of works in many different places. His five published books are *The Yellowstone National Park: Historical and Descriptive* (Cincinnati, Ohio, 1895; rev. ed., Cincinnati, 1903; 2d rev. ed., Cincinnati, 1915); *The American Fur Trade of the Far West,* 3 vols. (New York, 1902); *History*

of Early Steamboat Navigation on the Missouri River, 2 vols.
(New York, 1903); *Life and Letters of Father Pierre-Jean De
Smet, S.J., 1801-1873,* in collaboration with Alfred T. Richardson, 4 vols. (New York, 1905); and *War or Peace: A Present
Duty and a Future Hope* (Chicago, 1911). His annual reports
(although sometimes condensed or excised) are published in the
Annual Reports of the Chief of Engineers for the years 1887-
1908. His essays on conservation and on technical engineering
matters are contained in the *Proceedings* and *Transactions* of
the American Society of Civil Engineers and in the *Engineering
News* and *Engineering Record.* Specific citations to these
reports and essays may be found in the footnotes to this
biography. Chittenden's articles on matters of public policy
contained in several national periodicals, including the *Atlantic
Monthly, Forum,* and *Outlook,* are again specifically listed in
the footnotes, as are fugitive works on specialized engineering
topics, letters to the editor, verse, and other miscellaneous items
far too numerous to list here.

Printed Documents and Contemporary Accounts. For a student of the Corps of Engineers the *Annual Reports of the Chief
of Engineers* are essential. They contain annual reports of the
activities of each officer and of the work on all projects of the
Corps. Depending upon the generosity of Congress, they are
full or sketchy, but usually ample. Many reports of river and
harbor projects are published in the congressional documents
series as reports of Senate and House committees. *The Annual
Reports of the Secretary of the Interior* provide information
on the problems of the acting superintendent of Yellowstone
Park and his relationship to the engineer officer in the park.
Reports of congressional hearings contain much information
on the struggles over forestry, irrigation, the Weeks bill, and
general conservation policies. Publications of the Forest Service, the Geological Survey, and the War Department contain
data helpful in illuminating these problems, as do the *Proceedings* of the Trans-Mississippi Commercial Congress and the
Proceedings of the National Irrigation Congress. In Seattle,
the *Bulletins* and other reports of the Seattle Port Commission
are vital for understanding Chittenden's later career.

Newspapers. Indispensable for a study of the Seattle portions of Chittenden's life are such papers as the *Seattle Times* and the *Post-Intelligencer,* which provide news and editorials favorable to the business interests of the community. So also do the weeklies, the *Argus* and the *Town Crier,* although their views are not always uniform. On the Progressive side the *Star* and the *Sun* are invaluable. The *Seattle Municipal News* is also in this camp, but is more reliable and objective. The *Railway and Marine News* is the journal of the Pacific Coast shipping interests and contains much valuable information on port development. Curiously, the local papers fringing Yellowstone Park do not provide a great deal of data about the operations of the Corps of Engineers in the park. Major sources of information concerning engineering developments in the United States and the world are *Engineering News* and *Engineering Record.*

Books and Articles. There is no secondary work dealing adequately with the Corps of Engineers in its civil works in the West. One is badly needed although there are specialized studies on flood control. The history of the development of national irrigation policies and many specific projects in the West is unwritten. The role of the Corps of Engineers in the Spanish-American War is unworked. John Ise's monograph, *Our National Park Policy: A Critical History* (Baltimore, Md., 1961), is a most valuable pioneering study, and Duane Hampton has written a sound administrative history in *How the U.S. Cavalry Saved Our National Parks* (Bloomington, Ind., 1971), but much remains to be done in the realm of the history of national parks. Attitudes toward nature have been excellently treated in Hans Huth, *Nature and the American: Three Centuries of Changing Attitudes* (Berkeley, Calif., 1957) and in Roderick Nash, *Wilderness and the American Mind* (New Haven, Conn., 1967). In the realm of fur trade history Paul C. Phillips and J. W. Smurr have dealt with Chittenden's theme in *The Fur Trade,* 2 vols. (Norman, Okla., 1961), but have not superseded Chittenden's account. William E. Lass, *A History of Steamboating on the Upper Missouri River* (Lincoln, Nebr., 1962), has largely replaced Chittenden's study of that topic. The best account of Father De Smet's career is E. Laveille, *The Life of Father De Smet, S.J., 1801-*

1873, trans. Marian Lindsay (New York, 1915). The nature and components of organized conservation have recently become of serious interest to historians. The best survey is Frank E. Smith, *The Politics of Conservation* (New York, 1966). Outstanding monographs are those of A. Hunter Dupree, *Science and the Federal Government: A History of Policies and Activities to 1940* (Cambridge, Mass., 1956), Samuel P. Hays, *Conservation and the Gospel of Efficiency: The Progressive Conservation Movement, 1890-1920* (Cambridge, Mass., 1959), and Ashley L. Schiff, *Fire and Water* (Cambridge, Mass., 1962). Unfortunately local history in Seattle is largely untouched although several topics that illuminate national themes await the scholar, ranging from local politics to histories of journalism. The Progressive era in Seattle is particularly stimulating as a relatively unworked area.

Chittenden's career is illuminated directly or indirectly by a few articles. Noteworthy are J. Leonard Bates, "Fulfilling American Democracy: The Conservation Movement, 1907 to 1921," *Mississippi Valley Historical Review* 44 (1957); 29-57; Alan A. Hynding, "Eugene Semple's Seattle Canal Scheme," *Pacific Northwest Quarterly* 59 (1968): 77-87; and Dale L. Morgan, "The Fur Trade and Its Historians," *The American West* 3 (1966): 28-31, 35, 92-93.

Unpublished Dissertations. The following theses and dissertations have been most helpful in setting Chittenden's career against its national and regional background. Bob Randolph O'Brien, "The Yellowstone National Park Road System: Past, Present and Future" (Ph.D. diss., University of Washington, 1965), is scholarly and devotes a chapter to Chittenden and his influence. Charles D. Smith, "The Movement for Eastern National Forests, 1899-1911" (Ph.D. diss., Harvard University, 1956), deals in part with the stream flow controversy.

The following works all illuminate aspects of Seattle's economic and political history during the years of Chittenden's residence in the city: Keith A. Murray, "Republican Party Politics in Washington during the Progressive Era" (Ph.D. diss., University of Washington, 1946); Alexander N. MacDonald, "Seattle's Economic Development, 1880-1910" (Ph.D.

diss., University of Washington, 1959); Norman F. Tjaden, "Populists and Progressives of Washington: A Comparative Study" (Master's thesis, University of Washington, 1960); Wesley A. Dick, "The Genesis of City Light" (Master's thesis, University of Washington, 1965); William S. Forth, "Wesley L. Jones: A Political Biography" (Ph.D. diss., University of Washington, 1962).

Index

American Fur Company, 90, 99
American Fur Trade of the Far West, 72, 73, 74-91, 96
Anderson, George S., 11, 13-14, 15, 18-19, 20, 104, 162
Angell, Norman, 195
Appalachian National Forest, 158
Astor, John Jacob, 79, 85, 99

Ballinger, Richard A., 144, 145, 148, 153
Bancroft, Hubert Howe, 76, 77, 84, 102
Blethen, Alden J., 129
Bond, Frank, 60-61, 65, 66
Brainerd, Erastus, 129, 133, 136, 141, 142
Brice, Calvin S., 21
Bridges, Robert E., 187, 188, 193-95
Bryan, William Jennings, 41
Burke, Thomas, 136, 152-53, 204, 205, 207
Burroughs, John, 118

Cannon, Joseph G., 113, 114, 116-17, 153
Carey Act, 25-26
Carter, Oberlin M., 160
Carter, Thomas H., 40, 103, 109-10, 113, 114-15, 119
Chittenden, Clyde (brother), 2, 186
Chittenden, Eleanor (daughter), 14, 70, 186, 203-4, 208
Chittenden, Hiram Martin:
autobiography of, 73; as boundary commissioner, Yosemite National Park, 60-67; and Cascade tunnel plan, 149-52, 198; conservation theories of, 161-69, 171; at Cornell, 3-4, 72, 73; death of, 205; defense of Yellowstone National Park, 16-18; as engineer officer, Department of the Platte, 7-8; as engineer officer, Lake Washington Canal, 130, 132-42, 146; as engineer officer, Louisville and Portland Canal, 18-19; as engineer officer, Osage River project, 48-49; as engineer officer, Puget Sound, 147-48; as engineer officer, Yellowstone National Park, 9-10, 12-13, 103-13; at Engineer School of Application, 6-7; family of, 2, 8, 14, 20, 29, 47, 69-70, 106, 107, 116, 128,
139, 186, 199, 203-4, 206, 207-8; and flood control service, 42-43, 48, 68, 147; flood control theories of, 51-53, 201-2; and Floyd monument project, 49; foreign travel of, 9; "Forests and Reservoirs," 162-69, 171, 175, 177-81, 185; and Fort Washakie military road, 115-16; health of, 9, 54, 69-70, 119, 126-28, 130, 138-39, 142-43, 146, 148-49, 152, 154, 186-87, 197, 198, 208; historical writings of, 9, 19-21, 47, 70-96, 209; historical writings, criticism of, 80-83, 85-87, 90, 96; and Kansas River investigation, 50; and land suit, 142-46; marriage of, 6; as Miami Valley flood control consultant, 198-201, 209; miscellaneous writings of, 17, 38, 74, 197, 200-202; Missouri River Commission service, 8, 9; Mount Rainier National Park service, 146-47; navigation service, 43, 52, 89; Ohio canal survey service, 21-22; philosophy of history of, 97-102; poetry of, 13, 206; promotions of, 7, 20, 43, 54, 93; and reclamation report of 1897, 31; reclamation survey of, 26-41; reservoir theories of, 26-41, 50, 177-81, 198-202, 209; reservoir work of, 38, 54, 56, 57-59; retirement of, 148-49, 152-54, 185, 186; and road construction work, 68-69, 104, 105-6, 108-10, 111-12, 114, 115-16, 117, 120-21, 122-23, 125-26, 146-47; Seattle Port Commission service, 187-88, 190-95, 198; Spanish-American War service, 43-47; Spanish-American War, views of, 48; at United States Military Academy, 4-6, 72, 73; views on international affairs of, 196-97, 202-3; views on nature of, 16, 120, 123-25, 206; *War or Peace,* 195-96, 203
Chittenden, Hiram Martin, Jr., 20, 70, 186
Chittenden, Ida (sister), 8, 60, 199
Chittenden, Mary Wheeler (mother), 2, 199
Chittenden, Nettie (neé Parker) (wife), 2, 6, 8, 14, 69, 199
Chittenden, Theodore Parker (son), 116, 186, 206, 208